THE ART OF SEXUAL MAGIC

Also by Margo Anand

The Art of Sexual Ecstasy: The Path of Sacred Sexuality for Western Lovers

THE ART OF SEXUAL MAGIC

MARGO ANAND

ILLUSTRATED BY ATMA PRITI

A JEREMY P. TARCHER/PUTNAM BOOK
published by
G. P. Putnam's Sons
New York

Most Tarcher/Putnam books are available at special quantity discounts for bulk purchases for sales promotions, premiums, fundraising, and educational needs.

Special books or book excerpts also can be created to fit specific needs. For details, write or telephone Special Markets, The Putnam Publishing Group, 200 Madison Ave, New York, NY 10016; (212) 951-8891.

A Jeremy P. Tarcher/Putnam Book
Published by G. P. Putnam's Sons
Publishers Since 1838
200 Madison Avenue
New York, NY 10016

http://www.putnam.com/putnam
First Trade Paperback Edition 1996

Library of Congress Cataloging-in-Publication Data

Anand, Margo.
The art of sexual magic / Margo Anand.
p.   cm.
"A Jeremy P. Tarcher/Putnam book."
ISBN 0-87477-840-9
1. Sex instruction.   2. Sex—Religious aspects—Tantrism.
I. Title.
HQ64.A5   1995   95-11379 CIP
613.9'6—dc20

Design by Tanya Maiboroda
Illustrations by Atma Priti
Cover design by Lee Fukui
Front cover illustration, *Water Serpents,* by Gustav Klimt,
© Erich Lessing/Art Resource, New York
Photograph of the author by Max O'Neill

Printed in the United States of America
10 9 8 7 6 5 4 3 2

This book is printed on acid-free paper. ♾

To those who know that sex and spirit are one.

ACKNOWLEDGMENTS

I would like to express my gratitude and appreciation to the following people who have contributed to the realization of this book:

To my publisher, Jeremy Tarcher, for his unwavering support in the unfolding of the creative process, his wise counsel in many matters personal and transpersonal, professional and spiritual, his humor and intelligence . . . and his patience and trust.

To Azul, the wise Bodhidharma of Tantra, for his joyful friendship, inspiration, and creativity in embellishing this book with magic potent quotes.

To Subhuti, the best writer I have worked with, who proved that creating this book could be magic: easy and fun. I have especially appreciated his focus, concentration, and speed in helping me write, correct, and edit this book.

To Naomi Lucks and Laura Bellotti for their superb editing.

To my agent, Sandra Dijkstra, for standing behind me with great precision and clarity, even at the most confused moments; for her patience, her professionalism, and the help of her competent staff.

To Caroleen Green, aka Atma Priti, my talented illustrator, for her enthusiasm and artistic genius.

To Aman Schroeter and Deva Kosha, for sharing in the Tantric practice; magic explorations, and teaching of the SkyDancing Love and Ecstasy Training presented in my previous book, *The Art of Sexual Ecstasy*, as well as the Art of Sexual Magic training presented in this book.

To Kay Thompson, director of the SkyDancing Institute USA, for her dedication in organizing my office and my trainings with perseverence and multidimensional responsibilities.

To Betty Dodson for her inspiring research on female sexual anatomy in her book, *Sex for One*.

To those friends who have inspired some of the processes in this book: Gabrielle St. Clair and Michael Plesse, for the Chakra Wave; Mani Littmann, for the Fire Meditation; Terumi and Leonard Leinow, for the Chakra Rub; to Bob Hoffman, for the Quadrinity Process, which has clarified the nature of our wounds (see chapter 3).

To Gabrielle Roth and Constance Demby for their incredible music, which has pioneered a new interface between sensuality and spirituality.

To Dr. Dean Ornish, for being a great pioneer in healing the heart and inviting me to present to his heart patients the idea that sexual loving can be relaxing and fun, even when you have a delicate heart.

To Dr. Alan Brauer and his wife, Donna, for pioneering the research on extended sexual orgasm and being such welcoming supporters of my research.

To Marge and Lucas Hopkins, for unwaveringly battling the resistances against extended orgasm produced by the male supremacist influences in my life and psyche.

To Bob Hoffman for his contribution in healing the wounds with father and mother through the Quadrinity Process.

To those dedicated professionals and magicians who are leading the SkyDancing Institutes across the world, particularly Yatro Werner and Christiane Thomson (SkyDancing Germany); Nital Brinkley and Achintya Vasey (France and Switzerland); Aman Schroeter (Switzerland); John Hawken (England); Renee Koopmans (Holland); Robert and Lilianne Baillod (Canada); Kay Thompson (USA).

To all the SkyDancing teachers and practitioners who are part of the growing SkyDancing Tribes and who teach my work around the world and help to spread an orgasmic vibration of healing and joy around the planet.

On the invisible planes of metaphysical insight into the nature of awareness and the magic of synchronicity, my greatest source of teaching and inspiration has been the great mystic Osho.

Thanks also to those who teach his work in the USA: Kaveesha and Wadud. My grateful appreciation for the loving contribution of Ramanadass and Marilena Selby, who posed for many of the illustrations.

CONTENTS

You also learn to create a Magic Circle and are introduced to important elements of ritual that will help in your magical quest.

Having accessed your Inner Magician, you may discover—as many people do—that there are obstacles on the path of releasing your sexual energy for magic. These obstacles can manifest themselves in the form of doubts, shame, guilt, pain, or traumatic experiences recalled from childhood. This chapter gives you the tools you need to heal your sexual wounds. Like a true alchemist, you learn how to turn the base metal of your own energy into the purest gold.

Once your wounds have been healed, the next step is to explore and express your total energy resources by connecting with your Wild Self, bringing the creative impulse of Eros into your life. Through exercises like the Laughing Pelvis, you learn how to enjoy and celebrate your natural energy, giving it complete freedom of expression. An important dimension of your Wild Self is found in the raw, untamed animal within you, and this is awakened and released in a safe and creative way.

Now that you have reclaimed your energy, how do you wish to direct this power? What is your life's goal, or purpose? Who do you want to be? In this chapter you learn how to create clear, condensed visions for transforming yourself, your love relationships, and your environment. You are introduced to the act of creating a *Sigil* and other powerful Magic Symbols that will help you manifest your goals and are shown how to hold a magical vision during love-making.

In this chapter you learn how to circulate and transform sexual energy, paving the way for a full-body orgasm. This transformation of your sexual power happens by opening an energy channel through your body called the Inner Flute. You are initiated into the alchemy of carrying a vision, together with your orgasmic energy, up through the seven energy centers in your body, ultimately connecting with the subtle frequencies of the Astral Network.

In this chapter, the female partner, addressed as the goddess Shakti, learns how to access her full orgasmic power independently of sexual penetration, in new, exciting, and ecstatic ways. This orgasmic power will bring Shakti to new heights of pleasure in lovemaking and will be directed upward through the Secret Channel to create the highest possible form of magic.

8. SHIVA'S MAGIC: THE ALCHEMY OF
   MALE ORGASM 279

Now it is the turn of the male partner, addressed as the god Shiva, to learn how to increase his sexual sensitivity and responses, experiencing new forms of orgasm that enhance his manhood, increase his pleasure, and give him unique insights into the role of being receptive in sexuality. Shiva's expanded orgasmic energy will, like Shakti's, be channeled into sexual magic.

9. MAGICAL CONGRESS: FUSING SEXUAL
   ORGASM WITH MAGIC 319

Now you are ready to practice the full Tantric ritual of sexual magic with your love partner. Having aroused your orgasmic energy, you learn how to enter into Tantric union. Entwined together with your love partner, you bring a vision through your bodies, powered by your expanded orgasmic energy, and project this potent symbol into the Astral Network. This is the point at which sexual magic truly becomes a Tantric art.

CONTENTS

    How do you know that your magic is working? When will your desire for transformation be fulfilled? This brief postscript contains suggestions about what to do while awaiting the outcome of your magic.

As the river gives itself into the ocean,
what is inside me moves inside you. . . .
—Robert Bly
The Kabir Book

PREFACE
From Sexual Ecstasy to Magic

When I begin a seminar or a conference, I often ask the audience, "Who in this room has had a peak experience in sexual loving?" Many hands go up. Everybody knows, deep in his or her flesh and bones, that sexual loving can be a doorway to the most wonderful experiences. And when I ask them "How does it feel?" they invariably reply, "It's magic."

"What is magical about it?" I inquire.

Answers include:

"It's a feeling of being without boundaries or limitations."

"It's an exhilarating sense of infinite possibilities."

"It's a sense of joyful oneness with the divine."

"It's a feeling of creative power."

Those of you who have read my previous book, *The Art of Sexual Ecstasy,* will already know that sexual energy can be refined and expanded, transporting you to realms of orgasmic delight that offer an endless variety of exquisite experiences. This is a type of magic, a magic that is natural to good lovemaking.

As part of my quest for such magical experiences, I spent many years researching the cultural traditions and teachings of sacred sexuality all over the world, discovering new and different ways to transform sexual union into a blissful meditation, into a communion between body and soul.

In particular, I discovered Tantra, an ancient mystical path that offers an all-embracing vision of cosmic harmony. In the Tantric vision of the universe, apparently contradictory forces such as spirit and matter, good and bad, day and night, love and hate, are seen as complementary energies that weave and move around each other in an endless, dynamic, cosmic dance.

In Western countries, the word *Tantra* has become synonymous with sexuality. Yet the Tantric vision is vast, stretching far beyond the realms of love and sexuality, embracing body, mind, heart, and spirit, and, indeed, the whole universe and all its mysteries. Tantra is perhaps the most all-encompassing spiritual path that has ever existed.

After absorbing these sacred teachings, I started to share my insights and discoveries with thousands of people around the world in the form of workshops, seminars, and trainings. As I did so, a method emerged that I call SkyDancing Tantra. It is an initiation into the life-transforming power of love and ecstasy—a training that, while specifically designed for Western lovers, has its origins in the Eastern, spiritual path of Tantra.

The name SkyDancing Tantra expresses the feeling of lightness and joy that arises during ecstatic lovemaking, a sense of "dancing in the sky" that comes when we bring the quality of meditative awareness to our orgasmic power.

Over the years, my love affair with SkyDancing Tantra gradually and inevitably introduced me to the realm of magic. Slowly, almost by accident, I became aware that orgasmic energy could be used as a magical, transforming force, not just in lovemaking but in many areas of my life.

At first I sensed, then I experienced, how ecstatic states of deep sexual union provide a fertile soil in which creative seeds can be planted: seeds of personal transformation and transcendence, seeds of more fulfilling relationships with lovers and friends, seeds of material abundance . . . seeds that can sprout into reality because of the intense, orgasmic energy field in which they have been planted, nourished, and grown.

This book, *The Art of Sexual Magic,* is the result of several years of intensive research and practice into sex magic. My approach draws on many sources, but as a method it is new and original. You will not find it in the traditional books on magic, sex magic, or Tantra. This training weaves together three powerful elements:

1. Psychology as a means to healing
2. SkyDancing Tantra as a path to bliss
3. Sexual Magic as a path to transformation and manifestation

The message it teaches and the promise it holds are that now it is time—and now it is possible—to heal the guilt, the shame, the wounding that is imprinted on our sexuality. When this healing happens, sexual energy has tremendous power—a power that can transform the world, our relationships, and ourselves through love, delight, and harmony, giving birth to the magician within each of us.

In this book, I share my personal discoveries, offering a simple, practical, and yet powerful training in sexual magic—a training that can bring the liberating and transforming force of magic into the life of anyone who cares to practice it. And that is what I now invite you to do: to come with me on the great adventure of transformation through sexual magic.

Even though this book stands as an independent training in itself, it will be helpful to have read and familiarized yourself with my previous book *The Art of Sexual Ecstasy.*

HINTS ON USING THIS BOOK

This book is devised as a training manual for practicing sexual magic. It is a step-by-step guide for your empowerment as a master of magical transformation.

The training I have developed is not difficult. In fact, it is designed to yield the maximum results with the least possible effort, giving you the best possible opportunity to experience the joys and delights of sexual magic. It has been practiced with good results by many couples, and also by people working alone, without a regular partner.

The book is designed in the same style as a group seminar. Each chapter is a stage of the training, offering a stepping-stone to the next stage or practice. It is important to proceed sequentially, as each chapter gives you the skills and information you need to move successfully to the next. After completing the whole sequence, you are free to experiment and play with exercises from any part of the book, according to your inclination.

The chapters offer three or four major exercises and these, too, are to be done sequentially. Exercises may take anywhere from thirty to ninety minutes.

Timing

To complete a thorough training, you need to take about a month to practice the exercises in each chapter. This means that a full training in sexual magic will take nine months.

As part of your training, you may want to devise a monthly schedule: practice the first exercise in the chapter for one week, then move to the second exercise in the second week, then to the third in the third week . . . If there are only three exercises in a chapter, you can spend the fourth week practicing a combination of the exercises you have already learned.

If you have time available only on weekends, try allocating one weekend to each exercise. In this way, you can still complete a chapter every month.

The minimum amount of time that can be spent learning the contents of a chapter is one evening a week and one weekend a month. Less than this will set the practice periods too far apart to create the necessary continuity for learning and mastering the skills.

A more intense and speedy approach to the training would be to cover a chapter every two weekends, thus halving the time of your training. Or, if you want to work in a really intense fashion, you could try covering a chapter every weekend.

Patience

A word of advice, however, before launching into the exercises: be patient with yourself. The first time you try an exercise you may need longer than you think because you are stopping here and there, taking time to understand, and noticing when things seem easy or difficult. This is true of learning any new skill.

If you stay focused on your intention to learn these arts, moving step by step at your own natural speed, you will soon find that you are mastering the principles and developing a smooth, easy style of magical practice.

Commitment

The first step on the road to sexual magic is to make a commitment: to decide that you want to learn these skills and follow the training program.

If you are working with a love partner, you need to make this commitment together.

Regular Practice

It is very important to maintain a steady schedule of practice. If you are working with a partner, arrange to meet every weekend, or at specific times during the week, and encourage each other to stick to your schedule.

If you plan to do most of your training on weekends, I suggest that you try to meet in the middle of the week, on Wednesday evenings. A mid-week get-together lends a sense of continuity to weekend practice and also boosts your energy—even if the meeting is relatively short—which will help you carry the flavor of your new magical world through the working week.

Determining Your Progress

In this training, the first step is practice and the second is enjoyment. When you move beyond discipline and concentration into enjoyment and relaxation, you have mastered the practice and magic is at hand.

How to Practice

Because some of the exercise descriptions are quite long, involving a number of stages, the question arises: How can I do the exercise if I am trying to follow the guidelines in the book?

Here are some suggestions:

- Read the whole book, all the way through, so that you understand the basic principles, then come back to the first exercise and read it slowly and thoroughly, several times.
- If you are working with a partner, you can read the exercise together, or to each other, then you can discuss the steps to see whether you have understood them.

- You may want to make telegraphic, easy-to-read notes of the main stages of the exercise, so that you can glance at them during your practice.

- Put the book aside and enter into the practice, following the steps as you remember them. Don't be too concerned if you miss a step the first time you try a particular exercise. You'll pick it up next time, because you need to practice each exercise several times until you can move through it in an easy, relaxed, and skillful way. This repetition helps you to develop confidence, trust, and mutual cooperation.

- Another way to practice—one that can be fun to experiment with—is to record each exercise on audiotape, following the suggested timing given for the exercise, and then play the tape to yourself as you practice.

Single Practice

Because many exercises in this book can be done alone, you will be able to practice sexual magic even if you do not have a regular partner. In this case, you are both the lover and the beloved. It is a journey within yourself to connect your sexuality with your magical potential. It is a dialogue between you and your inner magician. And it works. Just remember to get a big mirror and lots of good music!

Sexual Preferences

This training is designed for anyone who is attracted to the practice of sexual magic, including heterosexual couples, same-sex couples, and singles. I have designed the whole training with this openness in mind.

Moving Beyond Resistance

There may be moments when, faced with a particular exercise, you find yourself shaking your head and saying "Oh my goodness, I can't possibly do this!" Such reactions are understandable, especially when exploring delicate areas like moving through sexual shame and learning to expand your orgasmic energy in preparation for sexual magic.

The important thing is to go as far as you can, knowing that even the act of reading the text is going to bring new understanding and insights to your sexuality and to your ability to bring magic into your life. It may take several attempts before you succeed in completing a certain exercise. It may take a little while before you say to yourself "I've been waiting all my life to find out about this, and I'm not going to stop now!"

Teachers and Friends

Doubt and fear are teachers and friends, not enemies. They are there to protect you from harm, so do not push beyond your boundaries by being too stubborn about your goals. Identify your discomfort, discover what your fears may be trying to tell you, talk about them, write about them, until such time as you feel ready to move through the barriers into the next level of the practice.

Language

During the training, I use a few foreign words. For example, I refer to the male partner as Shiva and the female partner as Shakti. I call the penis a Vajra and the vagina a Yoni. I will explain what these terms mean later on. My purpose in using such terms is to break out of the limiting mental associations that are conveyed by our normal, familiar, vocabulary.

Magical Journal

In preparing to enter into this training, it is a good idea to create a journal in which to record your experiences. Always keep it handy. It will be like a traveling companion, recording the progress you make, reminding you of your achievements and discoveries, and it will serve as a useful reference guide in the future.

Music and Energy

I recommend that you use music as often as possible during these practices, bringing aliveness, more energy, and a special atmosphere to the magical rituals. You will find some recommended music in the appendix.

Have a wonderful journey.

SEXUAL MAGIC:
My Journey and Yours

You probably already know that sex can be a magical experience, but you may not be aware that magic can be a sexual experience. It's true: magic that is charged with the orgasmic power generated by sexual loving acquires an intensity and potency unequaled by any other method. When you gain mastery over the art of sexual magic, you gain mastery over the most powerful form of magic there is.

Over the last few hundred years, magic has gotten a bad name. It's been shrouded in secrecy and surrounded by all kinds of charlatanism. Its reputation has descended from the spiritual realms of the shamans to the Las Vegas floor show. But sexual magic is not the trick of pulling a rabbit out of a hat, or the fairy-tale "abracadabra" of turning a frog into a handsome prince. Sexual magic is *real* magic: the power to make things happen, the art of harnessing personal and transpersonal sources of subtle energy to give shape, form, and substance to your ideas and visions. More specifically, it is using the power of your sexual energy as a vehicle for your will and imagination, focusing on a personal goal and then transforming your goal into reality by accessing higher states of consciousness.

Sexual magic is magic *par excellence*. In this book you will discover a natural, easy, yet potent method of practicing this apparently mysterious craft, using a source of power that lies very close to home: the primal energy of your own sexuality. This brings the art of magic within the reach of anyone who has the time and enthusiasm to learn a few basic principles and practices:

1. To create a vision of the goal you wish to manifest

2. To turn your vision into a potent symbol and blend it with your expanded sexual energy

3. To bring your symbol up through the seven energy centers in your body, thereby alchemically transforming your energy and your consciousness

4. To connect your symbol with universal fields of energy and intelligence in order to have your vision manifest itself as a reality in your daily life

One of the most important steps on this journey is to open yourself to the full power of your orgasmic potential, understanding that the more sexual energy available to you, the more powerful your magic is going to be. To do this, you must be willing to move beyond the sexual norms established by our culture. For example, most people in the United States experience orgasm as a ten-second event that happens once or twice a week. That's about twenty seconds a week, totaling roughly sixteen minutes a year.

The lover knows much more about absolute good and universal beauty than any logician or theologian, unless the latter, too, be lovers in disguise.

—GEORGE SANTAYANA
The Life of Reason: Reason in Society

Hence, our experience of the power contained in orgasm is fleeting, at best, even though we devote thousands of hours to thinking about our sexual pleasure, worrying about it, day-dreaming about it.

The purpose of this book is to take you into uncharted territory, where collective attitudes about sexuality are transcended. It is a world where you are a pioneer, breaking new ground to discover that your orgasm can be greatly expanded, and that your sexual vitality can become a motor for your magical transformation, helping you to actualize your wishes.

In the following chapters, I offer a complete training in the art of sexual magic. It will give you all the skills you need to ride the intense power of your expanded orgasmic energy as it rises through your body, carrying with it the vision of your desired goal. Passing through the body's seven energy centers, your orgasmic juices and your vision will merge, undergoing a profound alchemical transmutation. It is this inner alchemy, this powerful fusion of your sexual energy and your vision, that allows magic to happen.

RECLAIMING YOUR POWER AS A MAGICIAN

We begin this training by honoring and cultivating the Magician who is already inside you:

> The Magician who can step out of the social currents that normally swirl around you, pushing you haphazardly here and there
>
> The Magician who can decide, right now, to live life consciously, deliberately, through clear intent to manifest what is needed and desired
>
> The Magician who has the courage and determination to say:

From now on, I will be responsible for my life. I take back all the power that I have given away out of a desire to conform, please others, or do the "proper" thing. I no longer delegate my power to parents, to teachers, to priests, to politicians, to opinion polls, or to the media.

I take back the power to determine my own future. In particular, I will be responsible for my own love life. I reclaim the power to honor my sexuality as the deepest source of my creative energy, as a motor for my transformation. I take back the right to use this sexual motor to become a fully orgasmic human being, knowing that this is my door to sexual magic and the key to transforming my entire life.

Thus speaks the magician, the one who embarks on this exciting journey of self-transformation.

HOW I DISCOVERED SEXUAL MAGIC

The key to understanding sexual magic was revealed to me not, as might be expected, during ecstatic lovemaking, but when I was more thoroughly alone than at any other time in my life.

At the suggestion of an Indian Tantric mystic, I was participating with

13

a group of psychologists in an experiment of sensory deprivation. I was left alone in a quiet room in the countryside, blindfolded and with earplugs, for seven days and seven nights. Each day's nutrition consisted of water and a pound of grapes. There was no interaction with anyone else for the whole period.

In this state of isolation, deprived of external stimuli, I soon began to move inward, penetrating through layers and layers of my own mind. In doing so, I began to meet all the various people and voices of my past that had somehow given shape and substance to my personality. I had the feeling that I was going through crowded rooms filled with relatives, friends, teachers, priests, lovers, all standing around at one huge, chaotic cocktail party, spouting contradictory opinions about how I should live my life.

As I passed through these rooms, I tried to maintain a meditative awareness in which I could hear all these people without becoming trapped into remaining with any of them, or into believing what they were saying. In this way I could continue my journey, penetrating deeper and deeper toward the core of myself.

After several days, I arrived at a place of deep stillness and tranquillity. It was a strangely paradoxical sensation, because I could feel a tremendous amount of energy coursing through my body that would normally have made me very active—wanting to run around, make love, throw a party, anything to burn off the excess energy—and yet on this occasion I felt deeply relaxed, in an act of totally letting go, in a state of acceptance and trust.

I had the feeling that I had at last touched the depth of my being. It was a state of consciousness that not only conveyed an authentic sense of self, the essential "me," but also extended far beyond, linking me with the collective consciousness of all living beings, of the planet, and of the universe itself. It was a state at once luminous, ecstatic, universal, and peaceful.

Love is the connecting tissue of the universe.

—BARBARA BRENNAN

I had received glimpses of such states before, in sexual union and in meditation, but now for the first time I noticed a different quality arising. In that space, I began to connect with a source of great wisdom and clarity. I could ask the deepest questions about the meaning and purpose of my life and receive the most profound answers. I could see the steps of my life unfolding over the years ahead and I could see how to change my options, create new, alternative futures, accomplish long-held, heartfelt goals. In short, I felt that I was sitting under *Kalptaru,* the legendary wish-fulfilling tree of Hindu mythology that manifests people's longings.

This was my first real insight into a territory of magical consciousness that could be accessed to find answers, to visualize personal goals clearly, and to heal and transform myself and my relationships with others. It was a place where past and future seemingly collapsed into the present moment, allowing me to act upon the future, creating the best possible outcome for events that had not yet materialized. And the truth of my insight was verified for me when, during the following months and years, the steps of my life unfolded just as I had envisioned them during the seven-day sensory-deprivation experiment.

DEVELOPING A MAGICAL METHOD

Emerging from this profound experience, I understood that the sensory-deprivation experiment had helped me access a state in which I was deeply relaxed and yet at the same time filled with ecstatic energy. It was this unusual combination of deep relaxation and high energy that had created the fertile soil for magic.

My next step was to ask myself the question "Okay, how can I re-create these conditions in my daily life?" Clearly, it was not practical to try to incorporate lengthy periods of sensory deprivation into my crowded schedule. Nor was there any guarantee that such experiments would reproduce the magical state I had experienced on that first occasion.

The solution was obvious. Through the practice of SkyDancing Tantra (see preface) I had already become skilled in the art of transforming sexual energy, refining and purifying it, channeling it up through my body and accessing ecstatic states of consciousness. These states were very similar to the one I had experienced during the sensory-deprivation experiment.

What had been missing, until now, was the insight that this deeply relaxed state could also be a doorway to magic. Ecstasy could offer a blank canvas on which any personal vision could be drawn or painted. It could provide the soil in which to plant seeds of transformation, out of which my personal goals could sprout and grow.

Inspired by this insight, I began to experiment with creating ecstatic sexual states through the practice of SkyDancing Tantra, then planting the seed of a heartfelt wish in the expanded state of consciousness that had been created. Needless to say, I was immensely intrigued by these new experiments. Would they result in sexual magic? Would they hand me the key to opening new doors in my life?

The answer to these questions has been a resounding "yes," and that

The body is the supreme temple of transformation, the place where all the forces of the universe gather to be channeled and transformed into a higher integral order of nature and spirit.

—JEAN HOUSTON

is why I am now able to offer a complete training in sexual magic. But before I speak of the training itself, it will be helpful to look at the relationship between sexuality and magic.

MAGIC AND SEXUALITY: PARALLEL FORCES

Sexuality and magic have many parallels, many similarities. For example, they both involve altered states of consciousness. As far as sexuality is concerned, this is something that almost everyone can understand and experience.

Just pause and think for a moment about your own love life. You may have noticed that when you are making love, enjoying the arousal of sexual sensations, caressing each other, feeling turned on, alive, sensual, moving with your beloved in a rhythmic dance of pleasure, special moments arise in which you are not the same person as you ordinarily know yourself to be.

In the heat of passion, in the depths of orgasmic pleasure, normal ways of thinking and behaving change dramatically. You become so absorbed in sexual pleasure that you step out of time. Past and future disappear. This moment becomes all. You are brought into the now, the present, and this has a profound effect on your whole way of experiencing yourself. The usual traffic of the mind, the ongoing thoughts about what happened yesterday and what might happen tomorrow, simply disappears.

In this deep sexual embrace, the mind stops. Quite literally, you "fuck your brains out." Your consciousness becomes clear, innocent, fresh. Your body becomes relaxed, energized, filled with pleasurable sensations.

Scientific research demonstrates that orgasmic lovemaking releases a wide range of biochemical substances in the brain, including serotonin and endorphins, which create a natural high, causing the mind and body to relax, let go, and take you beyond any pain or tension into a state of profound well-being.

In this state, personal boundaries between you and your lover begin to dissolve. A warm, nourishing energy field surrounds both of you, as if you were bathing together in a deep, mystical pool of love. The psychological, emotional, and energetic barriers that normally keep two people apart become blurred and indistinct. This is one of the greatest joys of love—that,

Sexuality is not what separates us from enlightenment. Sexuality is an inherent quality of our earth experience which merges us into enlightenment!

—CHRIS GRISCOM

at least for a while, you can lose yourself in your beloved; you can become one with another human being.

This merger can open doors to even deeper mysteries. Through deep sexual union, you can feel oneness not only with your beloved but with all things. You can feel a harmony with the whole cosmos; you can fall in tune with the eternal dance of existence.

It is in these moments of expanded consciousness that you can project a vision of your goal, your creation, into the harmonious fabric of the universe that surrounds you. In ecstasy, you come very close to the universal source, the creative womb out of which all things arise. What better moment to make magic?

Study any of the traditions of magic, whether they have their origins in African, Native American, Egyptian, or Judeo-Christian cultures, and you will find that the process begins with entering into a state of trance—through drumming, dancing, chanting, repetition of sounds or words, whirling, special breathing techniques—in order to create an altered state of consciousness in which magic can happen.

In sexual magic, you create a trancelike state of consciousness by learning to relax in states of high sexual arousal, letting your whole body become flooded with orgasmic pleasure. Through special techniques of inner, alchemical transformation, you blend this orgasmic energy with your magical vision, rising to higher and higher levels of consciousness until you are able to release your vision into the cosmos. If done correctly, this alchemical process will manifest your vision in your life in a direct, specific, and powerful way.

MAGIC AND SEXUALITY: CREATIVE FORCES

Sexual energy is nature's ultimate creative force, the power through which it manifests new life. Magic is our own creative force, the power through which we manifest new options in our lives. These two creative forces can meet in sexual union. It is through lovemaking that we can merge with the source of nature's boundless creativity while at the same time exploring our own magical, creative abilities.

The creative energy of sex is not limited to producing children. It finds expression through many different avenues. It is no accident that many great artists and writers, such as Picasso, D. H. Lawrence, Anaïs Nin,

Entering into a state of
trance through drumming
and dancing

Henry Miller, Isadora Duncan, and Leo Tolstoy, were highly sexual beings.
Their art, their creativity, was an expression of their overflowing sexual
energy, and they used it to create a new and different world around them,
enriching our cultures with their masterpieces.

　　This creative ability is available to everyone. If you allow your sexuality full expression, if you go deeply into it, you are going to access your
creative impulses. You are going to want to renew your own life, giving it
some fresh, original expression that has never existed before.

　　You may not instantly be transformed into a world-class poet, musician, or dancer, but you will bring a new creative touch to your actions.
Simple tasks like cooking meals or polishing your car, will take on a joyful

quality, as if they were part of some private, personal celebration. Leisurely pursuits like listening to music, chatting with a friend, or taking a walk become more meaningful and fulfilling, as if they were elegant, artistic brush strokes on your personal canvas. Challenges in your job or profession that once seemed like obstacles in your path to success will bring a sense of exhilaration and triumph as you find creative solutions to them.

If you combine the creative power of your sexuality with a working knowledge of magical ritual and practice, you will find that you are able to manifest the deepest personal visions that lie within your heart. Your sexual energy is so creative, so powerful, that you can use it to make positive changes in every aspect of your life. All it takes is a little understanding, a little magic.

Most people live as if they are going to live forever.
I live as if I am going to die any day.

—NIKOS KAZANTZAKIS
Zorba the Greek

SHAMANS, HIGH PRIESTS, AND MAGICIANS

Before exploring the art of sexual magic, we need to place it in the context of its historical background and understand its roots.

The origins of magic are to be found in shamanic paths that were developed by our native ancestors in order to harness the natural and supernatural forces that surrounded them. To make these powerful forces seem more human and accessible, the shamans often gave them personalities as gods, goddesses, demons, and spirits.

For the shamans, magic and spirituality walked hand in hand. The men and women whose social function was to enter into mystical communion with their gods and goddesses were also the ones who could cast spells, manipulate the physical universe, manifest visions, and harness elemental powers for human advantage.

Although I use the past tense to describe such practices, they are still in widespread use today, not only in the shamanic traditions of tribal communities around the world but also in the Wiccan tradition of witchcraft and natural magic that is widely practiced in Europe, particularly in England, and in the United States.

When primitive shamanism gave way to more elaborate systems of religious worship, the distinction between spirituality and magic continued to be vague and elusive. For example, the yogic disciplines of the Hindu tradition were developed with the intention of helping people attain spiritual enlightenment, but they also conveyed a wide range of supernatural powers, or *siddhis*, including the ability to move between the material world

THE ART OF SEXUAL MAGIC

and the spirit world, to make the future happen in the present, to change shape, to fly—all of it pure magic, but set in a spiritual context.

In the spiritual traditions of Tibet, the famous buddha Padmasambhava and his enlightened consort, Yeshe Tsogyel, are honored to this day as great Tantric mystics. Legend has it that they also performed all kinds of miraculous and magical deeds, subduing rebellious gods and demons, resurrecting corpses, being burned alive and then reappearing floating on a lotus flower in the middle of a river.

In the pre-Christian cultures of Babylon and Egypt, ceremonial magic was an integral part of religious practice. The priests and priestesses used their magical powers to subdue malevolent spirits and also to seek help from friendly spirits through uttering their names—a practice that is still widely used in magic today. Many schools of magic believe that to name a spirit, angel, or deity is to call forth that particular entity and become one with it, thereby temporarily acquiring its attributes and powers.

Today, in our sophisticated, technologically advanced societies we never think of religion as magic. But if a sorcerer or shaman from some ancient tribal culture were to be transported into a modern-day church in America, he might be forgiven for seeing the whole Christian ceremony in magical terms.

"Aha, I see what is happening," he might muse. "A son of an all-powerful father who came from the sky was born without intercourse, walked on water, changed water into wine, fed thousands of people with a few loaves and fishes, magically healed the sick, resurrected the dead, escaped from a sealed cave after crucifixion, and flew back to heaven. Big magic! No wonder people pray to this mighty god. He will bring them good luck!"

PAGAN DEITIES, PAGAN MAGIC

Before the coming of Christianity, the pagan religions of Europe drew their spiritual energy from the vital life force of the earth, from nature. The gods and goddesses of those religions were very human, had quarrels, played political games, made love, enjoyed feasting, and did not expect their earthly subjects to behave much differently from themselves.

Magic was an accepted part of this pagan tradition and was practiced by a wide range of druids, sorcerers, oracles, healers, priests, and wise women. Because the deities they worshiped were symbols of natural forces, and because magic was a means of harnessing those forces, pagan magic and pagan religion went hand in hand.

Magic was the language of the Great Mother, the creator of the universe, whose spiritual influence dominated many cultures in Europe and the Middle East in pre-Greek times. Magic was the gift that descended on the Maenads, the wild Greek women who danced themselves into trance-like abandon in their ecstatic devotion to Dionysius. Magic was second nature to Pan, the horned god, who could tame wild beasts with his music and bestow sexual fertility and good luck on those who sought his help and counsel.

But when the Roman emperors converted to Christianity, a few hundred years after the crucifixion of Jesus, everything began to change. Once the persecuted Christian minority in Rome had the backing of the tyrants and no longer lived in fear of being fed to hungry lions, it was their turn to become the persecutors. The earthy, colorful pantheon of Greco-Roman gods and goddesses was one casualty of this new and vigorous holy crusade. Magic was another.

As Jerome Antoine Romy notes in his *History of Magic,* from the time of Constantine onward, the Christian emperors "showed an increasing tendency to draw no distinction between the crime of magic and the pagan forms of worship." Laws were enacted proscribing both activities, opening the way for the systematic slaughter of unbelievers and sorcerers alike. It was the beginning of a witch hunt that was to continue for centuries.

The world is its own magic.
—Sunri Suzuki

Under the whip of an unforgiving, moralistic, all-male Christian Trinity, women had a particularly hard time, for to demonstrate any gift for healing, psychic intuition, or even rebellious intelligence was to risk condemnation as a witch and a violent death through burning, strangulation, or drowning. It is a sad and terrible fact that in the fifteenth century alone more than thirty thousand women were burned to death as witches and sorcerers in Europe, while more than a million people were condemned by the Inquisition for similar crimes in the years spanning 1575 to 1700.

Magic Gets a Bad Name

In spite of its efforts to establish a monopoly of spiritual authority over its subjects, the Christian church did not attempt to wipe out all forms of magic. Of course, that is what the Inquisition's reign of terror looks like—a campaign to stamp out every kind of magic, sorcery, and witchcraft—but that is not the whole story.

Seen from a wider perspective, the church's main aim was to eradicate *rival forms* of magic. It did not deny the existence of magical powers and magical events but claimed to be the only legitimate source of supernatural power. In other words, it had its own brand of magic and was determined to enforce loyalty to its own rituals, superstitions, miracles, and deities.

The aim of life is to live, and to live means to be aware, joyously, drunkenly, serenely, divinely aware.

—HENRY MILLER

For example, the church encouraged its flock to pray hard and long for good health, good fortune, good harvests, miraculous cures for sickness and disease, victory in battle, and whatever else was urgently required in order to survive life's trials and hazards. Providing one held the right beliefs, worshiped the right deities, and followed the church's commandments, there was every chance that such prayers might be magically answered.

So the early church was never really against the principles of magic. It was only against non-Christian forms and expressions of this ancient craft. In order to make a clear distinction between the two, magical acts endorsed by the church, such as those recorded in the life of Jesus and those attributed to certain saints, came to be known as miracles. Other acts purporting to be supernatural in nature but without church authorization were condemned as magic, or, more virulently, as Black Magic.

Thus magic got a bad reputation. And, to set the seal of social condemnation on non-Christian magic, such acts were frequently attributed to the work of the one great cosmic scapegoat: Satan. They were said to be the work of the Devil.

BLACK MAGIC AND WHITE MAGIC

It is quite likely that there were people in the Middle Ages, as there are today, who worshiped the Devil in an effort to acquire magical powers. But, as Isaac Bonewits points out in his book, *Real Magic,* the charges of "Devil Worship" and "Black Magic" were used by the church authorities primarily as a convenient tool for persecuting and murdering unwanted minority groups.

The accusation of practicing Black Magic was leveled against anyone "not worshiping the Christian God in the Christian Way (which differed according to local politics), especially Jews, heretics, pagans, and anyone who was unpopular, eccentric, held property wanted by the Church, or would not sleep with the Inquisitors." In short, it was a convenient way of getting rid of the church's opponents.

Nowadays, Black Magic refers more specifically to the use of occult powers to dominate and manipulate people against their will, or to cause misfortune to people who, for some reason, have offended or displeased a powerful magician.

Set against such "black" practices is the rival tradition of White Magic, which is commonly seen as devoting itself to good deeds, bringing light, peace, and happiness to the earth, defending good against evil. Given such definitions, it seems natural to support White Magic against Black Magic, for this allows us to assume that there is a right way and a wrong way to use magic, and that we are going to follow the right way. Such assumptions reflect our general cultural tendency, originating in the Judeo-Christian concept of good and evil, to look at life as a duality, as a choice between black and white.

Rather than getting locked into dualistic arguments about right and wrong, good and bad, black and white, I find it more helpful to establish neutral principles and guidelines for individuals who wish to use magic for their personal transformation and growth. I offer three such principles, based on the fact that you, as a magician, embrace three fundamental qualities: You are a seeker, a lover, and a healer:

The Seeker

The true magician explores many magical paths in an open-minded, non-judgmental way, making a pilgrimage of self-discovery that is based on wisdom acquired from personal experience.

The Lover

Love needs to be at the root of all magic, especially sexual magic. When love is present, then respect for yourself, for your partner, and for other people is also present. The desire to control other people is nothing but a substitute for love.

The Healer

The true magician is a healer, someone who knows that it makes no sense to use magic destructively when it can be employed as a wonderfully creative, healing, and transforming force, bringing light, love, and happiness into the lives of those who are touched by it.

When these qualities are recognized as the keys to magical practice, your success and fulfillment are at hand.

THE MEDIEVAL MAGICIANS

Today, magic is more openly practiced and accepted. But during the centuries dominated by the Inquisition, the real magicians—as opposed to the

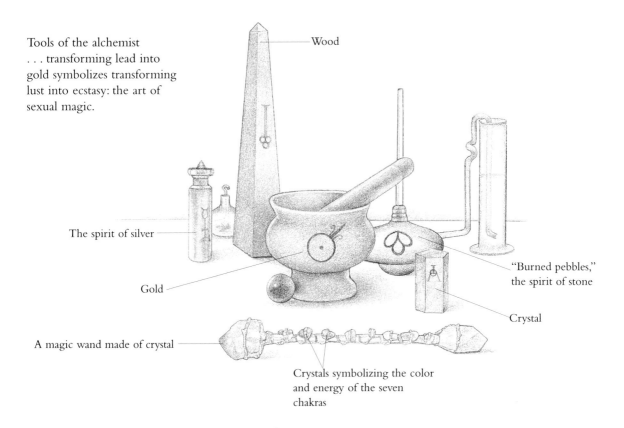

Tools of the alchemist . . . transforming lead into gold symbolizes transforming lust into ecstasy: the art of sexual magic.

Wood

The spirit of silver

Gold

"Burned pebbles," the spirit of stone

Crystal

A magic wand made of crystal

Crystals symbolizing the color and energy of the seven chakras

luckless minority groups who were labeled as such—had to find ways to conceal their craft from the suspicious eyes of prying authorities.

One classic disguise for magic was the medieval alchemist's quest to turn base metal into gold. Alchemists tended to be regarded as harmless eccentrics and were usually able to avoid persecution. After all, if they succeeded in changing lead or iron into precious gold, they would prove useful friends to the local nobility. And if, behind their strange crucibles, experiments, potions, and equations, they were really performing magic, who would ever know?

Here, again, the distinction between mysticism and magic was blurred, for the ranks of alchemists also included spiritual seekers, men and women who were in search of ultimate truths and whose practices took them far beyond anything permitted by Christian ritual and ceremony.

One secret practice was to ignite the fire of sexual energy in the genitals and circulate the energy up the spine to the brain, then down the front of the body, returning the transformed energy to the sexual organs before beginning a new cycle. This circulation was symbolized as Uroborus, the golden serpent that bites its own tail, refining sexual lust into pure spirit. The metaphor of an alchemist's furnace producing a circulating stream of molten metal provided a perfect cover for this practice.

Much of the magic practiced in the Middle Ages was based on the Kabbalah, a tradition rooted in ancient Hebrew texts. A basic tenet of this practice was that God had created the world by means of divine thoughts and words that found expression in sacred numbers and letters. Knowledge of these numbers and letters was believed to bring great power over manifest creation.

Kabbalistic influences continue in magic today and help to explain why so many rituals stress the importance of names, numbers, and the precise repetition of certain phrases or gestures.

SEXUALITY AND RELIGION

These days, it is difficult to imagine a religious practice in which a beautiful woman or man welcomes you at the temple and makes love with you, conveying through sexual union the spirit of the deity you had come to worship.

Yet in the goddess-oriented religions that existed before the spread of patriarchal faiths like Judaism, Christianity, and Islam, that is exactly what happened. Sexuality was embraced as a sacred act. For example, in the worship of Astarte and Ashtoreth in countries of the Middle East, the priestesses, or female custodians of the temple, would freely make love with men who came to worship the goddess. The experience of spiritual union with the goddess would be conveyed through sexual union with her earthly vehicle, the temple priestess, and through this act the goddess was honored as the one who had given to human beings the joy of sacred sexuality.

Even married women could serve in the temple. They could come there on special occasions and, as an act of worship, make love with any man who came by. The children born of such temple unions were respected, regarded as completely legitimate, and lived within the temple precinct, born and raised on holy ground. The priestesses had legal rights, could own property, and generally enjoyed equal status with men. They were multidimensional in their lovemaking skills and could later marry and have husbands. In fact, they were considered to make very good wives.

Similar customs existed in the Cretan culture that preceded the rise of Ancient Greece. It was the priestess who gave access to the "Great Mother," later to become known as Gaia, and who could convey, either through sexual union or through oracular vision, the message of the goddess to those who sought her guidance.

In Europe, the sexual dimension of religious communion was gradually curtailed by the Greco-Roman civilizations—priestesses and seers now had to be untouchable virgins rather than welcoming lovers—and when Christianity arrived on the scene, the sexual aspect of worship was snuffed out altogether. Even popular religious totems like the phallic pillars planted along Roman roadsides had their genitals chiseled off, to be replaced by crosses.

By the way, please note that when I talk about "Christianity" in this context, I am referring to the dogma created several hundred years after Jesus, pieced together in a Roman Empire that was undergoing a puritanical reaction to its own former excesses. This dogma, in my view, bears little or no resemblance to the mystical vision of Jesus himself.

The shift in moral and social values that accompanied the spread of Christianity was dramatic. Women were no longer permitted even to officiate at religious ceremonies, let alone offer themselves as sexual mediums for an incumbent deity. As for sex, it was not only desanctified, it was thoroughly condemned.

It is no secret that the early Christian priesthood despised life on

Earth. Mortal existence was regarded as a period of pain and suffering through which one had to pass, avoiding various temptations in order to qualify for admission to an eternal and far more enjoyable afterlife. Accordingly, all earthly forms of pleasure were either suspect, impure, transient, worthless, or a combination of all four.

Sex, the most available and potentially ecstatic of all earthly pleasures, was reluctantly accepted by the priesthood as a necessary activity for perpetuating the faithful and thereby the faith. But in order to receive the church's grudging blessing, sex had to be stripped of all ecstasy and reduced to the functional business of producing babies. It was not to be enjoyed as recreational pleasure, even by a husband and wife.

Spirituality is not primarily about the altered states of consciousness. It is about embodiment and grounding, or, as some theologians would put it, the incarnation of the spirit. The challenge is not to go out of the body, but to realize that it is the temple of the sacred.

—GEORGE FEUERSTEIN, PH.D.

As a result, sexuality was transformed into a medieval battleground between good and evil, especially in the minds of those unfortunate monks and nuns who, while sincerely striving for purity in thought, word, and deed, found themselves constantly distracted by perfectly natural but theologically undesirable sexual impulses. Those who gave in to these impulses could justify their carnal lust only by protesting that they had been tempted and possessed by the Devil.

Thus, sexuality was joined with magic as one of the chief threats to orthodox religion. In the war between god and the Devil, both sex and magic were delivered as weapons into the hands of the Horned Beast. But a neutral observer in this conflict might see that, beneath the rhetoric, magic was really a rival source of spiritual power that threatened the Church's monopoly, while sex was a rival source of ecstasy.

Miraculously, sex and magic have survived the crusades waged against them. After centuries of being condemned to live in the darkness of superstition, they are slowly beginning to reemerge into the light of understanding and appreciation.

Their struggle is not yet over. Even today, a large segment of our culture continues to condemn both arts, but I like to think the day is not far off when sex and magic will take their place in a more natural and compassionate conception of the universe:

A universe in which all opposing forces are seen as complementaries

A universe in which ecstasy and sexual orgasm are valued as transformative powers.

A universe that is, by its very nature, Tantric.

27

THE TANTRIC ATTITUDE TOWARD SEXUALITY AND MAGIC

It is said that when the god Shiva, the embodiment of pure consciousness, merged in sexual union with the goddess Shakti, the embodiment of pure energy, their Tantric embrace resulted in the creation of the Earth, the stars, the moon, the animals . . . in short, their lovemaking resulted in the creation of the universe itself.

This beautiful metaphor contains an important truth, for in our evolving understanding of this mysterious universe it has become apparent that all energy and movement, and therefore all life, occurs between the attraction of polar opposites.

It is the movement between the negative and positive poles that creates electricity. It is the attraction between the male and the female that creates new life. The dynamics of the universe are dialectical, apparently in conflict, but occurring within a larger context of unity and wholeness. This is the understanding of the Tantra vision.

Tantra, in essence, is the path of acceptance, of including the higher and the lower, the earthly and the spiritual. It allows God and the Devil to hold hands, as two poles, or two aspects, of a single energy. It encourages spiritual seekers to practice sacred sexuality as a means of self-realization. It embraces both sex and magic as valuable tools on the path of transformation.

In addition, Tantra recognizes the female principle as being equal to the male, an important step in the cultivation of sexual energy for magical and spiritual purposes. As Chogyam Trungpa notes in his introduction to *Women of Wisdom,* a fascinating account of six Tibetan female mystics: "Western culture splits the feminine between the prostitute and the madonna. In Tantra we see the emergence of female images which are sexual and spiritual, ecstatic and intelligent, wrathful and peaceful."

In Tibet, where the practice of Tantra reached its greatest heights, certain paths of spiritual development included, after long periods of preparation and purification, ritual sexual union between the teacher and the student. In this Tantric embrace, this merging of two bodies, two hearts, two spirits, secret knowledge would be magically transmitted from the master to the disciple.

Sexual energy would be channeled up the spine through certain forms of breathing and visualization, accessing higher and higher states of consciousness. At the auspicious moment, the secret teaching or knowledge would be transmitted energetically as the two beings merged in ecstatic union.

One aim of such sexual practices was, as Chogyam Trungpa describes it, to "dissolve the sense of inner and outer and plug into a sense of all-pervading energized space which is primordial wisdom and a kind of burning transcendental lust and bliss." Another, more specific, aim was to create a "rainbow body of light" that would endure after the physical body ceased to function. Still another was to access certain types of *dakini* energy—qualities of the divine feminine principle—in order to transcend the limitations of the human ego.

I once had the good fortune to work intensely for several years with a Tantric teacher in sexual magic. He would visit me unexpectedly, in the secret hours of the night, and would invite me to engage in intense breathing exercises that would quickly generate a fiery energy in my body. Then, making love with me in a very slow, conscious way, he would direct me to focus this fiery energy in the area of my heart.

After some time I would begin to have very powerful visions. I

Meditating inside the cave of the inner heart

remember one that was particularly strong, in which I saw myself as a buddha, or spirit being, sitting meditatively and blissfully in a cave. As I watched, the cave became red in color and started to pulsate, so that soon I became aware that my buddha-being was sitting inside the cave of my own heart. A feeling of heartfelt bliss began to expand, along with the size of the cave, growing bigger and bigger until it filled the entire universe. At this point, I was able to radiate love and compassion to all living beings, unconditionally.

Thus I received very special information about what my teacher later described as the "wisdom of the heart." The fact that I had been able to experience this wisdom made his teaching real, existential, instead of mere knowledge.

The emphasis in sexually transmitted Tantric teachings tends to be mystical rather than magical, but the same approach is used for both arts. It is a matter of choice: whether you wish to reside in a state of mystical union with the universe, or whether you wish to harness the universal powers deriving from that union for the purpose of earthly manifestation.

In the Tantric tradition of Tibet, magic and mysticism flourished side by side. It was left to the initiate to decide how to use such powers. It was really a matter of personal integrity and responsibility, an attitude that is as valid today as it was then.

Sexual Magic in the West

The man who introduced modern sexual magic in Europe and the United States was not, contrary to popular belief, the notorious English magician Aleister Crowley. It was an American of mixed racial heritage called Pascal Beverley Randolph.

Randolph, who studied magical traditions in Europe and the Middle East before establishing his own Brotherhood of Eulis in Boston in 1870, created a method of sexual magic that was probably drawn from Tibetan sources.

In his treatise titled *Sex Magic,* Randolph gives detailed instructions for creating the right atmosphere and energies between a man and a woman before moving into a magical ritual of sexual union. Then, during lovemaking, the magician is encouraged to "accentuate your desire to the instant of ejaculation and think energetically of the wished thing before

Love is the hardest thing in the world, the most arduous. It really needs guts to be in love. That's why for thousands of years people have escaped from the world in the name of religion.

—OSHO

and after the act." In other words, Randolph describes how to use the energy of sex to manifest magically a personal goal of desire.

Although he held liberal views about sexual freedom, there is an unmistakable undertone of male chauvinism in Randolph's writings, for he makes it clear that the magical practitioner is a man who uses the woman's energy for his own purposes. For example, he suggests, "As soon as the magical prayer is terminated, dismiss the woman. She must leave without saying a word."

This inability to honor the woman as an equal is, in my opinion, the main reason why initial attempts to practice sexual magic in Western culture have failed. It is the love between a man and a woman, working together as coexplorers, sharing together as intimate partners, that introduces the quality of the heart into sexual union. Without it, sexual magic tends to be used as a way of boosting the individual's sense of power, control, and sexual prowess, often becoming a self-destructive addiction.

Today, women have the opportunity to enjoy sexual magic on the same terms as their male partners. This is important in terms of engaging the sexual energy of both partners, for as long as either one plays a subservient role the creative power of their sexuality cannot be fully tapped, released, and channeled into magic.

Notwithstanding their chauvinistic tendencies, Pascal Randolph and Aleister Crowley both understood a powerful truth: that sexual union provides a wonderful medium in which magic can happen.

Crowley came to this understanding after first passing through various English magical orders that drew on Rosicrucian, Kabbalistic, and Masonic sources. It was not until he joined the Ordo Templis Orientis, founded in Germany, that he started to practice sexual magic on a regular basis. Interestingly enough, the O.T.O. is believed to have acquired its ritual sexual practices from the teachings of Pascal Randolph.

Although not directly concerned with sexual rituals, the Wiccan tradition of natural magic, currently enjoying a revival in Europe and the USA, is helping to bring about a more balanced attitude to the role of men and women in magical ritual. Wiccan is a broad tradition with many different practices, but one of its central themes is a stress on feminine qualities, such as the gifts of intuition and psychic "seeing," as aids to invoking the blessings of the ruling deity of nature, the Great Mother, or Earth Mother.

ACCESSING THE ASTRAL NETWORK

There is another element that plays an important role in the alchemy of sexual magic, which is elusive and therefore not well understood. It is a metaphysical realm that I sometimes call the "creative womb of the cosmos." Through it, we tap into a universal dimension that is infinitely creative, capable of giving birth to new realities. It is a transpersonal space that receives and responds to our visions, our requests for personal change.

Eliphas Levi, one of the most celebrated nineteenth-century authorities on magic, describes this dimension as a "natural and divine" force field, both physical and spiritual, which can receive and respond to human vibrations. He explains: "The existence and employment of this force constitutes the great secret of practical magic . . . this force warms, illuminates, magnetizes, attracts, repels, vivifies, destroys, coagulates, separates, breaks, and conjoins everything under the impetus of powerful wills."

Levi poetically names this magical force the "imagination of Nature." He further asserts that this force is neutral and its use a matter of personal responsibility. He adds: "To understand the use of this force, but never to be obsessed and overcome thereby, is to trample on the serpent's head."

The same force has been described by different magicians in different ways. Machig Lapdron, an enlightened woman in the Tibetan Tantric tradition who was famous for her magical powers, refers to it as the "basic ground" or the "mother principle." Isaac Bonewits lends a more modern flavor to this ancient phenomenon by simply calling it the "Switchboard."

However, even a switchboard sounds a little dated in this age of vast computer networks that can transmit and receive huge amounts of information at lightning speed over great distances. My feeling is that the term *network* can best indicate the nature of this infinite, invisible web that spans the cosmos. And, in order to convey the universal dimension, I would also like to add the word *astral* as an adjective. Hence, I offer the term *Astral Network*.

The existence of an Astral Network defies our commonly accepted ideas about how the universe functions. It is not a mere mechanism, like an oversized clock, ticking away according to rigid laws. Rather it is a complex and continuously vibrating web of gravitational and electromagnetic fields that includes not only all material objects *but space and time as well*. Within these fields, matter is not a permanent and solid affair but interchangeable with energy.

Building on this understanding, pioneering biologist Rupert Shel-

drake offers his concept of morphic fields, in which a universe of fixed laws is replaced by one of habits and tendencies. In Sheldrake's universe, events don't *have* to occur in a certain way. They do so largely because earlier, similar events happened in that way, creating a certain imprint in the cosmic energy fields. As these imprints built on one another, they created a morphic field, an energy pattern, that determines how present events occur and how future events will take place.

Morphic fields are also created by human beings. For example, Tibetan monks have for centuries been chanting certain *mantras*—special

The astral network is a multidimensional web of morphic fields vibrating at different frequencies.

33

sequences of sacred sounds or words—as a way of accessing heightened states of consciousness. One of the best known mantras is *Om Mane Padme Hum,* which uses the imagery of "the jewel in the lotus" to convey a mystical state of consciousness.

When thousands of monks chant this mantra over hundreds of years, a powerful morphic field is established. Today, an individual who chants *Om Mane Padme Hum* in the correct manner is going to resonate with the vibration, or frequency, of that morphic field, thereby greatly enhancing his or her experience of the associated state of consciousness.

Since the dawn of civilization, countless numbers of morphic fields have been created by human beings that vibrate with every type of experience and every state of consciousness—including states of joy, bliss, happiness, and spiritual fulfillment, including the most rewarding and nourishing states of love, material success, and abundance. These morphic fields exist within the greater force-fields of the universe and can respond sympathetically to our desires, providing we know how to project a vision that will resonate with the appropriate field.

One way of looking at the Astral Network is to see it as a multidimensional web of morphic fields, all vibrating at different levels or frequencies, capable of resonating with, and responding to, the visions that we choose to create. Knowing this, we can find ways to create potent, condensed visions that can be projected with great force into the Astral Network.

This is one of the reasons why sexual energy is so important in magic. It is a natural and abundant power source that can magnetize and charge a vision, allowing us to project it into the Astral Network with sufficient strength to create an appropriate and meaningful resonance.

Another way of understanding the Astral Network is offered through the writings of Deepak Chopra, an Indian-born medical doctor who has become one of America's leading advocates of the importance of spirituality and magic, as well as alternative healing techniques for the mind and body.

Offering a new worldview of mind and matter, Chopra states: "In their essential state, our bodies are composed of energy and information, not solid matter. This energy and information is an outcropping of infinite fields of energy and information spanning the universe . . . Although each person seems separate and independent, all of us are connected to patterns of intelligence that govern the whole cosmos. Our bodies are part of a universal body, our minds an aspect of the universal mind."

Before you can reach to the top of a tree and understand the buds and flowers, you will have to go deep to the roots, because the secret lies there. And the deeper the roots go, the higher the tree goes.

—NIETZSCHE

What Chopra calls "patterns of intelligence" and Sheldrake "morphic fields" comprise, in essence, the concept of the Astral Network. I will say more about this network in chapter 6, including insights arising out of Carl Gustav Jung's work on the phenomenon of synchronicity.

If you find the concept of an Astral Network puzzling, don't be too concerned. As in the physics of electricity, you do not need to grasp the scientific principles in order to utilize them. Once you have trained yourself in the art of sexual magic you will experience what it is like to move in harmonious rhythm with life, experiencing how everything seems to fall into place, as if the universe is working in sympathy with your aspirations and desires.

COMMON MAGIC ON THE ASTRAL NETWORK

There is a practice, common among many people in America and Europe, that influences the Astral Network: that of using affirmation as a way of changing one's habits and behavior.

For example, a person who constantly repeats the affirmation "I am ready to receive pleasure" or "I am an orgasmic person" is charging a particular thought-form with energy. When this happens, two separate but related events will probably occur:

1. The affirmation will create a new imprint in this person's subconscious mind, replacing old, unwanted, negative beliefs that have in the past inhibited his or her capacity to receive pleasure or experience orgasm.

2. The affirmation may also resonate with the Astral Network and create an appropriate response, so that events may occur in this person's life that will support the new understanding.

This element of astral support is, in my view, the main reason why many people who experiment with affirmations report surprisingly positive results, especially in the first few days of using the technique, when their enthusiasm and energy are at the optimum. As the days go by, however, their enthusiasm tends to diminish and old habits and beliefs fight to reassert themselves, thereby lessening the impact on the Astral Network.

35

Affirmations are one aspect of a much more widely held idea, namely, that a strong and clear intention is needed if you are going to succeed in making positive changes in your life. This is perfectly true. A clear intent, a clear vision, is crucial to self-transformation, and to influencing the Astral Network.

But there is an important question that most advocates of this idea fail to address, namely, How do you develop a strong intention? With what power? With what energy? The mere understanding that a strong intent is needed does not, by itself, create sufficient energy and drive to effect the desired change.

Some modern magicians advocate the use of emotional pain and pleasure as the best fuel, or power source, for "firing up" an intention to change one's life. To be sure, the pain of being confined to an old, unwanted type of behavior can provide a spur for change. So can the anticipated pleasure of being freed from it. But how many people are able or willing to sustain such feelings over any period of time? Emotional pain and pleasure tend to change rapidly, varying in intensity according to the individual's mood and circumstances. As a result, the "fuel" supply for the intention to change tends to be somewhat irregular.

In my experience, there is simply no power source that can rival orgasmic sexual energy for fueling personal transformation, for this is equivalent to harnessing the creative life force itself. This is the raw energy that, when alchemically refined and transformed, can manifest the new reality you are seeking to create.

REWARDS OF SEXUAL MAGIC

One of the great blessings of sexual magic is that the process of making magic is as delightful as the goal is rewarding. Through learning how to expand sexual pleasure you are reclaiming your orgasmic nature, not just in the sexual context but in all aspects of your life. On the path of sexual magic, each step can be a joy, each exercise can be an adventure in ecstasy.

When you regularly practice sexual magic, following the same ritual with the same partner while holding before you a clear vision of what you wish to manifest, then your vision becomes charged with all the sexual energy that you are generating with your beloved. The more sexual energy you generate together, the more orgasmic you feel, the sweeter your pleasure becomes, and the more powerfully you charge your vision for magical transformation.

By practicing over a period of several days, weeks, or months, you can give new shape and direction to your life. Old, unwanted habits and ways of living are discarded. New possibilities and opportunities are attracted.

Beginning with small matters, experiencing success, then graduating to bigger and more profound changes, you will find that sexual magic can be a powerful tool for self-transformation, manifestation, and fulfillment. The more proficient you become in this art, the more quickly transformation occurs.

For me, one of the most satisfying aspects of leading workshops in sexual magic is to hear the success stories reported by participants afterwards. For example, one couple, Bryan and Nancy, used the technique of sexual magic to fulfill their desire to have a child. Nancy explains:

> We wanted to create a child together, my husband and me. We tried everything possible for two years . . . nothing. Then we started to call the child to us through creating a magical vision. We gave her a name—we wanted a girl—and made different portraits of her that we used as visualizations during our lovemaking. We offered our orgasmic energy to our vision. One full-moon night we did a very beautiful magical ritual and, during lovemaking, visualized that she was entering into my womb. A month later, to my joy and delight, I found out I was pregnant.

Michael, another workshop participant, practiced the art of sexual magic in order to improve his love life. He reports:

> The most important thing for me has been to create a vision of sexual transformation and hold it before me each time I make love with my partner, Wendy. This gives me the ability to be totally present in the sexual exchange, paying more attention to the breathing, the feelings, the sensations. My mind isn't wandering all over the place as it used to. I'm really there, with my partner, each moment. Wendy loves it, because it's what she's always wanted from me, and what I've never been able to give until I started to practice sex magic. It gets better every time we meet. I can actually feel my body becoming a vortex of sexual energy, and I take my vision of transformation into the vortex with me.

Intercourse is not primarily an experience of personal love, but of the gods, which yet happens through the union of two. The partner is no longer felt to be limited to the familiar conscious personality, but has become also the gateway to the infinite mystery of life.

—ELEANOR BERTINE

Stephanie, a paralegal, applied her sexual magic in a material way:

There was a time, a few months ago, when I'd just moved into a new apartment in San Francisco and I had a lot of monthly payments to meet, including my rent and a recently leased car. An assessment of my income confirmed what I already suspected—that I couldn't cover myself.

So I sat down at my new kitchen table and created a blueprint for the coming year: how much I needed to earn, in addition to my existing salary, what my talents were, how I could best apply these skills without killing myself through overwork. Together with Ray, my boyfriend, I drew up a plan, then turned it into a Magical Symbol, which represented my vision of creating enough income to cover my needs.

I drew the symbol on paper, colored it in with a paintbrush, then I turned to Ray and said, "Okay, let's go for it." Over the next weeks and months we practiced sexual magic steadily, holding the vision during our lovemaking. I found that, for me, the most magical time came in the deepest moment of orgasm, when I could just let go of control, and it was in this moment that I would see our Magic Symbol most clearly, as if it was impregnating the deepest layers of my mind.

Somehow this gave me the support and trust I needed to believe that my vision really could work, and it did—I became a real magician. Within about three months the whole plan started to unfold as I'd envisioned it, down to the last dollar and cent.

The congruence between my original vision and my reality was truly remarkable. What was also important was the feeling of empowerment I received through this experiment. I felt it was a turning point in how I looked at myself and what I could do with my life.

It is easy for skeptics to attribute these goal fulfillments to nonmagical causes, including coincidence, ingenuity, hard work, and just plain luck; magic, by nature, cannot be scientifically proven. But the people who experienced these personal successes have no doubt that sexual magic is responsible for their good fortune. And if you practice sexual magic yourself, you will know what they mean.

Now you are ready to start the exercises. Enjoy yourself, practice well, and nourish the creative impulse of the Magician who lives within you.

EMPOWERING YOUR INNER MAGICIAN

Who is the magician? In answer to this fundamental question, imagine yourself standing on the peak of a high mountain, or in a clearing in the deep forest. You stand proudly erect, your body adorned with a long, flowing robe, your forehead decorated with a glittering diamond held in place by a silver band. One of your arms is raised toward the heavens, where an electrical storm is murmuring and flickering in the sky. Your other arm points down toward the earth, to the rich, moist, life-giving soil beneath your feet.

You stand exactly in the middle, poised between heaven and earth, a human conductor for the energy that seeks to flow between these two polarities of nature. You are the alchemist, the one who can invoke and channel the energy that pulsates above you, who can bring it down to earth and, in so doing, give it shape and form in accordance with your will and your intention. You have the power to make manifest that which is not yet visible, to create that which is still unborn, for you have learned the art of working in harmony with the elements that surround you.

Yes, this is you. It is not just your imagination. You are the magician,

The magician, either male or female (or both!), in full ceremonial robes, standing in nature, one arm raised to heaven to bring down heavenly energies and channel them to the earth through the left hand.

and you already have these powers. Just think back a little and you are sure to recall moments when you were aware of magic entering your life, when something happened that was so unexpected and so wonderful that you were transported into a state of consciousness where nothing seemed impossible.

Such moments are not usually planned, nor do you work for them. They come as divine gifts, joyful feelings of expansion and power: an unexpected promotion, a chance encounter with a very special person, a downhill ski run that took your breath away, a gathering of friends that became a celebration of joy and happiness. Often, these special moments come during lovemaking, when your sexual pleasure and your loving heart combine to create an alchemical flood of ecstatic energy flowing through your body. These magical experiences confirm a basic truth: We are all magicians, and we always have been.

In this chapter, you begin the adventure of empowering yourself as a magician. You will be guided through a process of initiation that will confirm your right and your ability to wield magical powers and challenge you to expand beyond previously held ideas about yourself. You will explore the personal qualities and attitudes you need in order to make magic, and you will also be introduced to ritual aspects of this ancient craft.

To those readers who expect to be immediately introduced to juicy, exotic sexual practices that create magical outcomes through orgasmic lovemaking I have to say "Please, wait a little." We are starting this journey not with sexual magic but with learning how to access the magician within ourselves, independently of the sexual experience, so that later on our lovemaking may become truly magical.

In my experience, the real secret of magic lies in creating an alchemical transformation within yourself, changing the way you see life and respond to its challenges. Once this inner transformation has begun, it will be an easy matter to apply your magical powers in the context of sexual magic.

The alchemical process of transmutation of lead into gold is simply a metaphor for the transformation of ourselves into awakened self-mastery. One way this is accomplished is by a deep yearning and a guiding passion for union with the Beloved or our soul.

—ELIZABETH KELLEY

THE QUALITIES OF THE MAGICIAN

As a magician, you are like a painter who holds in his hand a palette filled with many different colors. You are about to create a beautiful painting, and these colors are the raw materials out of which your masterpiece will take shape on the empty canvas before you.

The range of materials at your disposal includes a working knowledge of magical ritual, ceremony, and practice, but, in addition, you need to draw on internal qualities, inner resources that will prove essential to your success.

As I proceed to list these personal resources you may find yourself thinking, "Well, I have this quality, but I don't have that one, so what am I to do?"

You will find that, as you progress through the alchemy of this training, these qualities will be awakened in you, helping you to develop a broad sense of competence in your approach to sexual magic.

Here, then, are some of the main qualities required of a magician:

1. Inventing and Creating

Magic is a creative force. Understanding this, the magician learns how to heal, transform, improve, and enjoy life, how to push beyond the boundaries of any limiting ideas, how to break through any habitual negative attitudes such as tiredness, resignation, or disappointment. You are willing to create your life story anew, pursuing the unknown, welcoming change, inventing new ways to seek love, pleasure, ecstasy.

2. Observing with Awareness

With awareness, you bring the qualities of alertness and intelligence to focus on whatever is happening now, here, in the present moment. For example: "My beloved is angry and speaks harshly to me . . . my chest tightens . . . fear arises and I feel threatened . . . I cover this fear by reacting sharply . . . then I catch myself . . . understanding that we are caught in an old pattern of reacting to each other . . . I point this out and my beloved, too, sees what we are doing . . . we take space, allow things to settle . . . soon, when we are no longer in the grip of our emotions, we can forgive each other and become open to meeting again in a loving and supportive way . . ."

This is awareness. The magician watches everything that happens, inside and out, without judging it as good or bad.

3. Tuning In and Resonating

This is the ability to become one with the vibrations, the moods, the energies, the atmosphere that surrounds us, whether we are alone in the forest or at a lively cocktail party. Tuning in, resonating with the environment, we become sensitive and receptive to nature and to other people. To resonate means to be empty of preconceived ideas, judgments, and feelings, to bring ourselves in a fresh and neutral manner to each new situation. Thus, the magician feels what is really happening.

4. A Willingness to Dis-Identify

The magician knows how to resonate with the environment, but at the same time he or she can dis-identify with it. This seems like a paradox, but it is not.

We have all known moments, especially as children, when we were completely absorbed and identified with whatever we were doing: playing an enjoyable game, splashing happily in a pool of water, eating a delicious fruit . . .

The shaman and the magician also possess this quality, as they become one with nature spirits, with natural energies and powers, but they retain a separate sense of identity, an inner knowing that they are a separate consciousness. Even in ecstasy, they are not lost in the experience.

5. Imagination: Discovering New Possibilities

As magicians, we use our imagination not as compensation for what is missing in life but as a deeply creative impulse to manifest and realize all that we can become. Imagination extends before us as a creative thread, leading us from where we are now to where we want to be. Imagination allows us to wonder "What if I could expand my orgasm from ten seconds to ten minutes? What if I could transform my longing for love into a living, breathing experience of love?"

Imagination gives us a whole new style of magical thinking in which nothing is predefined or predetermined.

6. Living Your Wild Self

As a magician, you have the courage to live your Wild Self, to explore and release your own uninhibited impulses and energies. This freeing of wild energy brings you in touch with the vital power inside you.

Your body is part of the wild animal kingdom. Your instincts, your urges, your sexual drive are also part of this kingdom. The magician knows how to access these powerful energies, releasing and channeling them into creativity and manifestation. With wildness, your zest and enthusiasm for life return, banishing any old, lingering attitudes of dullness or weariness. Like an eagle soaring above craggy cliffs, like a bear charging through the forest, you reclaim the beauty of your own animal aliveness and strength.

7. Staying Centered

Here is an anecdote from my friend Melanie:

> I remember the day Danny, my six-year-old, was running downstairs, stumbled, dropped the glass he was holding, and fell facedown on the broken glass. The other kids were hysterical, Danny was crying. The other adults present were panic-stricken.
>
> I gently picked him up, carrying him to the bathroom, cleaning his cuts, comforting him, loving him, telling him that he would be okay and that we needed to get him to the hospital right away . . . Through it all I felt very calm and collected. I could feel my heart pounding, I knew I was worried sick, but I felt completely capable of doing whatever needed to be done. It had a very calming effect on everyone around me, especially on Danny.

The magician cultivates the art of staying centered, staying relaxed in the center of the cyclone.

8. The Magician as Lover

Sexual magic begins with love. As the magical lover, you are in love with making love. Through love, you can melt and merge with your beloved, tuning in to each other, moving together, allowing your two energies to expand in waves of orgasmic delight. And as a lover you are willing to forgive any mistakes or faults, willing to go beyond resentments toward your partner. When you know how to wipe the slate clean, you can begin anew each time you meet.

The best guarantee of magical success is to have a sense of trust in yourself and in your partner. Trust means that you are connected with your heart, your center of love.

9. *Persevering and Making a Commitment*

When you are clear about your direction as a sexual magician, you are able to move through obstacles and difficulties. For example, you may be involved in a magical ritual, joined in sexual embrace with your partner, holding a magical vision, channeling orgasmic energy, and then suddenly you are overcome by self-doubt, worrying whether anything is happening.

Ordinarily, these are times when you may be tempted to give up, thinking "Oh well, we tried, but it's no good, let's call it a day . . ."

In sexual magic, these are the moments in which to persevere, to whisper words of encouragement to each other, to stay committed to the practice, knowing that your perseverance is going to be rewarded.

THE ART OF THE SEXUAL MAGICIAN

Sexual magic is something that wants to happen to you; it is not a difficult art. The energy pathways and the ecstatic potential already exist within you, and all that is required is a willingness to explore and develop them. Sometimes these pathways reveal themselves without even being evoked.

Love is the only gold.

—TENNYSON
Becket

I remember an incident related to me a couple of years ago by Lester and Allison, two friends of mine who, although curious about sexual magic, had not yet begun to practice it. They were lying naked on a big, shaggy rug in their living room one weekend morning, having just made love, feeling very relaxed and good about themselves.

Lester recalls:

I hadn't come to a climax, but that was okay. I wasn't missing anything. It was just fine to lie there, curled up with Allison, feeling the sun on my body, not needing to do anything.

Then, in a slow, relaxed way, Allison started to play with my penis, which gradually became erect and stiff. Normally, that would be a signal for me to get back into lovemaking, to do something, start heading towards a climax, but somehow the mood was so relaxed I just kept lying there, feeling kind of dreamy and passive, enjoying this unexpected gift.

Allison started using her mouth on me, licking up and down my penis, then taking the head in her mouth and sliding me deeper into her throat. I could feel myself wanting to get tense, wanting to push, wanting to go quickly for my climax out of fear that she might stop before it happened.

But I didn't. The more pleasure I received, the more I challenged myself to stay relaxed and allow things to take their own course.

Allison was moving her mouth in a slow, sensual rhythm. I could feel my orgasm starting to build. Again, I felt an urge to take over, to push for release, to say 'okay, now I'm going to come,' but instead, maybe for the first time, I stayed totally passive.

The orgasm happened by itself, rising like a soft, breaking wave of energy that rippled through my genitals. As I started to come, this rippling feeling suddenly turned into a sharp, very exquisite orgasmic impulse that shot like a bullet all the way up my spine and into the center of my head, where it silently exploded in a burst of soft, white light."

It was such a surprise. I'd read about channeling sexual energy, but I'd never actually investigated it and I certainly didn't expect it to happen by itself, with no conscious effort on my part. So that's how I became interested in Tantra and practicing sexual magic.

Lester's experience shows the natural capability of our bodies to channel sexual energy, especially up the spinal pathway from the sexual organs to the brain. All that we need to do is trust, relax, and say "yes" to this pleasurable and exciting journey.

Sexual magic involves the following steps:

1. Creating and holding a vision of what you wish to accomplish
2. Condensing your vision into a powerful symbol
3. Awakening your orgasmic sexual energy
4. Empowering your symbol with your orgasmic sexual energy
5. Carrying your symbol on a wave of sexual energy up through your body, passing through the seven energy centers, or *chakras*
6. Releasing the symbol, with your orgasmic sexual climax, into the universe, connecting with the Astral Network
7. Allowing a new creation to be manifest in your life

As a sexual magician, you become capable of expanding, directing, and transforming sexual energy. By this I mean playing with your sexual pleasure, with your genitals, with body movements, breathing patterns, imagination, and visualization, gaining mastery over your own sexuality and also over the sexual interaction between you and your love partner.

This expertise develops into a Tantric dance in which you and your lover weave your sexual energy and your magical vision into one creation, one orgasm. Within this orgasmic experience you enter a deep communion with each other, your souls shining, your spirits meeting, enabling you to dedicate your orgasmic energy to a higher goal, to a vision of what you wish to become, to a manifestation of your deepest wishes.

THE IMPORTANCE OF RITUAL

I often tell people who attend my workshops that magical practice without magical ritual isn't really magic at all. Why? Because the act of magic occurs most effectively in an atmosphere that totally supports what you are trying to achieve, and it is ritual that creates this supportive atmosphere.

By ritual I mean a series of symbolic gestures, words, invocations, songs, movements, dances, all of which are intended to call forth the sacred, spiritual dimension of our lives—both outer and inner—in which deep mystical states can be experienced. It is through such rituals that the mind becomes clear, the heart opens, the senses become sharp, and the body tingles with aliveness and expectation.

In sexual magic, ritual serves as a bridge between sexuality and spirituality, between our tangible senses and the intangible mysteries that surround us. Ritual takes raw sexual energy and organizes it into a discipline of delight. Like the geometric arrangements of Eastern sacred *mandalas* and *yantras* (meditative symbols), ritual gives shape and purpose to human energy.

External ritual enhances internal preparedness for magic. In this way, the outer supports the inner. The creation of a Magic Circle, the invocation of certain energies, the wearing of ceremonial clothing, the proximity of power objects near you as you practice—all these can give a tremendous boost to your magical powers.

Later, when you have become a skilled magician, you may find that you have the ability to make magic in any circumstances, under any conditions, but now, while you are learning how to give birth to your latent powers, it is important to let ritual support your efforts.

Everything has its own natural virtues by which everything is the beginning of a marvelous effect, and magic is the art of bringing out these marvelous effects.

—ALBERTUS MAGNUS
Book of Secrets

THE MAGIC CIRCLE

One of the most important rituals for sexual magicians is the creation of the Magic Circle, a circular space that is protected and made sacred through various rituals and invocations, to establish a positive and supportive atmosphere for magic. You will be using the Magic Circle through this book, with every exercise.

By way of introduction, I want to tell you about my very first attempt to make a Magic Circle, an experience that turned out so successfully that it became an inspiration for the complete ceremony described later in this chapter.

I was in love with Keith, a magnetically handsome California businessman, and we had been apart for three months. I was in Los Angeles, writing a book, and Keith was away on a trip to Russia. Knowing that he was about to return, some friends told me they had a little cottage by the sea that I could use for his homecoming. Giving me the key they said, "Here, enjoy a wonderful honeymoon weekend."

I didn't have time to go to the cottage until the last minute. Keith was arriving at four in the afternoon, and I must have arrived at the cottage no more than two hours ahead of him. When I walked into the house I was dismayed to find that it was from another century, cluttered with the strangest furniture and with the kitschiest paintings on the walls. The sole concession to modern living was an ugly plastic sofa in the living room, and the whole house exuded an atmosphere of dust, cobwebs, gloom, and neglect.

I called my friends and exclaimed, "Are you crazy? What kind of place is this?"

They said, "Oh, we forgot to tell you. This was our grandmother's cottage, and she just died two weeks ago. We haven't been there since."

I thought to myself, "Well, thank you very much. Now what am I going to do with these weird vibrations? How can I prepare this place to be a honeymoon love nest for my sweetheart and myself?"

I didn't have time to find another place. Moreover, I'd already given Keith the address of the cottage, so I really had no choice but to try to transform the environment.

Clearly, I couldn't renovate the whole house in two hours, so I decided to focus all my attention on the bedroom. First, I cleaned the room as thoroughly as possible. Then I took the pictures off the walls and removed anything that could remind me of the presence of the grand-

I believe in the flesh and the appetites,
Seeing, hearing, feeling, are miracles, and each part of me is a miracle.
Divine am I inside and out, and I make holy whatever I touch or am touched from,
The scent of these arm-pits aroma finer than prayer,
This head more than churches, bibles, and all the creeds.

—WALT WHITMAN
Song of Myself

mother. (It's not that I had anything against her personally. She may have been a perfectly wonderful woman. It was just very clear that her energy wasn't conducive to a weekend of intimacy and passionate lovemaking.)

I sprayed the room with water mixed with perfumed oils to clear the atmosphere. Then I created my first Magic Circle.

I began by walking three times around the room, circling to the left, a ritual movement designed to remove all negative or unwanted energies. As I did so, I talked with the grandmother, saying "I'm grateful that I have your room, and I thank you for welcoming me here, and now I ask you to leave, to create a clear space for Keith and me to be together."

I'd already opened the door and windows, so now I made sweeping gestures with my hands and arms, intended to send the energy of the grandmother out of the room, together with anything else that was old and past, any lingering emotions, any sense of shame or guilt about things that may have happened there.

Having circled three times to the left, I then made three circles to the right, ringing bells, singing and chanting, looking toward the center of the

The Magic Circle: creates a positive and supportive environment for magic. Included are cloth markers around the mattress, stones, an altar to the east, power objects, and a burning fire.

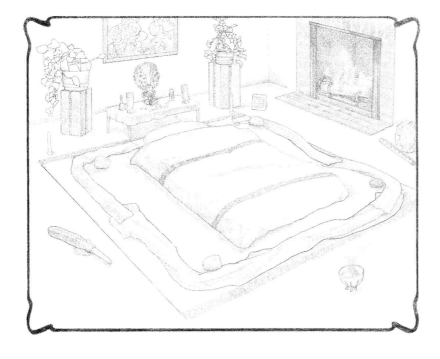

circle and inviting all kinds of positive energies to present themselves, declaring aloud "I invite joy here. May love, trust, sexual delight, great orgasms, and wonderful golden moments fill this room!"

After completing these circles I performed a series of invocations, calling upon the four directions, with their associated elements and qualities:

North, Air, clarity and vision.

South, Water, innocence and love.

West, Earth, vitality and strength.

East, Fire, spirit and passion.

I stood in the middle of the circle and raised my arms to the sky, inviting spirit-guides and teachers to bless our love meeting.

I lowered my arms toward the earth, inviting a sense of wonder and mystery to our coming union.

I invoked the energy of the center, the connection between Shiva and Shakti, the divine archetypes of the male and female principles enshrined within each human being.

It was a sincere and beautiful ceremony, which I virtually made up as I went along, based on my knowledge of magical ritual. By the end I could feel a tangible difference in the room, a feeling of a clean, virgin space that had been blessed with psychic protection and love.

My story has a happy ending. Keith arrived just as I had finished preparing the room and myself—I literally stepped out of the shower as the doorbell rang—and then we spent a delightful weekend together. Indeed, the energies I had invoked seemed to pulsate in the room, supporting and protecting our union.

It could be argued that it would have happened anyway, without the Magic Circle. But the strange thing was that whenever we wandered out of the bedroom, into the kitchen or other parts of the house, we immediately felt adversely affected, as if we had ventured into some dusty attic filled with morbid memories. So I really got to see the power of transforming the energy of a room by creating a Magic Circle.

Later in this chapter I will guide you through a ritual for creating your own Magic Circle. In the meantime, here are some suggestions for what you will need:

1. Stone Markers for Your Magic Circle

Many magicians advise the use of stones to create a Magic Circle. Stones resonate with the energy of the earth, giving a sense of groundedness and solidity. They are also very practical, being readily available, long lasting, easily moved, and easily stored. You can use as few as four, to mark the four principle directions, or you can create a complete circle of stones.

I suggest that you take a walk on the beach, or in the country, in the mountains, forest or desert, and select four round stones that appeal to you—stones that you enjoy holding in your hand—and use these as your markers for north, south, east, and west. You may want to choose a particular stone for each direction, or you may want them to be interchangeable. If you decide to use more than four stones, choose small ones that you can place easily in a ring between the big four.

2. Cloth Markers for Your Magic Circle

An easy and colorful way to mark your circle is to obtain seven long cloths, or scarves, made of silk or cotton. These scarves need to be made of natural fiber so that energy will pass through them. The seven scarves can be of different colors, like the seven colors of the rainbow. Intertwine the scarves so that the colors meet and merge as they weave the shape of the circle.

The symbolism of the seven colors is as follows:

Red: sexual energy

Orange: strength and balance

Yellow: power

Green: love and acceptance

Blue: authenticity of expression

Violet: clarity, intuition, and insight

White: ecstasy and cosmic consciousness

Later you will see that these seven colors correspond to the seven energy centers, or *chakras,* in the human body.

3. An Altar to the East

At the eastern point of your Magic Circle, in the direction of the spirit, you need to create a small altar, which signifies your devotion to self-transformation, your commitment to exploring your higher self. This altar can be made of a low table or box, covered with a beautiful fabric of any color—gold, silver, white, red, black, purple—that feels supportive to your magic.

There is a tradition in some schools of magic to use red-and-white cloth for the altar. White symbolizes the "white eagle" and red, the "red lion"—alchemical metaphors for male semen and female blood. When mixed, they were thought to create a magical elixir that would empower the alchemist's vision and help to manifest his goals and desires.

Because we live in a more enlightened age, there is no need to resort to such elixirs. Nevertheless, the red and white colors serve as useful symbols of male and female energies merging to create sexual magic, and you are welcome to use them to cover your altar.

On the altar you need to place a candle, symbolizing the light of your spirit, which you can light whenever you begin an exercise.

It is helpful to place a crystal on your altar. Crystals are receivers and amplifiers of energy. I remember that I once sat with a holy man in India for a week, keeping a crystal in my lap. When I returned to the U.S. and gave the crystal to a friend to hold, the energy was so strong that he fell off his chair and nearly passed out!

The crystal on your altar will steadily absorb the energy generated by your magical practices and will soon begin to amplify and transmit this same energy, thus helping you to generate a magical atmosphere each time you use your Magic Circle.

Talking about the use of crystals brings me to the subject of power objects, another important aspect of ritual magic.

Find ecstasy within yourself. It is not out there. It is your innermost flowering.
The one you are looking for is you. You are the traveler and you are the destination.
In experiencing the ecstasy of your own being, you have achieved the final goal.

—OSHO

POWER OBJECTS IN MAGICAL RITUAL

What is a power object? It is, quite literally, anything that gives you a sense of power. It is a catalyst that opens doors to your own sources of energy. When you hold a power object in your hands, it is a symbolic gesture that says "Through this object I am connecting with my inner power, with my inner strength, my magical energy."

In my workshops, when we come to this stage of the proceedings, I

The magic altar to the East covered with a white cloth. On it are two cups for white and red elixirs (for her and him); a bell (clear mind); a statue of a couple in divine union; feathers for air and spaciousness; a candle in a lotus holder; the passion of the heart; and other favorite power objects.

like to send the participants off for a leisurely stroll through nature, inviting them to "resonate" with the environment and see what objects attract their attention.

For example, you may come across a raven's feather, a brilliantly colored stone, a white piece of quartz, an antler, a branch, a twig, leaf, clump of moss . . .

Pick it up, close your eyes, weigh it in your hand, and sense whether this object feels good, strong, and helpful to you. Resonate with the object. See if it evokes any images, colors, symbols, feelings, messages. If it does, you have found a power object. Bring it back and place it in your Magic Circle, either on the altar or at some strategic point around the circumference.

In addition to objects found in nature you may feel drawn to crystal balls, magic wands, precious stones, special pictures or statues. When you go shopping for such objects, notice whether your attention is drawn strongly to one special item; whether your vision zeroes in on a particular stone or wand amid a whole display; whether your heart starts beating faster as you

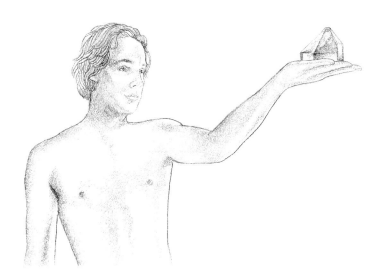

A crystal used as a magical power object for focus and strength

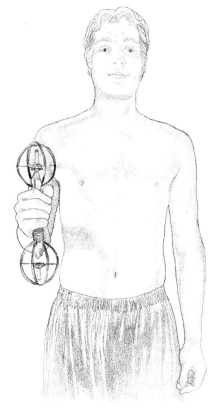

A power object from India reflecting meditation to open the third eye, the center of vision

A magic wand made from copper, silver, and crystal for telepathic transmission

A statue of a Buddha and Dakini in Yab Yum divine magic union. During sexual embrace all seven energy centers are joined. On the feet of Buddha, a crystal ball for clarity and completion.

A magic crystal wand

gaze at a particular crystal ball. These are signs that this object resonates with your energy and can be used to enhance your power, giving you a sense of harmony and support when you look at it or hold it.

Here are some more interesting ways to add symbolism and power to your Magic Circle:

- Paint symbols of the twelve zodiac signs on stone markers around your circle.

- Paint symbols of the sun, moon, stars, lightning, and other natural phenomena on your markers.

- Paint or draw symbols for Mars, Venus, Jupiter, Pluto, or certain auspicious planetary conjunctions on your markers.

- Adorn each marker with a small semiprecious stone such as quartz, citrine, garnet, moss agate, turquoise, rose quartz, amethyst, zircon, jade, or moonstone. All these stones act as catalysts for energy.

- Scatter flowers around the edge of your Magic Circle—to bring beauty, color, and fragrance to your ceremonies. In fact, if you wish, you can make a Magic Circle using only flowers.

Take time to decide which objects and symbols feel good, and don't be afraid to change your mind. If you feel uneasy about a certain object, get rid of it and find something else. Gradually, you will discover the power objects and symbols that enhance your magical rituals. Your main criterion should be that such objects help you to feel powerful and strong, yet at the same time allow you to be comfortable and relaxed.

Here, I must mention Klaus, a German businessman who took one of my trainings in sexual magic and who developed a passion for power objects. During his initiation ceremony as a magician, Klaus received a vision of a "magical toolbox" from which he could pull any tool that he needed, including a "laser beam distributor" for burning through his own negative feelings, a "magneto-come" and an "onlliner" to attract people who were far away whom he wanted to meet, and a "universo-meter" to measure certain aspects of time and space.

Klaus enthusiastically created his "power tools" out of a combination of natural and synthetic materials whenever he was faced with a situation that needed resolution. He swore they were of great assistance in both his private life and his business affairs, and his ingenuity and enthusiasm for

This very place, this is the lotus land, this very body, this is the Buddha.

—THIRD PATRIARCH

55

creating such tools contributed much laughter, playfulness, and positive energy to the group.

Klaus's approach to magic illustrates an important aspect of our work. His tools symbolize the magician's creative ability to find unexpected solutions in any situation. The magician is an inventor, creator, adapter, catalyzer. Even when life seems difficult or problematic, the magician can find unorthodox ways to undo the knot and release the pent-up energy. It is just a matter of widening our perspective and trusting our intuitive feelings.

Sexual Symbols in Magical Ritual

In sexual magic, some of the most important power symbols are those representing the male and female sexual organs.

For the man, a symbol of phallic power is needed, such as the carved wooden phalluses that are often wielded by African shamans. When the man holds this phallic power object in his hand, he is symbolically holding the creative, outgoing force of male energy that he is going to share with the woman. It is a fertility symbol, a magic wand, a representation of male sexual power.

Such a power object can take the form of a phallic-looking crystal, piece of wood, bone, metal, or even a dildo. It can be of any size. The important thing is that the man feel comfortable with this power object as a representation of his sexuality.

For the woman, a symbol of the female sexual organ is needed, representing the essence of female power, also known as *matrix* power. Although matrix symbols have not been as common in Western magical traditions as male symbols, we can now give this craft a timely injection of sexual equality.

When a woman holds a symbol of the female sexual organ in her hands, she is offering the secret of her womb, the juicy, receptive, and creative force of the universe. A power object of this nature can take the form of a seashell, a crystal cluster shaped in the form of a cave, or a piece of smoothly shaped wood that offers an opening in the center, or any object that conveys a sense of female sexuality. Again, the most important thing is that you feel comfortable with this object as a symbol of your feminine force.

For me, the crystal egg has been a powerful symbol of female sexual energy. Following an ancient Taoist teaching, I practiced placing a crystal

If this be magic, let it be an art, lawful as eating.

—SHAKESPEARE
The Winter's Tale

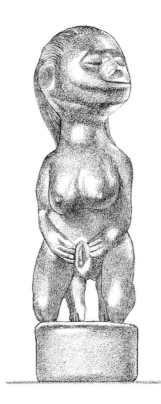

Example of a sexual power object: a statue from Bali of a woman opening her yoni.

egg inside my vagina, contracting and expanding my genital muscles around it for several minutes. This practice not only brought enhanced sensitivity and power to my genitals in lovemaking, it also strongly charged the crystal egg with female energy. Later, I held the egg in my hand while giving public lectures and interviews, and I felt very much empowered by this symbol of female strength.

These two sexual power objects, one representing the phallus, the other the matrix, or female power, should be placed upon the altar.

By the way, all these ritual objects, including the markers for your Magic Circle and your power objects, should be used only for your magical rituals and practices, not for any other purpose. In this way, they will gradually absorb the energy generated by your ceremonies and reflect it back to you, enhancing the magical atmosphere in which you work. Their use for other, more ordinary purposes would dissipate the energy.

Magical Costumes

Did you ever stand in front of the mirror, wearing for the first time a beautiful new garment? Do you remember admiring yourself, loving this graceful, gorgeous image of yourself?

When I was in my early twenties, I remember watching my boyfriend in Paris slip into a stunningly attractive, Renaissance-style shirt that I had given him. He looked so handsome and romantic in the open-necked collar, the billowing sleeves, the loose, hanging folds that revealed the firm muscles of his chest. To me, he was totally divine at that moment, and I could see that it affected him, too, raising his vision of himself to the status of a dashing lover, a daredevil adventurer, a magician.

I had a similar experience myself, when wearing a long, white, flowing debutante dress before my "coming out" ball in Paris. Gazing at myself in the mirror, I felt very proud of how beautiful I looked. I felt like a princess and had a sense of power, love for myself, and optimism about what I could achieve in my life.

It is good to remember such moments when you consider how to create your magical costume. It can be a great gift to yourself to choose the right clothes, the right style, color, and cut that make you look beautiful, give you royal dignity and stature, or convey an air of mystery, smoldering qualities of eroticism, and sexuality.

Your magician's costume has several functions. By discarding your ordinary clothes and putting on special ones you are acknowledging a transition from daily life to a totally different reality, a precious time of magical practice and experience. Changing your clothes invokes a new, expansive, magical way of thinking.

Moreover, if you continue to wear the same garments during your ongoing practices, they will absorb the energy of your magical experiments and resonate with this particular state of consciousness. Soon you will feel yourself entering a magical frame of mind whenever you put on these clothes.

Your chief magical garment could be a beautiful robe, gown, or kimono. Choose any garment that appeals to you, that feels sensual to your touch and endows you with a sense of magic and majesty. Feel free to decorate the robe with magical symbols of your choice, and remember that certain colors have special significance in magic: white for purity, purple for wisdom, red for vitality, black for mystery.

It is important that this garment open easily in front. Many of the

You will use the light of the Goddess to create a new world with futures filled with magic and miracles. You can also use that same light to create a brighter, more joyous reality right now.

—LAZARUS

A sexual, joyful magic-ritual costume inspired
from Balinese and Polynesian traditions

Another magician's costume. Note that they
are "unisex" costumes which can be worn by
men and women.

exercises in this book require physical or sexual contact between you and
your partner, and it is both enjoyable and practical to wear a robe that you
can open easily, suggestively, exposing parts of your body to your beloved
while keeping an air of mystery.

Belts are important in magic, especially those with a strong metal plate made of steel, iron, or copper that covers the abdomen, the balance center, or *hara* point. Similar types of belts were worn by Japanese samurai warriors and Arthurian-style medieval knights, to give a feeling of staying centered and grounded during combat. This support is important when conducting powerful experiments with magic.

In addition to your robe, it is good to have a colorfully patterned piece of cloth that you can wrap around your waist during less-formal occasions. This item is known as a *lungi* in India, and a *pareo* in Hawaii. It makes a graceful unisex costume for both men and women. With jewelry, or with a flower in your hair, this simple garment looks both exotic and erotic. It is a favorite costume for many people who practice Tantra because it is attractive and also easily removed. In Bali, where lungis are common, simple patterns with stark colors are worn by the men, while softer, more flowery styles are preferred by the women.

A third item that I recommend for your magical wardrobe is a sweat-suit, such as you may ordinarily use for jogging, stretching, or dancing. This allows freedom of movement in exercises that require physical activity and is a handy, general-purpose outfit. Choose one made of natural fiber.

These three types of clothing provide you with a complete magical wardrobe. Keep these items together with your ritual objects and symbols, separate from your other clothes, and wear them only for magical practice.

MAGICAL JEWELRY, ORNAMENTS, AND MAKEUP

The classic item of magical jewelry is a diamond, crystal, or precious stone held in place at the "third eye," located slightly above and between your eyebrows, which signifies your connection with your inner, psychic powers. Such jewels magnetize the psychic center of the brain, influencing our powers of insight and concentration. A diamond can symbolize the "diamond mind" of the Tibetan Buddhist tradition, meaning the mirrorlike luminosity of a meditative mind, holding on to nothing yet reflecting everything. Usually, this jewel is set in a gold or silver band that surrounds the head.

Alternatively, magicians use a crown or tiara that is worn on the head, symbolizing the opening of the crown center, or *chakra,* at the top of the head and the connection with heavenly powers.

Jewelry for magic can include charms and symbols such as a large jewel or stone worn over the heart, which confirms the presence of love, acceptance, and trust in yourself. This stone can hang from a gold or silver chain around the neck. An amulet or brooch in the form of a snake, the symbol of wisdom, is considered to be particularly auspicious.

Those of you who are interested in astrology may like to wear a symbol of the element associated with your sign, such as a fire symbol for Leo, Sagittarius, and Aries; a water symbol for Pisces, Cancer, and Scorpio; and so on. In addition, a system has been evolved that assigns certain types of semiprecious stones to each astrological sign. As a general guideline, choose jewelry that feels good on your body and enhances your sense of elegance and power.

The use of cosmetics and makeup is a matter of personal choice. Creative makeup can certainly enhance your transition from daily life to a private realm of mystery and magic. Drawing symbols on your body with body paint can also be a powerful support for magical practice. You can also use makeup and costumes to impersonate a particular deity, such as Venus, Mars, Shiva, Shakti, Kali, etc.

Men, if you feel shy about wearing costumes and jewelry, remember the divine incarnations of Eastern deities, such as Krishna and Rama, who wore splendidly decorated robes and covered their bodies with beautiful ornaments. They also used makeup, especially around the eyes. Men can find it extremely erotic and enticing to dress in this way.

The important thing to remember is that, as a magician, you are using all these external supports to enhance your sense of personal empowerment and the effectiveness of your magic.

Now you are ready to begin the exercises.

EXERCISE: CREATING YOUR MAGIC CIRCLE

Purpose and Benefits

This exercise will create a protected and energized environment in which you can explore sexual magic. You will be using your Magic Circle for every exercise in this training, thus ensuring that all your work takes place within a supportive magical context.

Preparations

- ❧ Gather the materials for your Magic Circle. You can create a Magic Circle out of stones, colored scarves, or some other materials of your choice.

- ❧ You need a cushion on which to sit. If you prefer, it is perfectly okay to use a chair.

- ❧ You need a low table or box for an altar, plus a cloth to cover it. If you sit on a chair, you may wish to create an altar that is high enough to reach easily without having to stoop down.

- ❧ Bring a candle, for use on your altar.

- ❧ Bring your phallic and matrix power objects, together with other items that empower your trust in your own magical abilities.

- ❧ You need a bell, chime, or gong. You can also bring a small drum.

- ❧ You can create your Magic Circle with your love partner, as a joint venture, or you can create it alone.

- ❧ Thoroughly clean the room in which you are going to create your Magic Circle. This will get rid of any "psychic dust" that may be lingering from past incidents that occurred in this space, enhancing the feeling of freshness and aliveness in the room. Then take a shower.

- ❧ For the moment, do not wear your magical robe. This item should be ceremonially worn for the first time in your Magic Circle only when you have completed your initiation as a magician, later in this chapter. Wear something loose and comfortable, such as a sweatsuit, kimono, or wraparound lungi.

- ❧ Allow one hour for this exercise, and make sure that you will not be disturbed.

Practice

STAGE 1: ADOPTING THE MAGICIAN'S POSTURE

Stand in the middle of the space where your Magic Circle will be.

Close your eyes and place your hands over your heart.

Take a few deep, slow breaths, relaxing as you exhale. Give yourself a few moments to forget about any daily concerns and to bring your attention fully here, now, to this moment.

When you feel ready, slowly raise your right arm toward the sky, index finger pointing upward, while letting your left arm fall slowly toward the earth, index finger pointing downward.

Imagine yourself to be at the midpoint between heaven and earth, a channel for energy to flow between the two. This is the position that I call the "Magician's Posture," and I will be referring to it again during this and other exercises.

Visualize energy, in the form of golden light from the sun, or silver light from the moon, raining down from the sky, entering through your right hand, passing through your body, out through your left hand and down into the earth. Do this for a few seconds, understanding that your true purpose as a magician is to establish a connection between the unmanifest and the manifest, between spirit and matter, heaven and earth.

It's time we saw sex as the truly sacred art it is. A deep meditation, a holy communion, and a dance with the force of creation.

—MARCUS ALLEN

STAGE 2: PLACING THE MARKERS

Remain in the Magician's Posture and declare aloud the purpose of this magical exercise:

"I, _____ (your name) am now creating the Magic Circle."

If you are creating the Magic Circle with your beloved, you may want to make a joint declaration:

"We, _____ (both your names) are now creating the Magic Circle."

You may continue to make joint statements with your partner throughout the practice.

Place your four marker stones in the positions of North, South, West, and East.

As you place each marker stone, say aloud:

"I, _____ (your name) dedicate this stone to the North."

"I, _____ (your name) dedicate this stone to the South," and so on.

Move slowly and consciously, so that you can give meaning and significance to each gesture. There is no hurry.

Removing negative influences and calling supportive positive energies into the Magic Circle

When the four marker stones are in place, create the rest of your circle, either with stones, scarves, or materials of your choice.

When you have completed the circle, stand again in the middle, adopt the Magician's Posture, and declare aloud:

"I, _____ (your name) dedicate this Magic Circle to my empowerment as a magician."

STAGE 3: DEDICATING YOUR ALTAR AND POWER OBJECTS

Bring the materials for your altar and construct it at the Eastern point of your circle. Cover the box or table with the cloth you have chosen, then place a candle on your altar. Place a bell or gong on the altar, and, if you wish, a crystal. Put some fresh flowers on the altar. Make it look beautiful.

Stand before your altar. Light your candle. Adopt the Magician's Posture, right hand pointing to the sky, left hand touching the altar, and declare three times:

"I, _____ (your name) dedicate this altar to support my magical powers, as a cornerstone of my magical ceremonies."

Now bring your power objects, including your phallic and matrix symbols, and place them carefully on the altar.

Standing, sitting, or kneeling—whichever is the most comfortable position for you—raise your right hand to the heavens and place your left hand on each object in turn, dedicating it to your empowerment as a magician. For example:

"I, _____ (your name) dedicate this matrix symbol to my empowerment as a magician."

Be sure that you dedicate each power object separately.

STAGE 4: ENERGIZING THE MAGIC CIRCLE

Before moving to the next step, make sure the windows of your room are open. Stand at the eastern point of your circle, pick up your bell or gong from your altar, and begin to walk slowly in a counterclockwise direction around your Magic Circle. If you prefer, you can use a drum for this part of the exercise.

As you walk, imagine that any old, unwanted, or negative energies in the room are being sucked out into space. Ring your bell or gong, beat your drum as you walk, declaring aloud "Let all unwanted energies depart from this place! Let any impatience, anger, sorrow, self-doubt, and other negative thoughts leave the room!"

Circle three times, arriving back at your altar.

Now change direction and circle three times in a clockwise direction. Imagine as you do so that all kinds of positive energies, such as light, joy, love, friendship, sexual pleasure, are being drawn into your Magic Circle. Ring your bell, beat your drum, declaring as you walk "Let wonder, compassion, patience, beauty, harmony be present here, within this circle! Let these energies gather here and sustain our magic!"

STAGE 5: INVOKING THE FOUR ELEMENTS

Move to the center of your Magic Circle.

Face north, ring your gong or beat your drum, and declare:

"I, _____ (your name) call upon the guardian of the north, the power of air, wind, and breath. Come, great eagle, guardian of the skies, open my mind to clarity, vision, and understanding. Give wings to my soul. Teach me lightness of being."

Turn, face south, strike your musical instrument, and declare:

"I, _____ (your name) call upon the guardian of the south, the power of water, ocean, emotion, fluidity, and feeling. Come, great dolphin, guardian of the oceans, open my heart to playfulness, joy, and innocence. Give me courage to let my feelings flow. Teach me depth of being."

Turn, face west, strike your gong or beat your drum, and declare:

"I, _____ (your name) call upon the guardian of the west, the power of Mother Earth, strength, fertility, and groundedness. Come, gentle deer and mighty buffalo, guardians of the hills and mountains, bring health, strength, and sexual vitality to my body. Teach me sacredness of being."

Turn, face east, and declare:

"I, _____ (your name) call the guardian of the east, the power of fire, heat, passion, and spirit. Come, great lion and mighty dragon, guardians of fire, bring me the flames of life and lust, so that my spirit may burn bright, be purified and transformed. Teach me passion of being."

STAGE 6: INVOKING THE ABOVE, THE BELOW, THE CENTER

Remaining in the center of your circle, place your musical instrument on the floor in front of you and adopt the Magician's Posture, your right hand pointing toward heaven, your left hand pointing toward earth.

Looking upward, invoke the powers of your higher self, declaring:

"I, _____ (your name) call upon my teachers, guides, and master healers. May they bring spirit and peace to this Magic Circle."

Looking downward, invoke the powers of your own subconscious mind, declaring:

"I, _____ (your name) welcome intuition, insights, visions, and all hidden aspects of myself that may be revealed to me as I continue on my journey."

Finally, gently place both hands over your heart, close your eyes, and declare:

"I, _____ (your name) call upon Shiva and Shakti, the divine principles of Tantric union, the male and female aspects of my being. May they unite in joy and ecstasy as the two merge into one."

STAGE 7: CONSECRATION: MELTING HUG
Stand for a few minutes in the center, eyes closed, feeling the power and support of this beautiful Magic Circle that you have created. This is the first step on your journey into sexual magic.

If you are with your partner, this is the right moment to consecrate your Magic Circle with love, in the form of a Melting Hug.

Turn and face each other. Come together slowly, opening your arms and embracing each other in a warm, nourishing hug. Gently wrap your

The Heart Salutation is a ritual way of beginning and ending a magic process. It means: "I honor you as an aspect of myself. I honor the divine spirit in you."

arms around your beloved. Without any undue pressure or discomfort, make sure your bodies are touching at the chest, belly, pelvis and thighs.

Breathe together in a relaxed, harmonious, easy way, welcoming and receiving the love of your partner, feeling the warmth of your connection expanding in your chest and spreading through your body. Continue the Melting Hug for as long as you both wish.

When you are ready, gently separate and take a small step back from each other. Look softly into each other's eyes, acknowledging the love that you have exchanged through this Melting Hug. You will be invited to experience the Melting Hug many times in this book.

If you are alone, you can also consecrate your Magic Circle with love. Stand in the center, place your hands over your heart and close your eyes. Breathe slowly and deeply, feeling your heart, acknowledging your love for yourself.

STAGE 8: COMPLETION: HEART SALUTATION
Finish your ceremony with the "Heart Salutation." This is a traditional way of honoring the divine presence that is to be found in every human being.

To do a Heart Salutation with your partner, face each other in the center of your Magic Circle, standing about eighteen inches apart. Bring your hands together in front of your chests, palms pressed lightly together. Bow to your partner, bending forward slowly from the waist, until your foreheads lightly touch.

Pause for a moment in this position, feeling honor and love for this beautiful, divine being with whom you are venturing into sexual magic. Then slowly straighten your back, returning to the upright position.

If you are alone, you can do the closing ceremony by making a Heart Salutation to yourself. Face your altar, press your palms together in front of your chest, and bow forward slowly, acknowledging the divine presence in your own heart.

You will be using the Heart Salutation to close each practice in this book.

Pointers

The ritual I have just described is offered as a general guide to creating a Magic Circle and should not be regarded as rigid or fixed. If you wish to add more elements, or leave some out, that is fine. Trust your own judgment.

Chanting from sacred texts, quoting from epics and dramas, improvising poetry, fashioning gold and silver are great sexual aids.

—*Kama Sutra*

It is not necessary to repeat the whole ritual each time you create a Magic Circle for an exercise. You can simply put out your markers, stones, scarves, altar, and other objects and begin your practice. However, you may wish to create a new ritual from time to time, as your practice of sexual magic deepens and matures.

Keep the materials for your Magic Circle in a special box or drawer where they will not be mixed with other things, so they will retain the energy of your ceremony. Wrap your power objects in silk.

Now that you have created your Magic Circle, you are ready to use it for magical training and practice.

EXERCISE: REMEMBERING TIMES OF MAGIC

Purpose and Benefits

This exercise is to acknowledge that you have experienced moments of magic in your life, thereby overcoming the tendency of the modern, skeptical mind to deny the existence of magic and personal magical powers.

Remembering times of magic deepens the understanding that we are all magicians. We all have a dimension of magic within ourselves that can be awakened and empowered.

In the second stage of this exercise, you are invited to act out your experience of magic for your partner, thereby confirming your magical abilities.

Preparations

- Create your Magic Circle.
- Assemble your power objects.
- Wear something loose and comfortable.
- This exercise is done best with your partner, although it can also be done alone.
- Allow 30–40 minutes for the practice.

Practice

STAGE 1: RECALLING A MOMENT OF MAGIC

Enter your Magic Circle.

Stand in the middle of your circle and adopt the Magician's Posture, right arm raised toward the heavens, left arm pointing downward toward the earth.

Declare aloud the purpose of this exercise:

"I, _____ (your name) will remember times of magic."

Sit or lie comfortably in your Magic Circle. You may wish to use a *zafu,* the traditional meditation cushion, or some other type of bodily support, such as a chair. The main thing is to be comfortable, relaxed, and yet remain alert.

Close your eyes and take a few slow, deep breaths.

Take time to center yourself and focus your attention on this, the present moment, allowing any thoughts and preoccupations to subside. Simply be aware of your own breathing, the rise and fall of your belly.

When you feel ready, let your mind begin to move back over your life, evoking memories. Without any hurry, see if you can remember moments of magic.

These moments may have had nothing to do with anyone else, or they may have happened in the presence of several people. What counts is your own personal impression that this was a magical event.

It could have been something simple, like following an impulse to go to the store and then meeting, seemingly by chance, someone who became very important in your life.

It could have been something dramatic, like miraculously avoiding an accident, or surviving some traumatic event.

It could have been a strong moment of self-affirmation and empowerment, such as participating in a fire walk, walking across a bed of burning coals on naked feet without being burned.

It could have been a feeling of joy and wonder that flooded through you while looking at a beautiful sunset.

It could have been a very intense sensation of passion or blissfulness that arose while making love.

Take time to evoke these incidents. Let your mind leisurely recapture the details of those occasions when magic entered your life.

When you feel that you have covered a wide-enough territory, focus on one situation in which you felt that you were responsible, or partly responsible, for the occurrence of a magical event. Perhaps you insisted on taking a friend to a certain place, where you both had a wonderful experience. Perhaps you had a strong intuition to do something that turned out to be exactly right.

Recall the situation in detail, remembering how it felt to be a magician: the feeling of pride in your accomplishments, the radiance surrounding you, the sense of wonder and creative power, the trust in your own unlimited capacity to create and transform your life.

Even if you did not think of yourself as a magician at the time, give yourself permission now. Own your magical influence on that particular situation, whenever it occurred in your life.

Spend a few minutes enjoying the experience of being a magician.

Then, when you feel complete, sit up and prepare for the second stage with your partner, in which you will act out the magical experience you have just recalled.

STAGE 2: ACTING OUT THE MAGICIAN
Decide with your partner who is A and who is B.

Partner A goes first.

Partner A: Stand in the center of your Magic Circle.

Assume the Magician's Posture, one arm pointing heavenward, the other pointing to the earth, and declare the purpose of this exercise:

"I, _____ (your name) am now acting out the magician."

Let your arms fall to your sides. Close your eyes, take a deep breath down to your belly, relax your shoulders.

Let the memory of your magical moment arise and flood through your body, your senses, once more. Relive the moment again. See all the details. Recall the feelings.

Begin to act out the magical situation you have recalled. Your challenge is to be as theatrical as possible. Walk around your Magic Circle, manifesting the magician you were in that moment.

Feel free to exaggerate. Be generous with yourself, using your colorful imagination and your flair for storytelling to communicate what happened.

Make sure you emphasize your personal role in the affair: how your magical abilities helped to shape the outcome. Don't hesitate to boast—that's what theatrics is all about.

Say "I am a magician because I totally transformed the atmosphere of the meeting and clinched the biggest sale ever."

Or "I am a magician because I alone prevented the accident in which several people might have been badly injured."

Or "I have this magical power because as soon as I walked in the room and looked at this attractive stranger, I knew the date would happen."

Partner B: Listen to Partner A's story with full attention. Be supportive, generous, enthusiastic. Clap, laugh, cheer. Say "Yes, good! You are a great magician! You are a gifted visionary! I believe in you!"

Partner A: When you have finished, sit down.

Partner B: Congratulate Partner A on his or her performance, saying "I acknowledge and honor the magician within you."

Now change roles. Partner A listens while Partner B acts out his or her experience of being a magician.

When both partners have finished, end with a Heart Salutation.

Pointers

You know the exercise has worked when you feel a sense of power in your solar plexus, a bubbling feeling of joy in your heart, and a newfound trust in your creative powers. It is rather like being a child at Christmastime, looking at all the presents beneath the tree and feeling that anything is possible in this magical moment.

If you find yourself telling your story in an ordinary, conversational voice, take courage and jump into theatrics. Dare to be larger than life.

If you cannot think of a real story, make one up, or come onstage and declare loudly, several times, "I enjoy the magic of being me!"

If you do this exercise by yourself, it will be helpful for you to imagine that you are acting out the magician in front of an audience of several hundred people, all of whom are enthralled by your story.

Now you know that magic is available to you, you can enter into a full ceremony of initiation as a magician.

EXERCISE: YOUR INITIATION CEREMONY: BECOMING THE MAGICIAN

Purpose and Benefits

Almost all magical paths require the novice to pass through an initiation ceremony as a way of demonstrating the strength of his or her desire to learn the secret, sacred ways of magic. Such ceremonies weed out the faint-hearted and the merely curious, permitting only brave-hearted souls to go into the unkown, to risk, to dare, to face whatever challenges the members of any particular magical order choose to place in their path.

In this exercise, you symbolically reenact this sacred initiation ceremony, meeting the challenge of the four elements that you must conquer in order to be empowered as a magician. You also encounter your Inner Magician, embracing his or her wisdom and receiving a magical talisman as confirmation that you are now a magician in your own right.

At the conclusion of your initiation ceremony you earn the right to put on your magician's robe for the first time, signifying that you have been admitted into the mysterious world of sexual magic.

Preparations

- You can do this exercise alone or with a partner.
- Create your Magic Circle.
- Bring your magician's robe into the circle, but don't put it on yet.
- Wear loose, comfortable clothing.
- This exercise takes the form of a guided visualization. As previously suggested, you can make an audiotape of the steps and play it back to yourself, or guide each other through it, or work from memory.
- Allow 45 minutes for the exercise.
- Make sure that you are not going to be disturbed; it is important that you complete this initiation ceremony in one session.

Meeting your Inner Magician in your sanctuary

Practice

STAGE 1: COMING TO THE GATE
Enter your Magic Circle.

Stand in the center of your circle, assume the Magician's Posture (left hand pointing to the earth, right hand and arm raised to the sky), and declare the purpose of this exercise:

"I, _____ (your name) am now becoming the magician."

Sit or lie comfortably. Close your eyes and take a few slow, deep, relaxing breaths. With each exhalation, let any concerns or preoccupations dissolve and disappear. Bring your total attention to this moment.

Imagine that you are walking on a path that is taking you into the countryside. It is a beautiful morning and you are walking at an easy yet purposeful pace, enjoying the sun and the breeze that is blowing across the fields.

After a while, you come to a long, high wall that seems to surround some secret place. Directly in front of you there is a gate. On the gate there is a notice that says "This is the Sanctuary of the Magician."

Cautiously, you push on the gate, and it swings wide open. You are the magician. This garden belongs to you. This is your secret sanctuary.

STAGE 2: ENTERING YOUR SANCTUARY
As you walk inside, your eyes are dazzled and delighted by vivid colors of beautiful flowers that dance before you in the breeze—purples, yellows, pinks, and golds. This place is a paradise. Your nostrils are filled with delightful fragrances of perfumed flowers. You hear sweet birdsong in the branches above your head. Nearby, a gentle stream is flowing. Gratefully, you sit on its soft, mossy bank, feeling the yielding turf beneath your body. You pluck a luscious fruit from a nearby tree and take a bite. Its nectarlike juices send your taste buds into rapture. Your skin glows with a golden light from the morning sun. You feel utterly content and at home.

After a while you get up and begin to walk through your sanctuary, feeling the springy earth beneath your feet, watching butterflies dance and weave through the shrubbery, listening to songbirds trilling joyfully. You feel light, relaxed, and happy. You could stay here forever. It is so pleasurable and you feel so at ease, both with your surroundings and inside yourself.

You stroll onward and eventually come to a small lawn where you see two elegant, comfortable chairs facing each other. You sit down in one chair, close your eyes, and wait. You know that someone is coming to meet you.

STAGE 3: MEETING YOUR INNER MAGICIAN

Now you sense the presence of a radiant being, approaching from a distance. Your heart beats stronger with excited anticipation, and you feel a big "yes!" inside as this being comes closer. You can hear the rustle of robes as someone crosses the lawn, and the moment of silence as this person stops and settles gently into the chair that is facing you.

Suddenly you realize: This is my guide, my higher self, who is going to initiate me into my own hidden powers. This is the one I have been looking for. This is the mirror of my own magical self. This is my Inner Magician.

Slowly you open your eyes and gaze at the being who faces you. Perhaps, in the beginning, you see no more than a shining light, a luminous glow—golden, silver, or rainbow colored—but then, as your eyes become accustomed to the radiance, you begin to see the shape and form of this being.

Take your time, allowing the image of your Inner Magician to slowly appear. Let the details emerge gradually and naturally. This is your friend, your ally, the one who is going to help you learn the art of sexual magic.

STAGE 4: CONFRONTING THE CHALLENGE OF THE FOUR ELEMENTS

When the image has become fully clear, your Inner Magician speaks to you, saying:

"I am here to help you through your initiation as a magician. Are you ready to meet the challenge of the four elements?"

You nod your head. Slowly, you both stand up and the Magician takes you by the hand, leading you through the garden to an open space between some trees. It is here that you will be tested, confronting the challenge of the four elements.

Fire The Inner Magician makes a sudden gesture and immediately flames appear all around, growing to form a huge wall of fire in front of you. The heat is so fierce that it almost burns your face.

Your Inner Magician declares: "Step into the fire and surrender to your inner fire, your passion. This is your initiation into courage."

You walk slowly toward the flames, facing the very real possibility that you are going to be burned alive. Then, impulsively, you leap into the flames and, as you do so, you feel an inner fire burst forth within you. Now there is only fire, within and without, purifying you, strengthening you, healing you. This fiery moment seems timeless, eternal, as if you have always been like this, a pure flame of being. . . .

Then, abruptly, you find that you have passed through the fire and the Inner Magician is there to welcome you.

Air   Your Inner Magician makes another gesture and you find yourself standing on a high mountain, on a tiny ledge above a deep abyss. The Magician declares: "Jump through air and discover your inner spaciousness. This is your initiation into freedom."

You take the leap of faith, jumping into the unknown, springing from the ledge and falling headlong through the air. As you do so, you feel a great rush of wind through your body, as if your body is swiftly dissolving into air. You are falling, you are flying, you are disappearing. You have never felt so free, so expanded. This moment of dissolving into air seems to stretch into eternity. . . .

You are gently slowing down, as if held by the strings of a parachute, and you land safely on the earth. Your Inner Magician is awaiting you.

Water   Again, your Inner Magician makes a gesture, and you see that the place on which you stand is surrounded by a wild, vast, fathomless ocean.

The Magician declares: "Dive into the ocean and discover formlessness. Flow and dissolve into the ocean of life. This is your initiation into love."

A huge wave rises up in front of you. You dive into it and are carried away into swirling, endlessly flowing waters that know no shores, no boundaries. As you relax, you feel your body begin to flow and dance with the underwater currents, as if you are becoming liquid, watery, formless. You have never felt so open, so willing to move and change, so in love with the endless flow of life. This moment, too, becomes timeless, eternal. . . .

Then you feel the soft touch of earth beneath your feet, and immediately the waters recede. You are left standing at the mouth of a deep, dark cave.

Your Inner Magician is waiting for you.

Earth   The Inner Magician gestures towards the tunnel ahead and declares: "Sink into the earth. Let your body guide you to the very roots of life. This is your initiation into strength."

You walk into the moist, womblike tunnel, moving into total darkness, unable to see, guided only by your intuition. You can feel the tunnel getting narrower. You can feel the rich, dark earth closing in around you.

As you do so, you feel your body getting heavy, dense, earthlike. You

Don't seek masters. You are the ultimate master magician in your own life.

—*The Book of Magic*

and the earth are becoming one. You have returned to the earth, to the very soil of life itself. You rest in the eternal, primordial, womblike silence of the earth . . .

STAGE 5: RECEIVING THE TALISMAN

Suddenly, as if waking from a dream, you feel a hand touch lightly on your forehead. You open your eyes to find that you are back in your Sanctuary, sitting opposite your Inner Magician, who smiles and says: "I salute your single-pointed desire to know yourself as a magician. Now, I give you this gift. This will be your talisman, your good-luck charm. It symbolizes the invisible, universal intelligence that lies hidden in all things. Hold it whenever you need me, and I will be with you."

Your Inner Magician gives you the talisman, which you hold gratefully in your hands, feeling its potency, power, and light. Perhaps it is a certain kind of stone, crystal, charm, or piece of jewelry. Look at it closely. See what it is.

Gently bring the talisman to your heart and allow it to sink into your chest, becoming part of you.

Thank your Inner Magician. Look silently into the magician's eyes for a moment. Then both of you stand up and come together in a deep embrace.

As you melt into this embrace, feel that you and your Inner Magician are becoming one. Allow this mysterious union to happen. Now you know: your Inner Magician is no one else but you. Now you are fully empowered to go into the world as a magician, capable of accessing the deepest, most creative powers of transformation in order to create success and harmony in your life.

STAGE 6: PUTTING ON YOUR MAGICIAN'S ROBE

Now slowly leave the garden, the sanctuary, and come back into your own world, this world, this room, taking a deep breath, stretching your body like a cat, awakening from this guided visualization.

Sit up. When you are ready, rise and go to your magician's robe. Slowly, and with a sense of dignity and ceremony, bring it to the center of your Magic Circle and put it on. This magical robe is a token of your initiation into magic.

Assume the Magician's Posture and declare three times:

"I, _____ (your name), am the Magician!"

Share the story of your inner journey with your partner. If you are alone, be sure to write it in your journal.

Pointers

When you meet with your Inner Magician, things may happen to you that are not included in the events I have just described. This guided visualization may open the door to unexpected messages and intuitive insights from your subconscious mind, in the same way that dreams can. Allow yourself to receive these teachings.

For example, one of my group participants, Roberta, found herself engaged in a sexual ritual with the god Pan. She describes the encounter as follows:

> When I opened my eyes in the Sanctuary, after being initiated into the four elements, I saw before me the unmistakable image of Pan. He was smiling and stroking a huge, erect penis. At first, I rejected this image and closed my eyes, thinking "This is not the kind of Inner Magician I am looking for."
>
> But then I thought to myself, "Here is a being who accepts his sexuality, his right to pleasure," which is something that has always been difficult for me to allow.
>
> I started to ask myself, "Isn't it about time you gave yourself over to pleasure? How long are you going to wait?" And with that thought I somehow yielded to the image of Pan, wanting to open myself to new experiences. The next moment, I felt Pan's penis stroking gently between my thighs, touching the entrance to my vagina. It was exquisitely pleasurable, but I couldn't accept this sensation for more than a few seconds before closing off once more.
>
> Then, again, I relaxed, giving myself permission to receive, and again I felt his penis stroking against my vagina. This time, after a few moments, he ejaculated strongly, his semen spurting over my belly. His penis was outside, but I could feel the sweet energy entering my body, filling my belly and pelvis, and it felt good.
>
> Again I relaxed, giving in to the pleasure, and this time Pan's penis pushed inside me, filling me. For a moment, I hesitated, but then decided to give myself fully to the experience, and Pan's penis swelled inside and pushed all the way up to my heart. I felt completely possessed by his pulsating penis, and when he came my whole body was filled with his semen, which tingled, glowed, and sparkled in all my limbs. It was a wonderful feeling of surrender to my own pleasure and to the dance of life.
>
> When it was over, I felt I had been initiated into sexual magic, and also that something very healing had happened to me.

We will make love an art, and we will love like artists.

—MARIANNE WILLIAMSON

HEALING SEXUAL WOUNDS

Now that you have been initiated as a magician, the time has come to enter the Magician's Crucible and heal any lingering wounds or energy blocks that may impair the free flow of your orgasmic energy. This important step on the path of sexual magic is dealt with in the following chapter.

PREPARING THE MAGICIAN'S CRUCIBLE
(Healing Sexual Wounds)

Whenever I introduce the art of sexual magic to seminar audiences and workshop participants, I am amazed by the variety of reactions. Some people see it as a mystical pathway leading to higher, more blissful realms of consciousness. Some think of it as a way to create an orgasmic, Tantric communion with their beloved. To some, something dark and dangerous comes to mind. To others, it conjures up images of unlimited power. Still others see it as a powerful method of self-development and personal growth.

In reality, the art of sexual magic can be all these things and more; and it is important to take in the whole picture, to understand the so-called "dark side" of your inner pilgrimage as well as the light.

The sexual magician is one who knows how to enter into expanded states of consciousness through channeling sexual power. But access to these expanded states is almost impossible if we do not, along the way, confront the dark side of ourselves, the "Shadow Side" of our being. It is almost as though, before soaring high into realms of heavenly bliss and enlightenment, we must first descend to the underworld and confront the demons that are hidden in the basement, in the subconscious part of our minds. Otherwise, the moment we let our defenses down, the demons will raise their ugly heads and obstruct our flight to magic and bliss.

To find out exactly who, or what, these demons are, and why they have decided to take up residence in the basement, I invite you to reflect on the way magic is popularly presented in fiction and fantasy—in novels, movies, television, and so on.

A favorite theme of such magical stories concerns the hunger for supernatural power by individuals who fall into the general category of "bad guys." Such people are portrayed as completely ruthless in their efforts to acquire magical powers, as madmen who are gripped by some kind of demented obsession.

The stereotype of this magical subspecies is often presented as a wild-eyed, scraggly-haired megalomaniac with a heavy foreign accent who summons demonic powers in order to destroy a sizable chunk of the civilized world. Meanwhile, bound and gagged in a nearby corner, a helpless and voluptuous maiden awaits her awful fate at the hands of this power-crazed magician.

But wait! All is not lost. Both the world and the maiden are saved by the timely intervention of an extremely handsome and heroic "good guy," or "white magician."

Human love is a noble surrogate for divine love, and the power of love serves as a bridge from the phenomenal world to the spiritual realm.

—JEAN HOUSTON

Cultural archetypes illustrating this kind of struggle between black and white magic include cartoon characters like Batman and his colorful enemies, such as the Joker. But perhaps the best—and easily the most popular—rendition of this mythological battle in recent years has been the *Star Wars* movie trilogy, in which the sinister black magician, Darth Vader, orchestrates the machinations of an Evil Empire and also tries to persuade hero-cum-white-magician Luke Skywalker to join "the dark side of the Force."

To me, the public's fascination with characters like Darth Vader indicates a widespread understanding that one of the principle "demons" lurking in our collective basement is the tendency to misuse power. This tendency is by no means confined to magic. Everyone knows that even the mildest-mannered clerk or secretary, when promoted to office manager, can quickly turn into a "little Hitler," and this seemingly universal trend may lead us to agree with Lord Acton's observation that "all power corrupts and absolute power corrupts absolutely."

That is why many people are afraid of magic, because magic greatly enhances personal power, and power is a double-edged sword. It can be used either creatively or destructively.

Does this mean that any attempt to unlock the secret doors inside ourselves that lead to our magical empowerment must be indefinitely postponed for fear of unleashing all kinds of aggressive, manipulative, and otherwise corrupt behavior?

I think not. Moreover, I feel that it is important for people who are genuinely interested in magic to arrive at a deeper understanding of what lies within themselves, if they are to break free of the restrictions dictated by popular superstition.

The tendency for people to misuse power is not, in itself, a real disease. It is merely a symptom of some deeper problem. In my experience, the desire to be powerful over others is actually a compensation for an inner sense of impotence or inferiority. It is a public demonstration of strength in order to hide underlying feelings of insecurity.

These underlying self-doubts are the real wounds that need to be healed if we are to become wise and powerful magicians. Once we feel good about ourselves, once we learn to love and accept ourselves, there will be no question of abusing our magical powers.

When participants in my sexual magic workshops express fears about unleashing "demons" that might be hidden within them, I guide them through a series of exercises to help them see what is actually the case.

An experience recounted to me by Roland, a young man who was experimenting with magic for the first time, is typical of the results of such self-inquiry:

> When I put aside my prejudices and looked at my deepest motivations and fears, I was surprised to be confronted by a rather sorry-looking individual, covered with bandages, limping along on a crutch, incapable of hurting anyone.
>
> I immediately recognized him. It was me. It was my wounded self, a symbolic representation of all those doubts and fears about myself that I had so carefully hidden from public view for so many years. And when I looked a little closer at this injured being, my heart was deeply touched. I wanted to reach out and help him to heal, because I could see, beneath the bandages, that he was only a small boy, a helpless, wounded child.

Roland's vision of a wounded child is significant because even though our personal demons come in many shapes and sizes—lust for power, anger,

Let your lovemaking be like a prayer between you, your God, and your Beloved. Talk to and make love to your lover as you would to God.

—ELIZABETH KELLEY

violence, greed, fear, sexual obsession, cunningness, deceit, and so on—they all have their roots in negative experiences that occurred during the tender years of childhood. It was then, when we were very young, sensitive, and vulnerable, that the damage happened.

To become a magician, we need to acknowledge these wounds, embrace them, bring to them the light of our understanding and heal them. Only then will our energy resources be available for magic.

In this chapter, you will be working on inner healing so that, having empowered your magician and healed your wounds, you will be ready to move wholeheartedly into the practice of sexual magic.

WOUNDING: THE GOOD NEWS AND THE BAD NEWS

The good news is: We are born ecstatic. As small babies we are open, sensitive, completely in tune with our own emotions. We are orgasmic beings, existing in a state of harmony with ourselves and the universe that surrounds us.

The bad news is: This blissful state doesn't last. Within a few years, we lose touch with our natural ecstasy. We become tense, contracted, fearful. Our energy gets trapped in artificial patterns of behavior that inhibit love, joy, spontaneity. We lose our innocence. We are cast out of our childhood Garden of Eden.

Why does this happen? Robert Hoffman, creator of the Hoffman Quadrinity Process and a pioneer in studying the origins of our negative behavior patterns, states that the basic wound is the same in all of us: a deep feeling of being unlovable. Hoffman says this feeling arises in our childhood, triggered not so much by bad intentions on the part of our parents but by the fact that they have the same problem. They, too, feel unlovable. And if they don't have love, how can they give it to us?

If you look back into your own childhood, you will probably recall many ways in which, as a child, you experienced the pain of not being loved: lack of attention at important moments, criticism that was intended to help but actually hurt, unspoken or overt hostility between your parents, unfavorable comparison with other siblings, and so on.

As a child, you were so sensitive and vulnerable that the pain caused by these incidents was devastating. You absorbed these negative messages like a sponge dropped in water. Even if they were not spoken to you directly, you heard them:

"You will never amount to anything."

"You can't do it right."

"You don't deserve to be loved."

"You mustn't touch yourself down there. If you do, you should be ashamed."

"Your sister did it better."

"Your brother is smarter."

"You're just not good enough."

It happens to all of us. As children, each time we experience the pain of not being loved, not being accepted for who we are, we go into a state of shock. We contract, physically, emotionally, and energetically in an instinctive reflex to stop the pain. Body muscles become tense, emotions shut down, energy flow is inhibited or blocked. Over time, with repeated wounding, this state of contraction becomes chronic and permanent.

Moreover, because we desperately need to be loved by our parents, we find ourselves invalidating our true identity, feeling ashamed of who we are, trying instead to match some image of an "ideal child"—maybe like a big sister or brother, a storybook hero, or the kid next door—in order to win back our parents' love. This further alienates us from ourselves, our emotions, our own natural sources of energy.

BLOCKING THE FLOW OF SEXUAL JUICE

The trials and traumas suffered in our childhood greatly influence our adult behavior, especially in the delicate area of lovemaking. For example, you and your beloved have decided to make love one evening, and at first everything seems to be going beautifully. Your sexual juices are flowing, you are moving deeper and deeper into pleasure, you are both enjoying the love play that is unfolding between you.

Then some small incident occurs—a word, a move or gesture, a distraction in the form of a ringing telephone or a noise in another room—and suddenly all the electric currents of your combined sexual energy are

Through lovingly embracing the full range of our experience—human and divine—we can heal the split that has existed between spirit and form, in ourselves individually and in the whole world.

—SHAKTI GAWAIN

turned off. You are still holding each other, but the power supply has been cut by some unseen hand. Seemingly for the most trivial cause, the whole mood, the whole sexual atmosphere, has abruptly evaporated.

Has this happened to you? If so, you are not alone. This is one of the most common problems mentioned by couples that I work with.

Not knowing why this occurs, many love partners mistakenly blame each other for the disruption, or else feel personally responsible and lapse into self-recrimination. But the truth, to quote Bob Hoffman, is that "no one is to blame." Rather, both partners need to understand that some inner wound has been touched, blocking the energy channels through which their sexual juices were flowing.

Another common manifestation of wounding occurs in the form of negative mental attitudes that tend to arise when two people are about to make love. Such attitudes include fears like "She's not going to be excited," or "I'm not going to turn him on," or "It's not going to be very pleasurable because I'm too tired." All sorts of excuses and scenarios are produced by our minds to justify an underlying fear that "it's not going to work."

Many people feel puzzled and frustrated by the sabotaging nature of this mental mechanism, because they want to make love, they are looking forward to a pleasurable experience, and yet these negative attitudes arise at the very time when sexual anticipation and excitement are beginning to stir. They do not realize that their awakening sexual energy is stirring up deep self-doubts and fears that have been carried inside since childhood.

These sexual blocks and negative attitudes, arising from the Shadow Side of our being, need to be healed if we are to access our full sexual energy and channel it into magic.

A HOLISTIC APPROACH TO MAGIC

There have, of course, been many people who have practiced sexual magic without healing their demons, or their Shadow Side. But if I pause to think about some of the best known sex magicians, such as Pascal Beverly Randolph and Aleister Crowley, it is apparent that they developed their magical powers, in part at least, as a form of compensation for some unresolved inner conflict, or sense of inferiority or inadequacy, that they chose not to look at.

The danger here is that the individual becomes addicted to, or dependent on, the practice of magic to provide a sense of power that he or she otherwise lacks. Indeed, Crowley strongly exhibited symptoms of an addictive personality, both in terms of his sexual indulgences and his reliance on drugs to maintain an expanded state of consciousness. Randolph, on the other hand, collapsed into depression and despair after his magical organization was discredited by negative publicity, a sign that he relied heavily on his status as a magician to compensate for an underlying lack of self-worth.

Rightly practiced, sexual magic embraces a holistic approach to life that integrates body, heart, mind, and spirit, embracing and healing all aspects of the human psyche, so that there is no need to become dependent on magic for a sense of self-worth or well-being. Instead, the journey into sexual magic becomes an authentic gesture of self-transformation.

From this holistic base, sexual magic can open the door to what I call "high sex," the art of learning how to "get high" naturally, rising in consciousness so that your sexuality ultimately becomes an expression of your spirit. In this way, you master the art of bringing the spirit back into sex. This is true magic.

GENDER ROLES: SELF–RAPE AND ANXIETY PERFORMERS

There are many negative experiences linked to learned gender roles that have a strong impact on our ability to experience sexual pleasure and orgasm.

A common negative pattern in women is the tendency to override their own sexual feelings in deference to the man, especially in regard to supporting the man's ego, his sense of virility and male power. This is done at the expense of the woman's own pleasure, which remains a secondary consideration. Inevitably, this is going to disrupt the natural flow of female sexual energy, inhibiting orgasmic pleasure and release.

In my work I find that the most common sources of sexual wounding in women are rape, incest, sexual abuse as a child, or being overpowered by an aggressive boyfriend or husband. But even when a woman is saying "yes" to the sexual act, she may still be creating problems for herself. As a general rule, it can be said that anytime a woman allows herself to be forcefully or prematurely penetrated, ignoring her own timing and pleasure, she is committing a kind of self-rape that is likely to reduce the sensitivity of her genitals and constrict the flow of her sexual energy.

In addition, experiences of difficult childbirth and painful abortion can put the female sexual organs and the whole pelvic area under severe stress, dulling a woman's genital sensitivity and reducing her orgasmic potential.

Lest you be left with the impression that being a man is a breeze compared to the hazards of being a woman, several male authors have in recent years come up with persuasive arguments to the contrary, illustrating the widespread nature of male sexual problems.

Bernie Zilbergeld, in his book, *The New Male Sexuality*, asserts that men in our culture have to walk a perilously thin line if they are to retain their sense of manhood. He explains, "It takes very little—maybe as little as one failure or one sign of weakness—to lose one's place in the charmed circle of men."

Zilbergeld lets the men speak for themselves. One thirty-six-year-old commented:

> I hear girls had it rougher, but you couldn't prove it to me. Growing up was the pits. Incredible pressures all the time. Had to do well at school, had to do well at sports, had to maintain my manly image and couldn't walk away from a fight, and later had to do well with girls and pretend I knew all about sex and was getting it regularly. I often wished the whole world would just go away and leave me alone. I don't know what I would have done, but it couldn't be any worse.

One of the most common forms of male wounding is what Zilbergeld calls the "anxious performers," men who are so worried about "doing it right" that they become very tense, especially around the genitals, concentrating exclusively on performance and thereby cutting themselves off from their true sexual energy. In addition, there is a recent tendency among men to become so concerned about giving their partners an orgasm that they forget about their own pleasure.

THE CRIMINAL AND THE POLICEMAN

Before looking at specific patterns of sexual wounding I would like to relate two stories told by participants in my sexual magic workshops. They will help to illuminate the territory we are going to cover.

The first concerns George, a thirty-seven-year-old journalist, who was experiencing difficulties in his sexual relationship with Lynne, his partner in sexual magic practice. When I introduced the delicate subject of sexual wounding to the group in which he was participating, George, showing great courage, admitted that he had never felt totally involved in his lovemaking. No matter how good it was, somewhere he felt that his energy was being stifled, held back. George said he didn't think it had anything to do with Lynne, but with his own attitudes and upbringing.

Who would give a law to lovers?
Love is unto itself a higher law.
—BOETHIUS
The Consolation of Philosophy

Over the next couple of days, I guided the group through a series of processes designed to awaken powerful energies in the pelvis and circulate this energy through the body, and on the second night George was awakened at about 3:30 A.M. by a vivid dream:

He dreamed that he was struggling with a criminal who lived underground in some kind of sewer. The criminal jumped on him as he was walking along a dimly lit street at night, and they wrestled furiously for a long time. After a while, George thought he'd mastered the criminal and brought him under control, but it wasn't true. As soon as he stopped physically subduing the man, he became dangerous again.

Suddenly George noticed a police officer standing on the far side of the street. He called for help and the officer responded, running toward them. The criminal started to run away and the cop chased him, but then, to George's shock and amazement, the criminal turned around, pulled out a knife, and slit the throat of the police officer, who fell on the sidewalk, dead. At that point, George felt he had no protection whatsoever from the criminal and was wondering what to do when . . . he woke up.

George sat up in bed feeling threatened, frightened. He was breathing hard and sweating. He had a feeling of being split inside.

As the impact of the dream subsided, he lay down again, closed his eyes, and soon became aware of a glowing warmth in his genitals. The warmth was spreading through his pelvis and into his belly, where it created a sharp pain, like an arrow sticking into his stomach. It became so intense that he woke Lynne, his girlfriend. She gently massaged his stomach and after a few minutes the pain subsided, but so, to his regret, did the warm feeling of expanding energy in his genitals.

For George, a revelation happened a few days later when it occurred to him that the criminal and the cop symbolized two conflicting aspects of his sexual energy. The cop represented the strict, puritanical attitudes he had acquired during his fundamentalist religious upbringing in Texas, whereas the criminal symbolized his longing to go deeply and freely into sex.

George's sexual energy had been heavily condemned and repressed in adolescence, which was why the criminal had to live underground. Then it occurred to him that perhaps the criminal wasn't trying to kill him but was struggling with him in an attempt to be accepted and acknowledged as having a right to exist outside the sewers, where he had been forced to live. Seen from this perspective, the death of the police officer wasn't a threat but a liberation, an opportunity to embrace his sexuality—hence the sensation of glowing, warm energy spreading through his pelvis.

I applauded George's new understanding and encouraged him to continue the exercises he had learned during the workshop to help him release and express his sexual energy. The result was a dramatic and lasting improvement in his ability to both give and receive sexual pleasure.

Love and meditation are like two wings. A bird cannot fly with one wing—and for thousands of years man has tried to do exactly that. Either they have chosen love and ignored meditation, or they have chosen meditation and rejected love.

—OSHO

THE HUSBAND AND THE LOVER

My second story concerns Camille, a thirty-one-year-old, French-born beautician and Mark, her American husband. They came to one of my workshops in the aftermath of an intensely emotional situation provoked by the fact that Camille, in spite of her attachment to Mark, had made love with another man while visiting her family in the South of France.

Camille had been thoroughly charmed by Jean-Paul, a friend of her brother, and one night, after a lively dinner party at her parents' house, she had been unable to resist his advances.

"I was having such a good time that evening and it all seemed such harmless fun," Camille recalled. "Jean-Paul skillfully got me away from the others, into my father's study, and in the first moments of a friendly hug had already slid the straps of my dress down from my shoulders and was soon caressing and kissing my breasts. I was half naked before I knew it, and although I made a show of pushing Jean-Paul away I didn't really want him to stop. I was very excited. My body was tingling with the same kind of sexy aliveness that I experienced when Mark and I first started dating.

"I was bit a drunk, but I held off Jean-Paul long enough to ask if he would use a condom. He assured me he would, then picked me up and lay me across my father's oak-paneled desk, sliding me out of the rest of my clothes until I was completely naked. I abandoned all reserve at that moment, wrapping my legs around Jean-Paul's back and even helping him to penetrate me. I don't think he was a particularly considerate lover, but the excitement of the moment—making love in my parents' house with the study door not even locked—more than made up for it."

The next day Camille left for Seattle, and Mark was waiting for her at the airport. At first, she decided not to tell him, but on the drive home she began to feel so heavy-hearted that she tearfully poured out the whole story.

"Incredible feelings of anxiety, shame, and guilt overtook me as I explained what had happened," said Camille. "Mark listened quietly, but I could see that he was very upset. And I felt doubly bad because I realized how much I had missed him and how glad I was to be back."

At first glance, this is not a story about sexual wounding but about a fleeting sexual impulse. However, as I encouraged Camille to explore the issue more deeply, a different picture began to emerge.

Although Camille was in love with Mark, she admitted that she had not felt sexually fulfilled by their lovemaking for more than a year. Most of the time, she felt that their lovemaking took place too quickly, not giving her enough time properly to "take off" into her sexual pleasure before her husband had already "landed."

Yet she felt unable to share her problem with Mark. Instead, she slipped into a habit of trying to please him, saying "yes" to him in the bedroom, hoping that her own desires would eventually be fulfilled. It didn't work. She felt loved by Mark, but sexually she became more and more frustrated.

"It took me awhile to realize that, at the bottom of all this, was my inability to ask Mark for what I wanted," said Camille. "In my childhood, my father was very domineering and also quite violent, so it was practically impossible to make my own wishes, needs, and opinions heard. In fact, I gave up asking him for anything, although I frantically tried to get his approval by doing small, helpful things that I knew he liked.

"My mother offered me a role model of quiet submission, giving way to the man, putting up with anything for the sake of domestic harmony, and so I must have unconsciously adopted the same role when I married Mark."

As she explored further, Camille also realized that she was afraid of Mark, even though he was a gentle, considerate man who rarely lost his temper and was never violent. This, too, she traced back to her wounded relationship with her father.

Once the pattern had been revealed, Camille, with the support of Mark, was able to begin the healing process. She began to express her sexual needs and desires, and this encouraged Mark to also be more communicative with his own needs. Over a period of several weeks, a new level of intimacy opened between them, accompanied by renewed sexual enthusiasm.

They also decided to go through a Tantric ritual that I suggested as a way to heal their sexual wounds, and to express their love and support for each other as magical lovers. This important and challenging healing ritual, which I call the "Shame Buster," will be introduced to you later in this chapter.

The only way to rid yourself of temptation is to yield to it.

—OSCAR WILDE

NEGATIVE PATTERNS IN SEXUAL RELATING

To give you some idea of the links between negative childhood experiences and adult sexual behavior I am going to describe some typical patterns of wounding. These examples by no means exhaust the list—that would take a whole book, perhaps several volumes—but they offer a rough guide for you to explore your own childhood experiences and see how they have affected your adult love life.

1. Not Being Total in Lovemaking

If you were raised in a family environment where one or both of your parents were uncaring or unloving—not being available when you needed them, not taking time to really listen to you, being away at work all day— one resulting behavior can be that you develop an inability to participate totally in the sexual experience.

You may *appear* to be involved in lovemaking, but mentally and emotionally you remain separate. You don't really trust your love partner enough to go any deeper.

Being totally immersed in the pleasurable sensations of lovemaking requires you to melt and merge with your beloved, and this feels threatening, because attempts to open your heart in childhood were rebuffed by a parent who was not available. As a result, you got hurt. Now you feel, "I have to take care of myself. I mustn't get too deeply involved."

2. Denying Your Own Sexual Needs

If, as a child, you experienced rejection by your parents, a feeling of low self-esteem is going to be an inevitable outcome.

Perhaps you were born as a girl, and your mother and father wanted a boy. Or perhaps you were born a boy but still didn't live up to your parents' expectations. In such circumstances, you instinctively feel that your parents are disappointed in you, and you attempt to regain their love by continuously helping, serving and being available.

In later life, this manifests itself as a habit of caring for your love partner while suppressing your own needs and desires, ignoring any feelings of dissatisfaction. In the bedroom, you find yourself saying "It's okay, I don't mind not having an orgasm," or "If you don't want to make love tonight, that's okay with me," when in fact you would love to be carried to the highest peaks of passion and sexual fulfillment.

You find it difficult to receive emotional nourishment from others. Acute feelings of discomfort may arise when you are praised and showered with love.

3. Difficulty in Allowing Touch

If you were brought up in a family where touching was taboo, or heavily restricted, in later life you will probably feel uncomfortable with prolonged sensual contact such as hugging, kissing, showing affection, and remaining physically close to another person.

Once lovemaking has resulted in climax, you tend to break away quickly, or else force yourself to remain close while distancing yourself mentally.

Physical intimacy presents a difficult challenge, making other forms of intimacy also problematic. Your basic defense strategy here is to demonstrate indifference. In effect, you are still saying to the parent: "See, I don't really care if you don't hold me. It doesn't matter to me." This attitude creates a protective shell that can be difficult for your love partner to penetrate.

4. Passive Yet Addicted in Lovemaking

If you grew up in a family environment where you were often made to feel inadequate, you may develop what is known as "passive/addictive" patterns of behavior.

In response to early messages that "you'll never amount to anything, you're no good, you don't even try, you're not worth it," you give up the struggle to succeed and retreat behind a wall of passivity. In the sexual context, you rarely express what you need, or what you want. Your strategy is to let the other person do it all.

At the same time, you are addicted to having more sexual contact, always wanting to repeat the sexual experience because your passivity never allows you to reach full satisfaction. In this way, you can become a sex junky, dependent on your partner for pleasure and yet unwilling to make the first move or "take" pleasure for yourself.

If you listen closely, you may hear a little voice in the back of your mind saying "Was that a signal? Is he going to make a move? Maybe I'll wait until he makes it obvious what he wants."

5. I'm Just Not Good Enough

This is such a common pattern that I call it a "root pattern," out of which scores of different self-destructive behaviors can arise.

As a child, you develop the feeling of "I'm not good enough" in response to the painful experience of being compared negatively with other children, or by failing to match up to some vision of an "ideal child" held out to you by your parents.

In the sexual context, this root pattern manifests itself as an inability to ask for what you want—as illustrated by Camille's story—and also as a fear to go into your own pleasure because of a preconceived notion that it probably won't be much good anyway.

You have a deep sense of resignation, of "Well, this is just the way things are, so there's no point in trying to make them any better. I'm never going to be a very orgasmic person, and that's that."

Your pattern here is to be habitually disappointed, reinforcing a "poor me" or "martyr" approach to life. In your mind, there is always some sexual fiasco lurking around the corner, and the possibility of something going wrong is strongly anticipated.

6. Fear-Oriented Approach to Lovemaking

If you grew up in a family atmosphere of fear and anxiety, where your parents were physically abusive or shouted at each other, you may have difficulty relaxing into the natural flow of lovemaking.

A great deal of your energy will be invested in "doing it right." You can be overactive and overly concerned with technique so that your lovemaking becomes mechanistic and rather rigid. You can also be obsessed about finding out if your partner had an orgasm, ignoring your own need for pleasure.

Even if your lover is bathed in a glow of total satisfaction, you can probably hear yourself worrying "Yes, but maybe it could have been better if I . . ." or "Next time I'll remember to . . ."

You have a general feeling of having to push through obstacles to arrive at sexual satisfaction. Men have a tendency toward premature ejaculation, caught between a strong desire for release and an inability to contain excitement.

UNWORTHINESS: AN OBSTACLE TO SEXUAL MAGIC

Although this chapter is concerned with healing sexual wounds in order to expand your orgasmic power, there is another reason why this healing needs to happen.

One of the biggest stumbling blocks facing those who seek to accomplish their personal goals through magic is an underlying sense of unworthiness—the "root pattern" of not being good enough, which I have just been describing.

This hurdle is of great significance, because, more than anything else, it can prevent magic from happening.

Your desire to transform your life may be strong, your magical rituals and ceremonies may be carried out with perfect precision, but if, underneath it all, you just don't think you deserve what you are trying to manifest, your magical efforts are sure to be sabotaged.

Why? Because the internal split between what you want and what you think you deserve keeps your energy divided. It will prevent you from being able to harness your total energy resources in a single-pointed creative act of manifestation. Part of your energy will be working against your vision, inhibiting your ability to attain your desired goal.

This problem is further complicated by the fact that, most of the time, the part of our psyche that is sabotaging our magical vision—"It's no good; it'll never happen to me"—is concealed from our immediate awareness, hidden within the layers of the subconscious mind.

CREATING THE MAGICIAN'S CRUCIBLE

How do we heal these wounds, these negative patterns? How do we begin to undo the damage that has been inflicted on us since childhood?

The first step is to look honestly and sincerely at the way these negative experiences have affected our lives. We need to see how we have cut ourselves off from our feelings and our sexual energy as a way of protecting ourselves from being hurt. We must gather courage to return to a more spontaneous, natural, authentic expression of who we really are.

This means that we need to validate what we are feeling and to share it, express it, regardless of whether this causes us to feel afraid, ashamed, or embarrassed. We need to take the risk of being vulnerable again, moving through the protective layers of our armoring, no longer willing to play it safe, because we know that to be safe in this context is equivalent to being cut off emotionally and sexually.

Only by taking such risks will we connect with our natural, orgasmic energy sources once more, waking them up, allowing them to heal and to move, helping the joy to come back, reconnecting step-by-step with the ecstatic self that we knew when we first came into this world.

Finally, we need to understand that any form of habitual resistance to love, to sexuality, to pleasure, is really a resistance to our own true nature.

I have called this chapter "Preparing the Magician's Crucible" because its purpose is to help you create an intense, hot, provocative situation—just like a bubbling witch's cauldron or an alchemist's oven—that will help you

The purification process:
healing and transforming
impurities (in the form of
lizards and snakes) into light
and clarity

to reexperience and burn away old patterns of fear, shame, and guilt, freeing your sexual energy for orgasm and magic.

Specifically, it will help you to heal three common areas of wounding that inhibit the flow of your sexual energy:

- The denial of your sexual needs

- The tendency not to be total in lovemaking

- The feeling of not being good enough

This deep, powerful process is presented in the form of three exercises, each building on the preceding one.

First, I guide you into an experience of Anchoring the Magical State, helping you remember that you have already experienced magical moments of ecstasy in your life. This gives you support and courage to look into the Shadow Side of your being.

Second, you are invited to perform Striptease Dancing for Your Partner, daring to show your body in a sexual, erotic way, breaking through any feelings of shame, guilt, and fear associated with being physical and sexual.

Third, in the Shame Buster exercise, you courageously show your genitals to your partner, exposing any negative feelings associated with your sexual organ and receiving healing, honor, and respect.

Through these three exercises you move in progressive stages from the spirit to the body to the genitals, creating an intense, alchemical crucible for magical transformation and healing.

EXERCISE: ANCHORING THE MAGICAL STATE

Purpose and Benefits

This exercise will create a broad base of positive experience from which to explore negative attitudes and feelings.

In certain schools of Tantra it is a basic teaching that seekers on the path of self-transformation should be encouraged to remember ecstatic and magical moments that have already occurred in their lives.

By reliving such experiences, you can generate a state of well-being, a positive and supportive attitude about yourself, opening the possibility for more magical states.

Anchoring a positive past experience in the present gives you the capacity and resources to access it at any time, helping you to feel magical, creative, confident, and good about yourself and your sexuality. In addition, knowing you have the capacity for ecstasy gives you courage to face less-pleasant experiences that may be encountered on the inward journey.

This exercise takes the form of a guided visualization, taking you back in time to a moment when you experienced deep contentment, deep ecstasy, or a moment of great magic in your love life.

You are going to connect with this magical experience in your own way. It may be kinesthetic, through feelings and sensations in your body. It may be visual, through mental pictures and imagination. It may be through thoughts, or tastes, or smells. Whatever way you choose, this will be your way, and it will be the right way.

In love there is no asking or not asking. Love is spontaneous joy.

—ANONYMOUS

Preparations

- ✎ This exercise can be done with your partner or alone.

- ✎ Create your Magic Circle.

- ✎ Wear your magician's robe.

- ✎ One way to proceed is to make an audiotape of the guidelines and then play them back to yourself as you participate.

- ✎ Or you can take turns with your partner, guiding each other.

- ✎ Or you may memorize the guidelines, having read the section two or three times.

- ✎ You may play soft, soothing music in the background.

- ✎ Allow 15–20 minutes for the practice.

Practice

Enter your Magic Circle.

Sit comfortably, close your eyes, and begin to breathe deeply and slowly. With each exhalation, feel you are letting go of any tensions or mental preoccupations.

As your body relaxes, imagine that you are sitting in a movie theater, getting ready to watch a movie. You are in front of a blank screen, which you may experience as a neutral, white, or dark space behind your closed eyes.

Breathing deeply, feeling relaxed, invite your memory to bring forth images, pictures, feelings, thoughts of a special time when you were making love. If you cannot remember such a time, let it be a memory of some other deeply sensual, pleasurable moment that you experienced, either with another person or by yourself.

Let it be a truly magical moment that you thoroughly enjoyed.

Scan through your memories until you find the right one.

As you focus on that sweet memory, let the images of that time appear on the screen in front of you.

Maybe you were naked in a field, by a river? Maybe it was on your honeymoon, or the first time you made love? Maybe you were on vacation by the ocean and unexpectedly fell in love with a charming stranger? Maybe you were making love with your partner, not expecting anything great to happen, when suddenly everything clicked, creating a magical synthesis of orgasmic pleasure?

Connect with a scene that feels particularly meaningful for you.

Take your time. There is no hurry.

Then, as you watch the scene on the screen in front of you, see your-

Breathing deeply and feeling relaxed, invite your memory to bring forth images, feelings, thoughts of a special time when you experienced a loving sensual moment.

self slowly getting up from your seat in the movie theater and walking toward the screen.

See yourself arrive at the screen, step into the screen, and again become an actor in this delightful, erotic drama, participating in it again, now.

As you breathe more deeply, let yourself be totally transported into the experience of this exquisite moment of love.

Let yourself again feel the pleasurable sensations in your body, the quickening of your heartbeat, the blood pumping in your veins, the electrical currents running through your sexual organs, your thighs, your pelvis.

Through your inner eye, see the scene unfold in vivid detail. Take in your surroundings . . . the room, the landscape . . . the time of day, the flickering light of the candle, the color of sheets . . . the beautiful shape of your lover's body.

Allow yourself to connect with the sounds of that moment: the whispered, tender expressions of love . . . the soft moans and sighs . . . Maybe you hear again the music that was played . . . or the sound of the birds by the sea, or in the woods. Hear it all again. It's there for you now. Enjoy it.

Connect with the smells of that moment. The scent of your lover's skin . . . the incense that was burning . . . the country smells as you lay upon the grass, or in the forest.

And the taste. The sweetness of your lover's lips . . . the kisses, the water you drank, the fruits you ate . . . the tang of the sexual juices that you shared. Taste them again.

Embrace all these sensual, sexual sensations and let yourself be fully absorbed by them. Amplify them with deep breathing. Live the magic over again. Live it totally.

When you are ready, when you feel that you have drowned yourself in this remembered experience, take your hand—either left or right—and touch your body in a special place that feels right for you. Maybe you touch your heart, or your belly, or your other hand.

Feel the touch now.

Let this touch be an anchor for the experience you are so vividly recalling.

Let this touch be a way of imprinting the experience in the neurological circuitry of your brain.

Let this touch be a confirmation of the magic that is waiting to be activated inside you.

Let this touch preserve all the sensations of love, so that, whenever you need confirmation that you have known pleasure, ecstasy, magic, you can reawaken this experience with a touch of your hand on this special place.

Then, when you feel ready, take a deep breath, let your hand fall back to your side, and let the images begin to fade. Slowly bring yourself back, coming back to this room, this Magic Circle, opening your eyes.

Shake your head, your body, bringing yourself into the present.

Spend a few minutes sharing with your partner the experience you have just had. Or, if you are alone, write about it in your journal.

End with a Heart Salutation.

Pointers

Now that you have anchored a magical, ecstatic state, you will find you have the ability to access it at will. Whenever you feel the need, take a moment to sit or lie comfortably, touch your body in the same place you touched it before, and allow the experience once again to flood your mind, body, and emotions.

In addition to being used as a preparation for sexual magic rituals, this practice can be very helpful when you feel nervous or unsure of yourself.

I have suggested sharing your magical state with your partner, but this raises a delicate issue: What if the experience you have recalled on your "movie screen" involves someone other than your partner?

Much depends on the nature of your relationship, and on the degree of trust and love that you feel for each other. To cultivate harmony, you may want to decide together, at the beginning of the exercise, that you will focus on magical states you have experienced together. Or, if you do broaden the scope to include experiences with other people, you may wish to do so on the mutual understanding that you would like to bring these magical states into your lovemaking with your present partner.

So long as men can breathe or eyes can see,
So long lives this and this gives life to thee.

—SHAKESPEARE
Sonnet xviii

THREE KEYS TO SUCCESS: BREATHING, MOVEMENT, SOUND

Before moving into the Striptease Dancing and Shame Buster exercises, I would like to give you three keys to success in these challenging practices:

1. Breathing: remember to breathe deeply, all the way down into your belly. This will connect you with your feelings.

2. Movement: let your breathing guide your bodily movements, so that it seems as though your breath carries your movements. This helps to spread sensation and excitement through your body.

3. Sound: use your voice to express what you are feeling. This awakens your vital energy and lets your partner know how you are feeling.

These three keys give you the energy you need to move through any difficulties and generate sexual arousal. I will be encouraging you to use the Three Keys in many of the exercises in this training.

EXERCISE: STRIPTEASE DANCING FOR YOUR PARTNER

Purpose and Benefits

This wonderfully erotic, suggestive, funny, and challenging exercise has four aims:

To help you feel comfortable about showing yourself—your body, your sexuality, your beauty

To generate an energy charge in your body that will stir up strong emotions, excitement, and pleasure

To encourage a sense of being centered and grounded in your body

To develop the art of seduction, artfully revealing hidden aspects of yourself, from the shy maiden to the slut, from the gentleman to the gigolo

The exercise is in two parts: a warm-up dance followed by a strip-tease. In the striptease you give yourself full permission to go wild, to show yourself, to be seductive, playful, naughty, and erotic.

Preparations

- Create your Magic Circle. Make it big, so that you have plenty of room to move around.

- Find an interesting theme for the warm-up dance that precedes your striptease. For example, if you are a woman, you may choose to appear as an exotic temple goddess dancing some sacred ritual. If you are a man, you could be a native shaman dancing to tribal rhythms or a rock star bursting with sex appeal.

- Devise a costume that reflects your chosen theme. One useful tip is to conceal sexy clothes underneath your warm-up dance costume, so that you can make a quick and humorous transition into your striptease.

- Women: for your striptease you can use feather boas, silk underwear, high heels, garters, bold makeup. Don't be afraid to look like a slut—it can put you in exactly the right mood. Men: take it as a challenge to see how sexy you can look. Wrap colorful scarves around your waist, use body paint, wear a G-string, be outrageous.

- Make a mental note not to rush this exercise. Experienced female strippers know that if their clothes come off too quickly, the men tend to lose interest. The same applies when the roles are reversed.

- Choose your music carefully. Sensual sounds with a strong beat or belly-dance, folk, or tribal music will set the right mood.

- Your audience is your partner, so create an area with pillows or a sofa where he or she can recline and watch comfortably.

- Decide in advance which of you will go first. For the purpose of describing this exercise, I will assume that the female partner goes first. I will address her as Shakti and the man as Shiva.

- Allow fifteen to twenty minutes for each partner in this exercise.

Practice

STAGE 1: SHAKTI'S WARM-UP
Shiva, enter the Magic Circle and sit down, preparing to watch the dance. Open your heart to your partner, feeling a sense of excitement at seeing her in a new role: as the seductress.

Shakti, when you are ready, enter the Magic Circle and begin your warm-up dance. Start slowly, with your eyes closed at first, so that you can connect with your inner sensations. Take your time. Flow with the music.

Move your body gracefully. Allow yourself to *become* your body.

If you feel nervous or hesitant, focus your awareness on your lower belly. Let your movements come from this region, which is the balance point of your whole body. Dance from your belly. Move from your belly.

Create a rhythmic movement that steadily increases in power and

Shakti, allow the sensuousness of your body to be expressed in a dance, a striptease . . .

105

intensity. Using the three keys that I have just mentioned, let your breathing carry your movements, amplifying your physical sensations. Make sounds—sigh, moan, or sing.

Gradually let the rhythm take you over completely. Become wild, passionate, abandoned. Release yourself into your dance, charging your body with energy.

STAGE 2: SHAKTI'S STRIPTEASE

Shakti, when you feel ready, allow your dance to become erotic, sexual. This can happen gradually or suddenly, depending on what feels right for you.

Feel the sensuousness of your body as it moves to the music, letting yourself be seduced into a mood of sexual anticipation. Let your hands gently caress your body through your clothing. Feel the softness of the fabric on your body. Feel the warmth in your belly, in your sex.

Open your eyes and look at your partner, as he watches you. You may feel fear in the pit of your stomach. Allow this contained excitement to be part of the game. Dance your way through it. Remember to breathe deeply through your mouth and let your breathing carry your movements.

As you get into the mood, begin to remove your clothing, piece by piece. Touch yourself erotically as you do so, sliding the zipper slowly down your dress, wriggling your buttocks out of your skirt or pants.

Trace your fingers lightly over your skin as you peel off each garment. Slowly undo your stockings, sliding them down your legs, throwing them playfully to your partner.

Feel the delicious sensation of becoming naked in front of another person. Allow any sense of shyness, shame, or self-doubt that may arise. Don't try to hide it. Make it part of your act. Enjoy the thrill of exposure, indulging what has been condemned and forbidden.

Yes, maybe you doubt whether your body is perfect enough to be so daringly revealed, but it's not society's notions about fashionable figures that count here. It's your willingness to love and accept yourself as you are, and to express it.

Stay in touch with your sexual feelings.

Caress yourself. Cup your naked breasts with your hands, lifting them and showing them, squeezing the nipples with just the right pressure to send tingles of sexual electricity through your body. Reach around behind you and slide your hands down the small of your back and over your buttocks.

Play with a long silk scarf, snaking it over your naked body, between your legs . . .

It doesn't matter what anybody else is thinking. You are more important. For once, give yourself permission to be totally shameless. What counts is your pleasure. Display it now. Show it now.

Peel off your last remaining garments. Slide your silk panties down over your legs and feet. Be totally naked.

Sink down to the floor and move around like a sensuous snake, or a like woman writhing in ecstasy, possessed by an orgasmic trance. Touch yourself. Love yourself. This is your moment to break all the rules.

Shiva, be an enthusiastic and supportive audience for Shakti. Clap your hands and shout, "Yes, go for it! You're beautiful! I love you!" Help Shakti break through any layers of embarrassment, guilt, fear, or shame that may be triggered by this exercise.

Shakti, when the music dies away and the striptease is over, remain quiet, with your eyes closed for a minute or two, one hand resting on your heart, the other on your sex.

Shiva, when it feels right to do so, go to Shakti and reward her courage with a hug. Tell her what you liked about her dance: "I loved the sexy way you slid out of your dress . . . it really turned me on when you played with the scarf . . ." and so on. Be generous.

Take a break, then change roles.

STAGE 3: SHIVA'S WARM-UP

Shakti, enter the Magic Circle and sit down and prepare to watch Shiva's dance. Open your heart to your partner, feeling a sense of excitement at seeing him in a new way.

Shiva, put on your music, enter the Magic Circle and begin your dance. You may be a shaman, a medicine man, or witch doctor, involved in some kind of trance dance. You may be a powerful magician, performing a ritual invocation through dance and movement.

You may want to close your eyes at first, as you tune in to your body. Stamp your feet flat on the floor, knees bent, to give yourself a strong sense of being earthy and grounded.

Let your awareness be focused in your belly. This will give you a feeling of power and centeredness.

Raise your arms aloft and look toward the heavens, invoking the powers you need for your dance, but stay rooted in the earth, through your feet.

Fear is our greatest killer. It keeps us from love and hardens the heart.

—CHRIS GRISCOM

Let the rhythm of your dancing intensify and grow stronger. Use the three keys of breathing, movement, and sound to energize your body.

Feel your body heating up. Feel the energy starting to flow through your legs, arms, and torso.

Chant a war cry. Utter the words of spontaneous incantations: "This is the power of Shiva, and I celebrate it!"

Let the rhythm of your dancing overwhelm you.

Let the dance become wild. Pour your total energy into it.

STAGE 4: SHIVA'S STRIPTEASE
Shiva, when you are hot, energized, excited, let a sexual feeling begin to invade your dancing, your body, your movements, and gestures.

You may feel like pushing your pelvis forward in rhythmic spasms, emphasizing your male sexual power, initiating this new phase of your dance. Or you may start to dance with slow, snakelike eroticism.

Sex has been called original sin, but there is nothing original about it, nor is it sinful.

—OSHO

Free yourself from any limiting ideas about how your sexuality should be displayed. You may feel feminine and sensual one moment, masculine and aggressive the next.

Give yourself permission to do anything, be anything. Let the dance be a sexual discovery, a spontaneous happening.

Make eye contact with your partner, as she watches you.

Begin to remove your clothing. It may happen in a sexy way, or more directly and boldly, as a display of male sexual arrogance. Feel free to switch back and forth. Follow your feelings.

Stay connected with your bodily sensations as you strip away your clothing, piece by piece. They will guide your actions, showing you what to do.

Reveal more and more of your nakedness. Show your chest, legs, buttocks. Enjoy the sense of sexual liberation, the freedom to behave in the most provocative way.

Peel away the last remaining layers, displaying your sexual manhood. Touch yourself. Show yourself. Run your hands over your body. Feel the freedom of being totally naked and exposed.

If you have an erection, dance it, display it. Caress yourself. Roll around on the floor. Imagine you are making love. Become lost in the sensations of your body.

When the striptease is over, lie quietly on the floor for a few moments, taking time to absorb the experience, one hand resting on your heart, the other on your sex.

Shakti, when it feels right, go to Shiva and reward his courage with a hug. Tell him what you liked about his dance: "I loved the power of your dance . . . the cute way you showed your buttocks . . . the way you looked at me . . ." and so on.

Pointers

The more you charge your body with energy in the warm-up dance, the easier it will be to give this energy sexual expression in the striptease.

The first time you do the exercise, you may find that you are not capable of completing a full striptease. Shyness may hinder your performance. You may suddenly freeze and lose contact with your energy, experiencing the actor's ultimate fear of "dying" onstage in front of an audience.

If this happens to you, there is no need to feel that you have failed. Go as far as you can, then wait a few days and try again. Have the courage to repeat this exercise until you feel you have mastered it. You will experience a tremendous healing when you are able to go the whole way.

When you are the audience, you may feel excited and want to join your partner in the dance. Enjoy the feeling, but please remain where you are. This is an important process of self-exposure designed to provoke and transcend sexual fears, shame, or guilt. Any kind of interruption, however pleasurable, will lessen the impact of the exercise.

You can do this exercise alone, imagining that you are dancing in front of an audience. You can also use a mirror to watch yourself as you dance.

There is no need to have a fancy costume. You can wear your ordinary clothes. But in my experience, creating a sexy outfit intensifies both your sexual feelings and your enjoyment.

NAMING YOUR SEXUAL ORGAN:
VAJRA AND YONI

Before moving to the third and final exercise in this series, spend a few moments reflecting on the way we address our sexual organs. Our language has crude or derogatory names for these parts of our anatomy, which reflect the condemnatory attitudes we carry toward our sexuality.

In the following practice you will be given the opportunity to create a beautiful name for your sexual organ, one that you can continue to use throughout this book as a gesture of reconciliation and healing, which will help you to view your genitals in a new and positive way.

As an example, I have chosen the name Vajra, a Tibetan term meaning "thunderbolt," to refer to the male sexual organ, and Yoni, a Sanskrit term meaning "cosmic womb," for the female sexual organ. I will be using these names on many occasions in the chapters ahead.

Now you are ready to begin the Shame Buster exercise.

EXERCISE: THE SHAME BUSTER

Purpose and Benefits

This is a powerful practice designed to heal any wounding related to your sexual organs. It will prepare you for an expansion of your orgasmic power.

In this exercise, you give a name, voice, and personality to your sexual organ, allowing it to speak as an independent individual. If you are a man, you may choose to call your penis Vajra, Golden Rod, Thunderbolt, Happy Jack, or some other name that appeals to you. If you are a woman, you may decide on Yoni, Heavenly Lotus, Hidden Garden, or Pussy Willow, for example, as a name for your vagina.

When your sexual organ speaks, he or she will describe what it is like to be part of you, to live in your body, to participate in your sexual experiences.

As you will see, this simple device is very effective in exposing and healing any conflicts that may exist between you and your natural sexual energy.

The exercise also shows you how to develop an intimate language for lovemaking that reduces the emotional charge and pressure around sex, helping you and your partner to be more humorous, compassionate, and understanding in the way you relate sexually.

Preparations

- Have plenty of massage oil handy.

- Take turns to be active and passive in this exercise. In my description, Shiva goes first.

- The active partner is naked. The passive partner can be either naked or clothed.

- Allow forty-five minutes for this exercise.

Practice

STAGE 1: SHIVA'S SELF-MASSAGE

Enter your Magic Circle together.

Begin the session with a long Melting Hug, creating a deep heart connection and a supportive atmosphere.

Sit comfortably, facing each other.

Shiva, remove any clothing you may be wearing and begin to caress your body gently. Close your eyes and focus completely on the sensations you are creating as you touch yourself.

Shakti, sit quietly, close your eyes, and leisurely recall the times when

111

The Shame Buster Exercise: Shiva shows his genitals to Shakti, who observes lovingly.

you have been penetrated by Vajra, the sexual organ of your partner. Recall how it felt: the times when you were wet, juicy, and eager to have Vajra inside you; the times when it didn't feel so good. Recall the first time, the best time, and the most recent time. Forgive Vajra for any rudeness or indiscretions and appreciate the pleasure he has brought to you.

Shiva, take some massage oil and caress your skin with it, covering your body, starting at the feet and working your way up your body.

Maybe this is something you're not used to giving yourself. Perhaps you're more used to touching your partner. Take this opportunity to focus on your own sensations as you caress and massage yourself. Breathe deeply, connecting your caresses with your breath.

STAGE 2: SHIVA CONNECTS WITH VAJRA

Shiva, when you have massaged your whole body, let your hands slide onto your belly, then down between your legs. Begin to caress your Vajra, your sexual organ.

Move your hands all the way under your penis and testicles, pressing the soft perineum point between your scrotum and your anus. Take your balls in your hand, gently squeezing them, then stroke and caress your Vajra from base to tip.

There is no need to prove yourself by being stiff and erect. Let Vajra have his own moods. He is perfectly okay the way he is.

When you feel that you have connected with Vajra, tell Shakti she can open her eyes.

Shakti, look softly into Shiva's eyes, then allow your gaze to wander down his body to his Vajra.

Look at his male sexual organ. Observe Vajra in all his aspects. Look at the shaft, the tip, the balls. Look underneath the balls at the perineum. Look in silence, with reverence.

Shiva, lean back and spread your legs so that Shakti can have a clear view of your sexual organs. Allow yourself to be vulnerable and open. You may feel many different emotions arising as this exercise progresses. You may feel embarrassed, or ashamed. You may feel scared. Your body may feel clammy or cold. You may even start to lose enthusiasm for continuing.

When these things happen, breathe deeply and rock gently back and forth with your pelvis. This will keep your energy moving.

Keep looking into the eyes of your partner, accepting your emotions, accepting any difficulties or anxieties as part of a deep cleansing and healing process.

STAGE 3: VAJRA SPEAKS

Shiva, from now on, you will be giving Vajra your voice, allowing him to speak through you. Let this happen as honestly and sincerely as possible.

Shakti, look at Vajra and address him as if he were a person in his own right. Ask: "What is your name?"

He may say: "My name is Vajra," or "My name is Cherry Picker," or "My name is Lightning Rod."

Once Vajra has given his name, ask him to talk about his life with Shiva, inviting him to speak freely.

He may say: "Shiva is a nice guy, but we have had our difficult moments. For instance, it took Shiva a long time to figure out that he could trust me to know when it is appropriate to be sexual. He used to think I had to stand up and go down according to all kinds of strange ideas. That made life difficult for both of us. I remember one time . . ."

Vajra may continue: "He used to worry that I was too small, which felt kind of bad, because really I'm exactly the right size and in perfect working order. He was really surprised when a woman said to him for the first time that she liked his penis . . ."

Shakti, encourage Vajra to express himself fully, covering the territory of his sexual history, describing moments that are vivid in his memory.

Ask him whether enough attention is paid to him, whether his owner listens to his advice, or whether he feels ignored.

You may also ask Vajra: "Is there anything you want to say about the way Shiva and I make love?"

Vajra, express how you feel about this delicate topic.

Shakti, listen to Vajra with appreciation. His words may reveal important clues to more ecstatic lovemaking.

You can also ask him: "Is there a gift that you would like to receive from Shiva that would make your life together more harmonious?"

Vajra may say, "Yes, I want Shiva to give me his exclusive attention for half an hour a day," or "I want Shiva to switch from cotton briefs to silk shorts," or "I want Shiva to let me talk with Shakti's Yoni when we are making love, saying what I want and what I am experiencing."

When Vajra has expressed himself fully, he can say, "Vajra wants to stop talking now. Good-bye."

Shakti, make a Heart Salutation, pressing your palms together. Take a deep breath and begin softly to make the sound "Om," slowly bending forward until your head rests on Shiva's pubic bone. Chant "Om" in this position, sending blessings to Shiva's sexual organ.

Existence is a play of sun and shade, of hope and despair, of happiness and sorrow, of life and death. So existence is duality, a tension of opposite poles, a music of contrary notes.

—OSHO

113

When you come back to a sitting position, tell Shiva what you like about his sexual organ. You may say, "I like the color of the skin; I like the firm, round, mushroomlike head; I like how you touch yourself . . ."

Shiva, when Shakti has finished speaking, place both hands over your sexual organ, close your eyes, and sit for a moment in silence. This is called "closing the door." It allows the energy in your sexual organ to rest and relax after this challenging exercise.

Take a short break, then change roles.

STAGE 4: SHAKTI'S SELF-MASSAGE
Begin with a long Melting Hug.

Shakti, now it is your turn to be active.

Remove your clothing and sit comfortably in front of Shiva.

Begin to caress your body lightly.

Shiva, sit quietly, close your eyes, and begin to recall the times when you visited Shakti's sexual organ. Remember the times when it was magical, ecstatic, when it was like entering a dark, warm, nourishing womb. Remember the difficult times, when you felt rejected or misunderstood, or when you felt lost inside her. Remember the first time, the best time, the most recent time. Forgive Shakti's sexual organ for any transgressions, and appreciate the pleasure she has brought to you.

Shakti, while Shiva meditates, take some massage oil and gently massage your whole body, starting at the feet and working your way upward.

As you touch yourself, feel that you are giving yourself love and tenderness. Touch yourself from your heart.

STAGE 5: SHAKTI CONNECTS WITH YONI
Shakti, when you have finished massaging yourself, bring your attention to your Yoni. Slide your hands down over your belly, in between your thighs, placing your hands over your sexual organ.

Breathe deeply, letting the energy of your breath flow all the way down inside your body to your Yoni, giving love and energy to this place.

Until now, Yoni was almost always hidden, behind closed doors, a mysterious, veiled woman, not worthy to show herself in public. Now times are changing and it's her moment to be proud about who she is, and to show herself.

Tell Shiva that he can open his eyes.

Shiva, look into Shakti's eyes, then allow your gaze to travel slowly down her body to her Yoni.

Within our darkest moments, our brightest treasures can be found.

—MARCUS ALLEN

Shakti, lean back and spread your legs so that Shiva can have a clear view. Spread Yoni's lips, showing the inside of your secret garden. You may also like to turn over and show yourself sexily from behind. If difficult emotions arise, such as embarrassment or shame, give yourself permission to show them. Let everything be the way it is. Breathe deeply. Gently rock your pelvis. Keep your energy moving.

Shiva, look at Yoni. Observe her in all her aspects. Remember with reverence that you were born out of such a Yoni.

STAGE 6: YONI SPEAKS

Shakti, now you are going to give Yoni your voice, allowing her to speak through you as if she were a real person.

Shiva, ask Yoni: "What is your name?"

She may say: "My name is Yoni," or "My name is Precious Jewel," or "My name is Very Cherry," or "My name is Mossy Cave."

When Yoni gives her name, ask her to talk about her life with Shakti, encouraging her to speak frankly.

Yoni may say: "My life with Shakti has been full of adventures. I remember one of the first times she made love, we had this great experience and she immediately understood that I can be a door to exquisite pleasure if I am approached rightly.

"But I've also had hard times, too. For a long time I think she felt ashamed of me, not wanting anyone to see me, and that didn't feel good at all. Also, when she was using an IUD for birth control I felt very uncomfortable and wanted her to change methods but she wouldn't listen to me, so we got pregnant anyway!

"Then there was a period in her life when she was into dating and moving around. She let guys just fuck her, pounding away without much sensitivity. Sometimes I enjoyed this wild stuff, but at other times it didn't feel so good. I'm glad she eventually realized that I need a more sensitive approach if I am going to relax, trust, and take off into ecstasy . . ."

Shiva, you may ask Yoni: "Is there anything you want to say about the way Shakti and I make love?"

Listen to Yoni with appreciation. This is an opportunity to receive new insights into your lovemaking. Yoni, speak as you truly feel, so that new doors of understanding can open.

When Yoni has finished, ask her: "Is there a gift that Shakti can give you that would make your life together more harmonious?"

Yoni may say, "Well, she could put me more in the sun and let me be naked more often," or "She could pay more attention to my voice. I want her to listen when I call, to know that, when I tickle inside, this is an opportunity for her to get in the mood for lovemaking . . ."

Yoni, when you feel that you have fully expressed yourself, say "Yoni feels like stopping now. Good-bye."

Shiva, make a Heart Salutation to Yoni, pressing the palms of your hands together. Take a deep breath and begin to make the sound "Om," bending forward until your head rests on Shakti's pubic bone. Sing "Om" in this position, sending blessings to Shakti's sexual organ.

Sexual wounding is like a claw caught in the primordial genetic strands of the male and female twist.

—ANICCA

Come back to the sitting position and tell Shakti what you like about her sexual organ. You may say, "I love the shape. It's so delicate, petite, and pink . . . I like the shy way it opens to your touch . . . I like the curve of the outer lips; it looks like butterfly wings . . ."

Shakti, when Shiva has finished speaking, place both hands over your sexual organ and sit for a moment in silence, "closing the door," allowing your sexual energy to rest and relax.

End with a Melting Hug.

Pointers

This is a very powerful exercise, triggering strong emotions. Sexual healing takes place when we give ourselves permission to show these feelings in an atmosphere of trust, love, and acceptance.

However, if at any point you feel unable to continue with the exercise, do not force yourself to go on. Stop, tell your partner what is happening, and ask for a Melting Hug. Wait a few hours, or a few days, then try the exercise again.

The partner who is listening can give support in difficult moments by saying "I am touched by your courage, your sincerity. This is a beautiful exercise, and I know you'll feel wonderful after you pull it off. Let's keep going. I love you; I'm here with you . . ."

It is very important that the supporting partner not say anything that is critical or negative during this exercise, or afterwards.

From Healing Wounds
to Celebrating Wildness

The healing of sexual wounds gives you the confidence you need to explore your hidden wildness. In the next chapter, you discover ways to connect with the full power of your wild energy, releasing it in an exciting and pleasurable way. This, in turn, opens the way for developing full orgasmic power in sexual magic.

AWAKENING THE WILD SELF

When I introduce people to the idea of the Wild Self, I almost inevitably start talking about the divine madman, Drukpa Kunley; and when I talk about him, I always have to smile. Drukpa Kunley is the epitome of uninhibited, free-flowing energy, the personification of a truly wild being; and some of the ways in which he expresses this wild energy are really quite extraordinary.

Drukpa Kunley is a Tibetan mystic, magician, and folk hero who lived in the fifteenth century. Songs and stories about his exploits are still uttered today in Tibet, Bhutan, and Nepal, for he wandered all over the northern Himalayas dispensing a kind of crazy wisdom, enlightening spiritual seekers, shocking followers of traditional religion, defeating demons, and making love with a truly prodigious number of women.

Buddhist scholars acknowledge him as an enlightened master, an exponent of Buddha-nature and a reincarnation of the Tantric master Saraha. But, reading their commentaries on Drukpa Kunley's sexual deeds and extraordinary behavior, I sense the underlying bewilderment and embarrassment of these scholars at having to create orthodox, scholastic explanations about the activities of such a wild and untamed spirit. Yet Drukpa Kunley's seemingly eccentric and outrageous deeds contain important keys for embracing the Wild Self, as you may discern from the following three anecdotes.

In one of his tales, *The Divine Madman*, Drukpa Kunley is wandering through the marketplace of Lhasa, the Tibetan capital, which is filled with people from all over Central Asia including many pilgrims, monks, and nuns. Suddenly he shouts: "Listen to me, everyone! I am Drukpa Kunley and I have come here today, filled with compassion, to help you attain spiritual salvation. Now tell me, quickly, where can I find the best wine and the most beautiful women?"

There is a shocked silence, then one old woman informs the divine madman that the best women live in the Land of Kongpo, including a lovely young virgin called Sumchok. Immediately, Drukpa Kunley heads for that kingdom, where he finds Sumchok serving food to a powerful tribal chieftain.

He sings songs to her with hidden meanings, offering the promise of deep spiritual insights. She sings an enthusiastic reply, indicating her eagerness to penetrate beyond *Samsara,* the veil of worldly illusion, and attain to Buddhahood. Having lured the chieftain away from his castle by tales of hunting, Drukpa Kunley is then able to meet the beautiful Sumchok. She offers him tea, but he has other activities in mind . . .

> And he caught her by the hand, laid her down on the chieftain's bed, lifted her skirt, and gazed upon her nether *mandala.* Placing his organ against the piled white lotus *mandala* between the smoother-than-cream white flesh of her thighs, and having seen that their connection was tightly made, he consummated their union. Making love to her, he gave her more pleasure and satisfaction than she had ever experienced.

Afterwards Drukpa Kunley was about to leave, but Sumchok begged him to take her along. He agreed, then took her to a nearby cave, instructed her in meditation, and left her alone. Sumchok devoted herself to meditation and after four days "gained release from all frustration in a Body of Light, attaining Buddhahood."

Do what thou wilt shall be the whole of the law.

—ALEISTER CROWLEY

DEMONS AND LAMAS

It seems that Drukpa Kunley enlightened many women in this way, either during or shortly after sexual union, but he had other talents, too, including a knack of subduing demons. In fifteenth-century Tibet any hardship, difficulty, bad luck, or misfortune was usually attributed to the work of malicious demons—supernatural beings that could take any shape or form—and Drukpa Kunley, when not busy making love, spent a good deal of time defeating them with his magical powers.

His method of conquering demons was unique. He would either ram them in the mouth with his "flaming thunderbolt of wisdom," which was the term given to his penis, or spray them with his gushing semen. This sudden assault with the divine madman's total sexual energy never failed to quell, and even totally transform, a troublesome demon.

In one hilarious anecdote, a family whose house is plagued by demons begs Drukpa Kunley for help. He agrees and orders them to drill a hole in the front door, at approximately the height of his pelvis, then asks them to leave him alone in the house with a couple of kegs of wine. That night, he gets thoroughly drunk and begins loud, raucous singing that soon attracts the demons, but he has performed a magical ritual and they cannot get through the door.

The demons start pounding on the door, saying "Let us in! This is our house!" Finally, when they are desperate to come inside, he orders them to assemble in front of the door. Then he thrusts his "flaming thunderbolt of wisdom" through the hole and sprays them all with his mystical semen. Covered with this radiant, divine fluid, the demons immediately become peaceful, helpful creatures, and the family can safely return to their abode.

Many of the stories told about Drukpa Kunley have an irreverent, antiestablishment slant, especially with regard to the orthodox Buddhist priesthood. In one such tale, Drukpa Kunley is refused audience with a famous lama because he doesn't have enough money for an offering. In response, our intrepid hero quickly acquires a large amount of gold and returns to the lama's temple, where he is instantly admitted.

The lama gives him a traditional red thread to wear around his neck, but instead, the Drukpa Kunley ties it around his penis and rushes to the marketplace crying "Look at this! For fifty gold pieces you can also get one from the holy lama!"

What is the meaning of all this outrageous behavior? First of all, it is clear from these stories that the source of Drukpa Kunley's power and

Many waters cannot quench love, neither can floods drown it. If one offered for love all the wealth of his house, it would be utterly scorned.

—*Song of Solomon*

magic is his sexual energy. Harnessing this vital energy presupposes a positive attitude toward sex that runs contrary to the conventional morality of many major religions, including both Buddhism and Christianity.

This is why Drukpa Kunley's behavior is so antiauthoritarian and antiestablishment. It is designed to liberate the Wild Self from the stifling moral codes that curb our sexual expression, cut off our free-flowing energy, and inhibit our spontaneity and passion. He encourages us to rebel against these restrictions, to free the wild energy that is essential for our growth and fulfillment.

Moreover, the divine madman's power to subdue demons is a perfect metaphor for confronting and transforming those energies inside us that have been condemned as bad, evil, or undesirable. Our demons are really nothing but denied energies, denied parts of ourselves. These rejected parts need to be contacted and reembraced if we are to become whole and integrated human beings.

Much of what is told about Drukpa Kunley is obviously pure myth, but I love the man because he demonstrates how we can reembrace the whole of life, with all its juices and spices. I am not suggesting that we go around seducing young virgins, subduing demons, and tying red strings to our sexual organs. But I am saying that if we want to celebrate our total energy all the way to sexual magic, then, like Drukpa Kunley, we need to awaken the Wild Self that lies within us.

WILD WOMEN

There is no female equivalent of Drukpa Kunley, for patriarchal societies have not permitted women to celebrate their sexual wildness with the same degree of freedom as men.

There are, however, feminine archetypes that contain elements of wildness, such as the Hindu deity Kali, an incredibly powerful, fire-breathing goddess who dances wildly on the body of the male god Shiva, holding the severed head of a man in one hand, a sword in the other, and wearing a necklace of fifty human skulls.

Through this startling image, Kali is seen as representing the vital principles of the visible universe, the cycles of birth and death, the giver of life and also its destroyer—gracious, cruel, creative, destructive, loving, indifferent. But this wild, uninhibited goddess seems far removed from the meek, subservient role of women in Indian culture.

In Europe, myths and legends have tended to portray wild women in a negative way. For example, in the classical Greek drama *The Bacchants,* by Euripedes, a group of wild women called Maenads dance in ecstatic abandon while serving Dionysius, the god of ecstasy. Through their dancing they experience freedom, joy, and fulfillment and also exhibit magical powers. Left to themselves, they are a beautiful expression of unrestrained female passion, dancing barefoot in the woods, honoring the life force, entering into mystical, orgasmic states of consciousness.

However, Pentheus, King of Thebes, disapproves of their behavior and tries to prevent women from leaving his city to join the Maenads' celebration. In response to the king's intervention, the women's wild and ecstatic energy turns to rage and madness.

Medea is another Greek archetype of a wild woman. She is the beau-

"The Kali" in a modern woman: allowing anger and wild energies to be expressed so they can be released and transformed

The Goddess Kali. The lotus is the symbol of creation; cutting off the head symbolizes the sword of truth severing the illusion of the ego.

123

tiful sorceress who falls madly in love with Jason, the Argonaut. With her magical powers, Medea helps Jason perform the almost impossible tasks set by her father, King Aeetes, as conditions for giving Jason the legendary Golden Fleece. Without her aid, Jason could never have hoped to succeed in his quest.

But when Jason returns triumphantly to Corinth with the Golden Fleece, he betrays Medea by wooing the daughter of the king of Corinth. In her grief and rage, Medea exacts a terrible toll, killing the king, his daughter, and her own children in an orgy of bloodthirsty revenge against Jason.

From the perspective of the Wild Self, the main point to grasp about these tragedies is that the passion, ecstasy, and magical powers of both Medea and the Maenads began as a tremendously alive and creative force until it was confronted with male rejection and suppression. Only after it was blocked did their wildness turn into destruction and madness.

The sect and the cult of lovers is different from all others. Lovers have a religion and faith that is all their own.

— AZUL

The lesson is not, as some might suppose, that women should carefully control their passions, but rather that they should not be prevented from seeking freedom, love, and ecstasy through wildness. Until now, such a message would have fallen on deaf ears—male and female alike—but the emancipation of women has created an atmosphere in which these things can finally be said.

ORIGINS OF THE WILD SELF

When we look at archetypes like Drukpa Kunley, Medea, and the Maenads, we see the reflection of our own Wild Self, a self that has been with us, inside us, from the very beginning of our lives. It is a self that knows how to dance ecstatically, love passionately, live totally, burning the candle of life at both ends.

As very young children we were in perfect harmony with this natural expression of wildness. If you doubt what I am saying, just spend a few minutes watching a young child at play and you will see how much energy is available, enough to exhaust any adult athlete who might try to match the child's antics.

Or you can watch the child's moods, and you will see what happens when human energy becomes totally involved in laughter, anger, tears, screaming, and relaxation. It is as if the body's energy leaps spontaneously into action, springing from some hidden source that is utterly free of confinement.

The Wild Self has its origins in this childlike energy, in this raw, innocent, and vital power as it is expressed naturally before being filtered through the civilizing codes of social education. This civilizing process takes many forms. For example, a child is playing and the parents tell her to come in and eat lunch. Perhaps she is not hungry; perhaps, even if she is hungry, the game that she is playing is so enjoyable that she does not want to stop. Nevertheless, she is forced to abandon her natural impulses, come inside the house, sit quietly at the table, and eat with good manners. In these simple ways, wild energy is tamed and directed.

With the best of intentions, children are gradually taught to consider each natural impulse and weigh its implications before allowing themselves to follow it. Is this really the right time to laugh, to cry, to say what I think? Should I try to hold my urine until the end of the class, or ask for permission to go to the toilet now? Can I run and jump now, or will I be admonished for doing so?

Pretty soon, every spontaneous impulse arising out of the child's raw energy is forced to make a detour through the interpretive and analytical processes of the mind. A natural urge to express a feeling or emotion has to struggle through a labyrinth of parentally instilled "do's" and "don'ts," "shoulds" and "should nots" before it can be allowed to leak out.

This transition from childhood innocence to adult sophistication constricts the energy of *Eros,* the affirmative life force that is present in all of us. At root, *Eros* is a sexual force, a creative and dynamic drive that contains within itself an unconditional "yes" to life. Colliding with society, however, this force becomes perverted into a "yes, but . . ."

Yet not all our wildness is lost. For myself, I always managed to retain a glimmer of that early flame, which somehow saved me from being totally emasculated by the discipline and etiquette that was heaped upon me as I grew up. Climbing alone in the mountains, crossing the foaming torrent of an icy stream, racing through the trees in pursuit of a wild deer, I could relive and recapture a sense of my unbounded spirit, feeling a sudden rush of exultation and defiance through my body that made me want to shout aloud to the forest "This is who I really am, and nobody is going to take it away from me!"

Later on, in my late teens, I discovered the same exciting force through lovemaking. The rising tide of my own vital, sexual energy pushed me to defy all the rules concerning the behavior of "nice girls." I wanted to discover everything about my *Eros,* my sensuality, my libido; and the more I dared to explore, the more certain I became that the element of wild spontaneity was essential to my sexual fulfillment. After a beautiful afternoon of lovemaking in which I had successfully confronted some lingering sense of shame or sexual guilt, I would lie content on my bed feeling tremendously reinforced in my sense of "who I really am" and who I wanted to be.

A few years later, as part of my continuing exploration of Tantra and the Wild Self, I met a contemporary version of Drukpa Kunley, a controversial teacher of crazy wisdom in India called Osho who has devised all kinds of novel methods to help people break out of their civilized straitjackets and reclaim the power and passion of their natural wild energy.

Although widely condemned as a "sex guru," Osho's vision of life stretches far beyond the bedroom. To him, the Western obsession with sex is a product of centuries of repression and denial. Releasing and healing sexual energy goes hand in hand with expressing held-back emotions, dancing madly, breathing dynamically, speaking nonsense, laughing uncontrollably . . . in short, using any method to clear out the inhibitions that stand in the way of the natural flow of human energy. Only then, according to Osho, is an individual ready to sit down, close his or her eyes, and begin the inward journey of meditation.

I remember with great clarity one extraordinary meeting with this maverick mystic. Sitting in front of Osho, gazing into his twinkling, smiling eyes, I suddenly felt this rumbling laughter starting to arise, as if coming from deep in the center of the earth, then penetrating deliciously inside my body. Helpless, I burst out into uncontrollable laughter, and soon everyone present was infected by it. It was so contagious, the whole room was laughing.

Minutes passed and I just couldn't stop, so eventually I had to be gently carried back to my place. Afterwards, for a whole month, every day at the same time—seven o'clock in the evening—the laughter would return. No matter what I was doing—reading, praying, dancing, making love, cooking—this incredible laughter would bubble up inside.

The experience allowed me to discover the healing power of laughter, because whenever it would happen I had no choice but to stop taking myself seriously. Whatever I was worried about, the laughter would simply burst through it all, giving me a distance from my mental preoccupations.

I could laugh about my life, clearly seeing that "this isn't really me. These are the things with which I am identified, attached, but in reality I am pure consciousness, pure awareness, separate, free, untouchable, far beyond all these things."

It was a tremendously powerful experience, a gift from a unique mystic who has helped many people to move with meditative awareness into the dimension of the Wild Self.

IS THE WILD SELF DANGEROUS?

Almost every culture in recorded history, including our own, has perceived the Wild Self as a dangerous and threatening phenomenon. In a sense, this perception is correct, because every society has tried to create the so-called "civilized" human being at the expense of suppressing the natural, animallike energy within us.

The net result is that whenever our basic drives succeed in breaking through the veneer of civilized behavior, these energies tend initially to manifest themselves in a destructive and negative way. Long imprisonment has perverted the natural energy to such an extent that it cannot easily move in a creative direction.

It is no accident that the violence is so popular in movies and on television, for it is through the media that people vicariously live out their suppressed wildness, killing and maiming and striking out in a romanticized rebellion against a social morality that has castrated them, imprisoning them in a cocoon of niceness and politeness. Through fantasy, at least, the civilized man and woman can break out of their dreary nine-to-five servitude and shoot their way to freedom.

In recent years, the men's and women's movements in America and Europe have come close to recognizing the value of reclaiming the Wild Self. In their search for authentic gender values, these movements have understood that both sexes have been somehow robbed of their primordial, vital power, and that this loss is partly to blame for the frustration and dissatisfaction experienced between the sexes.

Traditionally, men have been permitted to express a certain amount of wildness in the area of sexuality, especially in terms of "sowing their wild oats" before settling down to wedded domesticity.

For women, even in these heady days of relative liberation, there are greater taboos around sex. For example, one of the most common problems

He who realizes the truth of the body can then come to know the truth of the universe.

—RAT NAS TANTRA

127

I encounter when helping women to discover their orgasmic potential is their fear that "if I really let go and express my orgasmic self when we make love, then I'm going to be too much and he's going to get scared and cut off from me." Rather than take such a risk, women tend to check any impulse toward wild sexual abandon.

Many people fear the expression of wild emotion in the form of anger. For example, in my workshops, there will occasionally be an angry eruption from a man or a woman who, sharing feedback with his or her partner, suddenly shouts, "Shut up! I don't like what you are saying!" Immediately, most of the other people in the room start to feel uncomfortable, or even afraid. Everyone wants the incident to pass as quickly as possible.

The tendency of both sexes, even in workshop situations, is to try to avoid the expression of what they perceive as unpleasant emotions, not realizing that these outbursts are crude signposts pointing to a potent wellspring of natural, vital energy.

Healthy mysticism is pantheistic.

—MATTHEW FOX

There is a way out of these difficulties. I am happy to say that it is perfectly possible to release the energy of the Wild Self in creative and playful ways that enhance intimacy and love between men and women, while at the same time denying none of the power and passion that are the Wild Self's essential qualities. My method for doing this constitutes the basis of this chapter, and you will have the chance to practice a series of intriguing and stimulating exercises designed for this purpose.

DISCOVERING SEXUAL WILDNESS

Before doing so, I want to address a very basic question: Why does a sexual magician need to discover the Wild Self? What is the connection between magic and wildness?

In chapter 1, I said that any vision or desire that you wish to manifest in your life needs to be charged with your orgasmic sexual power. But this orgasmic charge cannot be created unless you first connect with your wild energy. Sexual ejaculation can happen, sexual climax can happen, but real orgasm needs the presence of wildness in order to charge the body with ecstatic energy.

Let me explain what I mean by "wildness" in the sexual context. When sexual arousal begins during lovemaking it can, through certain techniques, be helped to rise in a slowly building, ever-climbing curve of intensity that injects more and more energy and pleasure into your body. If this exquisite buildup of arousal is allowed to continue without climaxing, there comes a point when your sexual energy moves beyond the point of your control.

The charge becomes so strong that the energy takes over. Sexual sensations begin streaming through your genitals and perhaps through your whole body in a series of involuntary, ecstatic responses that are not a "doing" but a "happening." This is an experience of your wild energy.

There is another type of sexual experience that is also associated with wildness, something that many people have experienced. It happens when two lovers are together, not particularly orienting themselves toward sexual union, when a sudden surge of sexual energy sweeps through them, pulling them into lovemaking. The impulse may be initiated by the lightest touch of a hand on the back of the neck, or a hug, or a gentle kiss, or perhaps through some hidden current of electric energy that passes between them without their knowing. This, too, is part of the Wild Self.

I am reminded of a story told to me by Jenny and Ken, two experienced teachers of the Tantric arts who have been friends, co-workers, and lovers for several years. There came a time when, for a number of personal reasons, Ken told Jenny that he no longer wished to be her lover. Many months went by, during which Jenny grudgingly tried to adapt to the new situation while still maintaining her teaching partnership with Ken.

Then, about a year later, just before leading a big workshop together, Jenny went to stay at Ken's apartment for three or four days in order to prepare their new program. Day after day, they went through their exercises, including the three practices that I will be describing in this chapter: the Laughing Pelvis, the Fire Meditation, and Connecting with Your Wild Animal.

Jenny found herself stretched between the twin poles of agony and ecstasy, not really knowing if she had been plunged into the deepest hell or raised to the highest heaven. She was spending twenty-four hours a day with the man she loved with all her heart. They were talking, touching, dancing, playing, hugging . . . doing everything together except making love. Jenny told me afterward that she ached to pull Ken to her and wrap herself around him as in the past, to feel his male sexual power growing stronger and stronger and then penetrating her, filling her, overwhelming her, but Ken doggedly stuck to his guns that they were no longer lovers.

Then one evening, when their plans for the workshop program were almost complete, they were just lying around, doing nothing, watching a little television, talking about this and that. Their conversation turned to the subject of animal imagery as a way of provoking healthy sexual aggression, and pretty soon they started playing like wolves, yipping and snapping at each other, frolicking on the rug, pushing each other around without hurting or being hurt.

Suddenly, out of nowhere, a sexual fire started burning in their loins—a fire so wild, unexpected and bright that there could be no resistance to it. Jenny explained afterward:

> There was this enormous heat that started in my sex and spread out through my body like a summer wildfire sweeping through dry brush. And I could tell from Ken's excitement that it was happening to him at the same time. My guess is that all those exercises we'd been practicing had somehow cleansed us, charged us, allowing this incredible new energy to come rushing through. There was no way we could ignore it, control it, or judge it. There was no way we could do anything but go to bed!
>
> Tickling, chasing, pushing, we ran for the bedroom. God, I was so happy to get my clothes off, I just tore them away! Then I caught Ken half undressed and pushed him onto the bed. He growled and jumped up, pushed me over and tried to keep me on the bed like the dominant alpha male of the pack, while he stripped away the rest of his clothes. I was getting very excited, grabbing at his jeans, snarling and jumping around naked on the bed like a she-wolf in heat.
>
> Then he leaped on me and we rolled around, snapping, growling, snarling at each other, digging with make-believe claws into each other's flesh, gripping each other's necks with our teeth. It was such a turn-on! He tried to mount me from behind, but I wouldn't let him. Instead, I tried to mount him! I was burning to make love, but at the same time I was tuned in to this strong animal feeling that . . . well, you know, if you've ever watched wild animals, the female doesn't let the male mount her until he's put on a big mating display, strutting up and down, showing his stuff, and in this way she gets him really, really excited.
>
> So I kept acting seductive and willing, like I wanted Ken to penetrate me, but then rolling away at the last moment, or turning around and growling and trying to push him over. If he looked as though he was giving up, or starting to get frustrated, then I would whine and softly lick his body in the most erotic places, which would instantly reawaken his enthusiasm for the mating dance, and off we'd go again. This seemed to go on forever. When he finally trapped me, pushing me down into the pillows and spreading my thighs from behind, we made love with such a totality, such an intensity that it seemed as if a whole new level of orgasmic energy opened up for both of

us. And I was so relieved to be back in that wonderful flow of sexual passion we'd known before.

Jenny and Ken made love all night, spurred on by an intense mutual desire to know each other again, to rediscover themselves in a new and innocent way, free of the past. Jenny said afterwards that it was one of the most outstanding sexual experiences of her life, for they both managed to stay on that delicate edge where aggression threatens to be too much yet stays in the realm of pleasure, where passion threatens to explode yet somehow continues to build and build.

"I realized that it is love that allows people to be wild while holding aggression in check," Jenny explained. "If there is a strong, deep heart connection between two people, then you can go totally wild and yet at the same time remain sensitive enough to stay playful and not hurt each other."

Jenny and Ken's story is an illustration of the Wild Self in action, finding natural expression in a sexual context. This is when the mind stops planning, controlling, and calculating, and the individual becomes totally merged with his or her bodily sensations, allowing the energy to flow without obstruction in an authentic and spontaneous expression of wildness.

I found God in myself and I loved her. I loved her fiercely.

—NTOSAKE SHANGE

CATHARSIS: THE CONTROLLED EXPLOSION

The release of our wild energy is a delicate affair, for we need to feel safe while at the same time unleashing an internal explosion of energy, letting go of control mechanisms that would normally keep such energies in check. In the following exercises, you will be invited to release your energy and emotions in a playful way, for in my experience playfulness creates an atmosphere in which wild energy can flow in a positive direction.

Nevertheless, catharsis is a type of explosion and, however safe we make the situation, you must be willing to let go of control, to go beyond the known, the safe, the secure, and, in the words of D. H. Lawrence, "to risk your body and your blood and your mind, your known self and to become more and more the self you could never have known or expected." This can be either a wonderfully cleansing experience or a scary one. Or, it can be both.

Some exponents of modern therapy say that catharsis has no real value because "it doesn't get anywhere." For example, if you feel anger arising in you and you release the anger, there is no guarantee that you will not feel angry again tomorrow. This is true but misses the real point. Whether it is expressed or suppressed, anger continues to exist as a fact of life. Just as clouds pass over the sun and bring rain today, they may bring rain again tomorrow, but that is part of the cycle of life. The same is true of anger or any human feeling.

Moreover, I am convinced that the suppression of strong emotion contributes to the stifling of our life energy, while catharsis, if it is sponta-

Imagine that you have become the hairy, goatlike male god Pan and that you have a giant erection.

132

neous, contains an element of wildness that can clean out and empower our energy systems, making room for a greater sense of vitality and enthusiasm for life. Emotional expression, if it is handled creatively, can be a very life-affirmative statement, while suppression is almost always a statement of self-denial.

Now we are ready to move into a series of three exercises that will help you discover and express your Wild Self.

EXERCISE: THE LAUGHING PELVIS

Purpose and Benefits

In this exercise you will come in touch with your wildness in a way that is gentle and fun, using laughter as a catalyst to vibrate and awaken your hidden sources of energy. At one stage of the practice, you will be directing your laughter into the pelvic area where it can help to break down the "psychological chastity belt" that has formed around your primal sexual energy—ideas about what is forbidden, indecent, immoral, and so on.

For some people, laughter may seem like an odd way to confront demons and act as a catharsis on suppressed emotions. But if you participate in this exercise with wholehearted enthusiasm, you will see laughter as a very effective and powerful tool to cut through layers of social conditioning and release a wellspring of energy.

You will meet the pagan god Pan, who lives in a state of continual sexual readiness, and his Greek counterpart, the goddess Baubo, a sexual jokester who sees through her nipples and talks from between her legs. Both these archetypes are earthy spirits who connect people with sexual energy; they can also help you to link sexuality with humor, joy, and laughter.

Pan and Baubo will help you experience how expressions that we normally dismiss as vulgar can, in the right context, produce a release and healing of suppressed energy. By "letting it all hang out" you will feel the healthy glow of unconditional acceptance and embrace long-forgotten aspects of your being.

This part of the exercise is especially good for women, many of whom have been educated to believe that they must at all times be sweet, composed, smart, and sexy—never allowing the "coarse," "vulgar" side of human nature to show itself.

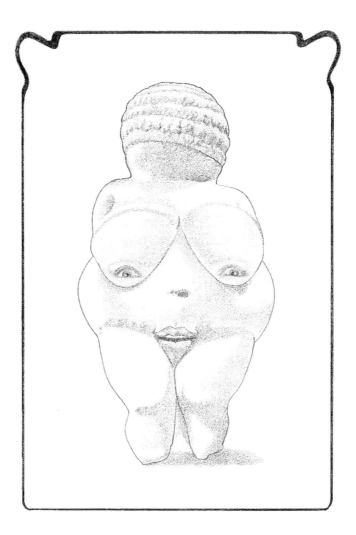

Imagine that you have become the goddess Baubo who sees through her nipples and speaks through her vulva: the joking, carefree goddess of obscenity.

Preparations

- ☙ The Laughing Pelvis can be done alone, but is more effective when practiced with a partner.

- ☙ Prepare your Magic Circle.

- ☙ Wear loose, comfortable clothing.

- ☙ As a first step, take time to gather any material that is likely to provoke laughter in you. For example, you could rent a movie that has a particularly funny scene in it, or you may find pictures, postcards, or passages in a book that make you laugh. Maybe you have some favorite jokes, or an audiotape of stand-up comedy, or perhaps a recording of someone's laughter that is infectious (my favorite approach). Whatever you find funny, prepare this material in advance and then bring it to your Magic Circle.

✍ Here is a joke that you can add to your collection:

A smart New York career girl marries a handsome young farmer from Vermont. Finding that his social manners lack the big-city polish to which she is accustomed, the girl begins to improve his style even while the wedding reception is in progress, telling him what to say to the guests, how to eat correctly, which forks and knives to use, and so on. The young man willingly obliges his new bride, but her advice slowly begins to erode his self-confidence. Finally, when the festivities are over and the honeymoon has begun, the couple retire to the bedroom. As they lie naked beneath the covers, the young man hesitantly asks: "Er, darling, w-would you mind p-passing the p-pussy, please?"

✍ Don't worry if at the beginning of this exercise your laughter sounds a bit forced and hollow. This is understandable, because laughter is usually experienced spontaneously while here you are deliberately creating a situation in which you expect to laugh. Moreover, many people just aren't used to laughing very much, because for them life has become a rather serious affair.

✍ You will soon see that anything can provide an excuse for laughter. For example, if you feel the whole situation is ridiculous—laughing as an exercise, whoever heard of such a thing?—then you can laugh at the ridiculousness of it all. Be creative, enthusiastic, and you will be surprised how easily the laughter will come.

✍ Allow twenty to twenty-five minutes for this exercise.

Practice

STAGE 1: LAUGH WITH EACH OTHER
Enter your Magic Circle with your partner.
   Greet each other with a Heart Salutation.
   Sit comfortably and begin to explore ways of provoking laughter in

Spend five minutes laughing
in your pelvis.

yourself and in your love partner. Tell jokes, watch scenes from movies, read passages from books.

Laugh at every opportunity. Be supportive to each other. Make funny faces; tickle each other.

Spend about five minutes laughing in this way, or, if you find that your laughter is rolling along nicely, keep going with this stage of the exercise for as long you like.

STAGE 2: BRING THE LAUGHTER INSIDE

When you are both ready, come to a standing position in your Magic Circle. Make sure your feet are shoulder width apart, with your knees slightly bent. Allow the muscles around your pelvis and your sexual organs to relax. Close your eyes.

Begin to laugh by yourself, bringing all your attention inside your body. Feel what happens to your body when you laugh. Feel the ripples of energy, where they go, what parts of your body are vibrating. Relax into these vibrations and allow them to spread.

Experiment with a range of laughter, moving from a loud, theatrical "ho, ho, ho!" to soft, gentle laughter. There are all kinds of qualities that can be present in laughter; it spans a wide range of human experience. See how many types of laughter you can create by yourself. Do this for about three minutes.

STAGE 3: LAUGH IN YOUR PELVIS

After a few minutes, bring your attention to the area of your pelvis, including your genitals, hips, and lower abdomen. Feel the laughter in this area. It may be just a small vibration, but that's fine. Let it be there. Encourage it, amplify it, combining your laughter with deep breathing. Imagine, as you inhale, that the air is traveling all the way down to your pelvis, opening and relaxing it.

As you laugh in your pelvis, you may begin to recall images or memories of situations in which your natural, wild energy was inhibited or condemned in some way. You may remember early masturbation experiences, or toilet training, or strong parental messages about sexuality, or being told not to laugh.

Let yourself laugh at these images, as they arise, dissolving the psychological and energetic armoring around them. Feel free to change these old scenes so that they now seem absurd or funny to you. Be imaginative.

Spend five minutes laughing in your pelvis.

STAGE 4: BE AS SEXUALLY OUTRAGEOUS AS PAN

To prepare for the next stage, open your eyes and make contact with your partner. Now it is time to behave in a thoroughly outrageous manner.

Continuing to laugh, imagine that you have become the god Pan. It doesn't matter if you are a man or a woman; just imagine for a moment that you have become the hairy, goatlike male god and that you have a giant erection.

We have to be careful that in throwing out the devil, we don't throw out the best part of ourselves.

—NIETZSCHE

With mime and movement, show your partner the dimensions of your sexual equipment, how long, how wide, how thick it is. Move around the room. How does it feel to walk with such a large penis? How does it feel to have so much sexual energy throbbing in your pelvis? Keep laughing.

If you are a woman, this is a golden opportunity to experience, in exaggerated form, what it is like to be a member of the opposite sex. Feel the male energy pulsating between your legs. Feel the male laughter that accompanies it. If feelings like guilt or shame arise, or thoughts like "This is too much," use these as opportunities to laugh.

Play the god Pan for three minutes.

STAGE 5: BE AS SEXUALLY OUTRAGEOUS AS BAUBO

Now, imagine that you have both been transformed into the goddess Baubo. Remember, she is the one who sees through her breasts and speaks or laughs through her vulva. Become this strange, bawdy archetype of a joking, carefree female deity, the goddess of obscenity.

As you laugh, feel that you have been endowed with huge breasts through which you see the world, that you have a huge opening between your legs out of which your laughter can bubble and flow. With mime and clowning, show each other what it is like to be Baubo.

Men, this is a great opportunity to experience what it is like, in comic form, to be a woman. Walk like a woman, feel the roundness, make exaggerated female gestures.

Both partners, encourage each other to be lewd, coarse, and vulgar, while continuing to laugh. Let everything hang out; hold nothing back.

Do this for three minutes.

STAGE 6: BRING THE LAUGHTER INSIDE ONCE MORE

Return to your Magic Circle and lie down on your back with your knees up. Keep laughing. Close your eyes and experience the laughter inside. Focus your attention on your pelvis. See if there is a difference in the sensations that are flowing through this part of your body, now that you have been clowning around as sexual gods and goddesses.

After a few minutes, slowly and gently allow the laughter to subside.

Lie still for a moment, eyes closed, enjoying the sensations in your body. You may feel that a great cleansing has taken place, with the laughter washing away many old cobwebs inside.

Sit up and share with your partner what you experienced during the exercise.

End with a Melting Hug and Heart Salutation.

Pointers

In the early stages of this exercise you may feel like taking short breaks in your laughter, but it's important to continue nonstop. Be total in this exercise. Stay focused on the physical sensations that you feel in your body. You will find that the laughing grows easier the more you do it.

A valuable key to releasing laughter is to be found in the motto "Fake it 'til you make it." In other words, just laugh and don't worry about what it sounds like. Or, if you really want to worry, laugh about the fact that you are worrying!

Now that you have loosened up your pelvis, you can explore awakening energy through your whole body.

EXERCISE: THE FIRE MEDITATION

Purpose and Benefits

In the Fire Meditation you connect with a fiery energy that heals, purifies, and enlivens your whole body, awakening the energy of the Wild Self. You combine strong breathing with visualization to create a sensation of fire that rises through your body, bringing with it a healing flame of energy that can open up energy channels, burn through blocked or suppressed energy, and release your wildness and your power.

Life is wild. Love is wild. And God is absolutely wild.

—OSHO

It also offers an opportunity for vocal release, screaming and shouting, and for letting go of whatever hinders you from feeling good about yourself.

When I guide people through this practice in my workshops I find that many of them have visions of the Wild Self during the meditation, receiving images or impressions of themselves as free and uninhibited human beings. Welcome such visions if they come to you during the exercise, or even afterwards, for they can help you get a taste of the aliveness and joy that the Wild Self brings.

This exercise is a useful preparation for opening the Secret Channel through the body's seven energy centers, a practice that will be introduced in chapter 6.

Preparations

- Prepare your Magic Circle.
- Wear a minimum of clothing because you are likely to become quite warm during the exercise.
- It is helpful to do this exercise to music (see appendix for suggestions).
- This exercise can be done alone or together with your partner.
- The meditation lasts thirty minutes.

Practice

STAGE 1: SHAKING YOUR BODY
Enter your Magic Circle.

Put on lively music and dance vigorously for a few minutes, moving your whole body, stretching, jumping, shaking, loosening up your joints and muscles, breathing through your mouth to activate your energy.

When the music is finished, stand comfortably with your feet shoulder-width apart. Unlock your knees and let them be slightly bent. Let your shoulders relax and your arms hang loosely by your sides. If your pelvis is held back, let it drop forward into a more relaxed position. Feel that your feet are planted firmly on the floor.

Begin to shake in a relaxed, loose way. Start with your hands, then bring in your arms and shoulders, making the sound "Aaaah" out loud as you do so.

After a few moments, bring your neck and head into the shaking.

Now start shaking at the knees. This will bring your whole body into the shaking movement. Loosen up everywhere. Shake everything.

Stop. Relax. Be still for a moment.

STAGE 2: BEGINNING THE FIRE BREATH
When you are ready, begin to breathe deeply and slowly through your mouth.

Move your hands in a rhythm with your breathing. Exhale, opening your hands wide. Inhale, closing your hands into fists.

Let the rest of your body join in the rhythm. Exhale, feeling your shoulders drop forward and your belly drop down. Inhale and feel your body come upright again.

Bring your head into movement. Exhale, letting your head fall forward. Inhale, raising your head, looking up to the sky.

Let the rhythm of your breathing and body movements become more intense.

STAGE 3: VISUALIZING FIRE

When you are ready, bring in the element of visualization.

Exhale, sending a stream of energy from your chest and belly down through your legs and feet, into the earth beneath you. Take time to develop a strong feeling, image, or thought of sending your energy down into the earth with each exhalation.

Each time you exhale, let your energy move deeper and deeper into the earth, penetrating down through the soil, down through the rock, as if growing deep roots.

Keep going until you can penetrate the Earth's fiery core, until you connect with those liquid, molten flames that burn eternally at the planet's center. See the red, molten lava, burning, gurgling, a huge ball of fire in the belly of the Earth.

As you connect with the Earth's core, evoke a vision, a memory, a feeling of fire. Remember when you last stood by a burning-hot fire, or when you watched flames leap into the sky, or felt heat penetrating your skin, warming your bones. Remember how you sweated from the heat. See the red and orange flames in your mind's eye.

Remember, too, the fire of your own passion, the rushes of red hot anger, the heat of sexual passion, the fire burning in your loins, letting all these images merge and mingle in a concentrated vision of fire.

STAGE 4: BRINGING FIRE INTO YOUR BODY

Now you can begin to draw the fire upward from planet's burning center.

Inhale, sucking the fire up through the earth toward the place where you stand on the surface.

Exhale, sending your own warmth down to meet the rising flames.

Inhale, feeling the flames reach the earth's surface and begin to lick the soles of your feet. It is pure, flaming energy. It is the fire of life itself.

Exhale, sending your energy down to meet the rising fire, feeling the soles of your feet getting warm.

> *Lovers don't finally meet somewhere. They are in each other all along.*
>
> —RUMI

Feel that your energy is
sinking into the earth as if
you were growing roots.
Connect with the fire at the
center and let it grow and
move through your body,
cleansing your being.

Inhale, feeling the red, molten fire flow up into your feet, ankles, and lower legs. Let your legs become warm. Feel the heat rising into your knees.

Keep breathing deeply, making bodily movements to help the flow of energy. With each inhalation, let the fire rise higher, into your thighs, pelvis, hips, buttocks. Visualize the fiery color of red spreading through these areas, purifying them, healing them, energizing them.

As you feel this energy burning in your pelvis, begin to make sounds. Give a voice to your instinctual self, to the fiery energy of your wild, primal roots. Growl, grunt, shout, express yourself in whatever way feels natural and appropriate.

Feel the fire rising into your belly, releasing the animal energy that is now awakening in your guts. Breathe deeply, fanning the flames of your passion, igniting a red hot fire in your belly. You may receive sudden glimpses, visions, or insights into your Wild Self. Use them to bring even more totality to the exercise.

Feel the fire rising into your solar plexus and chest area, filling your lungs, giving you power, radiating heat from your torso. Feel this energy in your heart, releasing emotions of sadness or joy. Allow your hands and arms to move, expressing these feelings.

Your body is becoming a pillar of flame, setting you afire with unknown energies. Welcome these sensations of new strength, new life. Give them a sound, a voice. Keep breathing.

Let the fire rise into your throat and mouth. Now you are breathing fire, like a dragon. Breathe the flames through your mouth; express the energy through sounds in your throat. Let the Wild Self come out in cries and different voices. You may even wish to speak gibberish or nonsense. Give yourself full permission to express the energy in whatever way feels good.

Now the fire rises all the way through your head. Here, it may become subtle, like small blue flames in your forehead, burning away any mental tensions, any cramped-up thoughts, worries, doubts, shadows, confusion. Let the fire revitalize your brain, clearing your head, energizing your mind.

Finally, let the flames rise through the crown of your head and beyond, rising higher and higher. Let these flames connect you with the universe surrounding you.

STAGE 5: BECOMING THE FIRE

Now your whole body is a column of fire, from head to foot. Inhale, feeling the flames swoosh upward through your body, cleansing every part of you. You are an open channel, a hollow stick of bamboo, letting fire stream from the center of the Earth all the way to the sky.

Enjoy this wild energy that rushes through you. Let your body, your arms, dance the fire. Let the fire purify your body, burning away any impurities, any old, stuck energy. You are being healed. You feel lighter, more radiant, golden. Open yourself to any visions, images, symbols that arise from within the flames.

Improvise a "fire dance," celebrating the purification that you are receiving. Move your body, make sounds, dance, go wild.

When you feel that the fire has reached every corner of your being, start to slow down your breathing. Feel the fire gradually sinking back down through your body, leaving your head, neck, chest, abdomen. Visualize the flames receding, leaving your pelvis and legs, draining out through your feet into the earth, sinking down into the planet's core from whence it came.

Feel how the fire has taken with it any old attitudes or blocks that you don't wish to carry anymore. Let them go. Give them back to the earth.

Lie down on the floor for ten minutes. Relax.

If you have done this exercise with a partner, sit up and share your experiences. If you did it alone, you may wish to write your experiences in your notebook.

End with a Heart Salutation.

Pointers

The Fire Meditation is a popular exercise in my groups and workshops because people find it challenging yet at the same time easy to do, with concrete results:

"I saw myself as a dormant volcano in which little tremors began to awaken my sleeping energy," reported one participant. "In my imagination, lava started coming up through passages in the earth and these passages extended into my body like channels of fire. Suddenly, as the heat reached my head, it was as if I erupted!"

You may perhaps feel that nothing is happening in the early stages of the exercise, but don't be discouraged. Be alert for small tremors of energy and other sensations in your body, especially in your legs and hips, and associate these sensations with images of heat and fire. Amplify the sensations with your breathing, while imagining that the fire in your body is getting stronger and hotter.

Rhythmic breathing is an important key. The more strongly you breathe, the more you will fan the flames of your Fire Meditation.

EXERCISE: CONNECTING WITH YOUR WILD ANIMAL

Purpose and Benefits

This powerful exercise is similar to the practices used by shamans to unite with a "power animal" for the purpose of gaining strength, wisdom, and secret knowledge of occult and natural forces.

However, my exercise is slightly different. Most shaman rituals embrace the belief that there is one type of animal that is closely aligned with your spirit, and that once you have discovered this animal—be it wolf, bear, or eagle—the association is permanent. You do not shift from animal to animal.

In my exercise, I invite you to connect with whatever animal appeals to you at this moment, in this particular exercise, so that you can use its image to awaken wild, instinctive energies that are dormant in you.

Repeating the exercise on different occasions may invoke different kinds of animals. You may find yourself running with the wolves, then flying with the eagles, then powering through the underbrush as a grizzly bear. Let yourself be available to these possibilities, but do not explore more than one type of animal per session as this can be confusing and dilute the impact of the exercise.

It is also fun to mimic animals like dogs, deers, and goats, copying their movements and cries, to attack abruptly like the horse or arch your backs like two voluptuous cats.

—Kama Sutra

Connecting with your wild animal gives you and your partner an expanded sense of freedom and playfulness, widening the parameters of your relationship and releasing any pent-up aggression in a safe and creative way.

In this exercise, you begin with visualization, imagination, but then you switch to real-life drama, acting out your animal self.

Preparations

- This exercise can be done alone, but will be described with two people participating together.
- Create your Magic Circle.

145

◈ Wear loose, comfortable clothing that will not restrict any animal movements you may wish to make as the exercise progresses.

◈ You may want to play music, particularly deep, rhythmic drumming, or you may prefer to do this exercise without music. Either way is fine.

◈ Resist the temptation to select an animal beforehand, so that deeper experiences can be revealed to you through the unexpected. Be completely available to the unknown.

◈ The exercise takes the form of a journey, or guided fantasy, which I have divided into six stages. Move through each stage, acting out the roles as I describe them, while the story unfolds. You and your partner are actors in a play. Enjoy the drama!

◈ One useful way of experiencing this exercise is to make an audio recording of my guidelines, which last about forty-five minutes, then play it back while you act out the various stages.

◈ This guided journey begins in the same way as your initiation ceremony in chapter 2, but, as you will soon see, it ends very differently!

Practice

Enter your Magic Circle.

Light a candle, burn incense, lower the lights—to evoke a mood of mystery and wonder.

Sit or lie comfortably. Close your eyes.

Take a few deep breaths, relaxing your body, getting rid of any tension, bringing yourself here, now, in the present moment.

STAGE 1: THE QUEST

Imagine that you are walking along a hiking trail in open country. It is a clear, sunny day and you are enjoying the breeze on your face and the warm sunshine on your body. You take pleasure in the swinging movement of your legs and arms as you walk at an easy pace.

The trail is climbing higher and, as you look back, you see that you are leaving civilization behind you. The neatly plowed fields, the highway cutting through them, the distant town . . . it's all being left behind as you turn your eyes again to the trail ahead.

Soon, the path begins to wind through trees. You are entering a beautiful forest. Unhesitatingly, you walk forward, and, as you do so, an

In your sleep you enter into the body of your power animal. Here, the wolf.

exciting feeling arises within you that something wonderful is going to happen inside this forest, something very significant and personally meaningful.

You follow the trail through the trees as the sun gently sinks in the West. You can hear birdsong and the occasional sounds of rustling in the undergrowth, but you do not see any animals as you wind your way through the old-growth forest that has stood here for thousands of years.

It is getting dark, and you begin to feel tired. Seeing an inviting hollow formed in the middle of three ancient trees, you decide to stop, stretch out, and rest. You are not afraid of spending the night here. The air is warm, and the feeling of the forest is mysterious but welcoming. Pretty soon your eyelids become heavy and you fall asleep.

Sex lies at the root of life, and we can never learn reverence for life until we learn reverence for sex.

—HAVELOCK ELLIS

STAGE 2: THE DREAM

As you sleep, you hear a voice, like that of some old, wise teacher, quietly speaking inside your head. The teacher is explaining something you already seem to know, that you have been here before, in this magical forest, long, long ago. That you have lived many lives as a human being, but before that time, long before that, you were a wise and powerful animal . . .

The voice drifts off and, in your dreams, you seem to be floating away from your cozy hollow in the trees, floating toward the mouth of a dark tunnel that sucks you into its womblike depths. Human faces flicker in the shadows as you are swept swiftly through the tunnel, faces that may have been you, in some other time, in some other life, faces that seem to grow more ancient, more primitive, more animallike as the tunnel deepens and then, abruptly, there is total darkness and stillness and peace.

Rest in this primordial stillness while a magical, mysterious transformation comes over you . . .

(From this point, you combine action with visualization, beginning to act out and express the animal you have become.)

STAGE 3: THE TRANSFORMATION

There is the sound of a bird, then a feeling of early-morning light flickering on your eyelids. You know that you are back in the hollow, underneath the trees, and you also know, instinctively, that something profound has occurred. This is not a human body that you now inhabit.

Be still, keep your eyes closed, and slowly explore the sensation of being in this strange new body. What kind of body is it? Is it big? Is it small? Does it have fur? Does it have feathers? Does it have four legs? A tail?

Speak softly to yourself, describing the different parts of the body you now inhabit. Go into as much detail as possible.

Sense the muscles of this body, how they will move once your sleep is fully broken. Sense the smell of this body, the aroma of fur or feathers. Don't be in a hurry. This is a precious moment of creativity that you are experiencing. Understanding and recognition are dawning inside you. You have become an animal. This is your reality. This is you.

The morning light gets steadily brighter, urging you to open your eyes. You get up slowly, stretch, maybe lick your paws, scratch your back, peck with a sharp beak into your feathers, preening yourself in preparation to meet the new day. You look around, smelling the wind, listening to the forest awakening around you. You feel a thirst inside your belly. You need water. It is time to move out of your lair and go down to the river for a morning drink.

In your own animal style, you make your way to the river. If you are a large bear, you amble along, sniffing this and that, careless of whatever creatures may be near. If you are a smaller animal, like a deer, you may move more alertly, on the lookout for predators or rivals. If you are a bird, you may glide from branch to branch. Feel the natural animal grace and power that courses through your veins as you walk toward the water.

Remember, this is now more than a visualization. Open your eyes and move your body as if you have become your animal. Crawl across the floor, imagining that you are on your way to the water hole or stream, while your partner does the same.

STAGE 4: THE ENCOUNTER

Water holes and drinking places are shared by lots of species and it is here, this morning, that you will meet another animal. See, over there, through the bushes, another creature is heading toward the river (this is your partner, with whom you will now interact).

Drink, but watch carefully. This is your water hole. You may want to utter a warning growl, bark, or screech.

Aha! The other animal is barking back! Now you feel the time has come to make a show of power. You go to meet the challenge, approaching the other animal, even if it is much bigger, smaller, or very different from you. There is no intent to hurt or maim but simply to show your strength, your animal power.

Face this intruder. Show your teeth, your claws. Show your powerful body. Make threatening sounds. Bark, grunt, growl, squawk. Make mock

The ritual of mating begins.

attacks, feinting retreats, sudden lunges, but do not actually touch the other creature. Feel your power, show your power, but do not use it in actual fighting.

After a few minutes, you have made your point. This intruder knows whom he or she is dealing with! Now you have gotten some respect, you can allow things to get more friendly. Perhaps there is room for two animals at this drinking spot after all.

STAGE 5: THE MATING DANCE

Let your sounds, your behavior, become less threatening, more accommodating. Sniff around this other animal. Explore its scent, its odors. Lick its face. Nuzzle its neck. Give it a friendly nudge in the shoulder.

Suddenly you smell a musky scent arising from each other's sexual organs. Hormones are being released. Lust is stirring powerfully in your loins. Yes, this is the mating season, and in this magical forest even creatures of different species can develop a healthy sexual interest in each other.

The ritual of mating begins. One animal is male, the other is female (you can begin with your own gender, but you get to play both roles).

The female is in heat. The perfume from her sex glands calls to the male and awakens his desire. See, he is already sniffing around her pleasure center, his own hormones responding to the invitation.

Now the mating dance can start. The male parades back and forth, puffing out his chest, showing his manhood, ruffling his feathers, making loud, conquering calls, dancing around in a ballet of movement designed to impress the female.

The female is interested, but she rarely looks at the male directly, pretending to lick her paws or chew some morsel of food, provoking even greater displays from the male in an effort to get her attention.

Now he advances, ready to mount the female. She snarls, or squawks, rebuffing his advances, further increasing his excitement. The fur and feathers fly as the male repeatedly struts and postures before the female, theatrically demonstrating his lust, then leaps upon her, while she, though secretly knowing the way things will end, keeps fighting him off, snarling, squawking, or yapping, making him more and more excited.

He performs another ballet then tries again, grabbing the female by the neck in an attempt to hold her steady while he mounts. Aha! This time he is successful, sitting astride the female and humping her with urgent muscular movements from his loins.

Go deeply into these sensations. Allow yourself to experience fully these animal energies, even though you have clothes on. Play it out. Be totally sexual until the mating ritual is complete.

STAGE 6: CHANGE GENDER ROLES

The mating done, the two animals separate and rest for a few moments. Lie down and close your eyes. Take a few deep breaths.

In this moment of relaxation, imagine that you magically change your gender. Now the female becomes the male. The male becomes the female.

Slowly, the mating dance begins anew, with each of you experiencing the opposite sexual polarity.

Feel the fun, as a woman, to be a male animal with a penis. Check out what it feels like. Strut your stuff. Be proud of your new sex.

Enjoy the novelty, as a man, to be a female animal. See if you can attract the attention of this cocky-looking male, but don't be too eager to please.

The new male parades and dances for his intended mate, then attempts to mount her. She may resist, once or perhaps several times, before succumbing to his advances. Enjoy the grunts, growls, cackling, and squawking. Make sounds you've never heard before as pure animal lust fills your body.

STAGE 7: THE RETURN

With the heat of the mating over, the two animals relax, lying lazily and peacefully side by side, their energies spent. After a while, they close their eyes and drift easily into dreams, strange dreams for animals because they see themselves floating into the mouth of a long, dark tunnel, being carried on the winds of time into a faraway future, until at last they find themselves at the other end of the tunnel, emerging into soft daylight.

Sleepily, they open their eyes and miraculously find themselves in human form, lying together in a Magic Circle. What a surprise. They are sexual magicians, practicing exercises from a book of magic!

When you feel ready, sit up and share your experiences.

End with a Heart Salutation.

Pointers

At first, you may feel that connecting with your Wild Animal isn't real, or seems silly, or does not give you the powerful feeling you had expected. If so, remember that we have been taught to play safe, to stay in control, to use our skeptical minds to dismiss things that seem strange and unfamiliar.

Have the courage to throw yourself totally into this exercise, breaking through to an experience of your animal wildness in a playful yet enthusiastic way. Remember, every one of us carries in our cells the genetic memories of our animal heritage. It is there, waiting to be awakened. Use the Three Keys of deep breathing, movement, and sound to awaken your energies and bring out the animal within you.

Conscious growth, conscious life, means becoming wiser, more intelligent, more fulfilled, more powerful, and happier.

—OSHO

Access your wild energies in a way that respects your partner's sensibility. Your challenge, here, is to stay on the edge: being wild yet playful without intimidating or hurting your partner.

During the mating rituals, you may feel like really making love to your partner. If so, enjoy the innocent lust of your Wild Animal in heat. Stay in character and don't slip into old, familiar patterns of sexual union. If you don't feel like making love, this is also perfectly okay.

In the mating rituals, make sure you experience both roles, the male and the female. In my workshops, many women say they experience a strong release of wild energy and also a sense of sexual healing when they give themselves permission to play the male totally and mount their partners.

Some people like to become fish during this visualization exercise, but it can make things rather problematic during the mating stages. For example, it is difficult to imagine a bear diving underwater to mate with a dolphin, or a killer whale coming on land to seduce a reindeer. If you feel drawn to such challenges, please go ahead. But generally I guide people into choosing land animals or large birds for this exercise.

If you do the exercise alone, you may choose to visualize an animal intruding at your water hole and act accordingly. You may even decide to invent a mating dance with an imaginary partner—something to try out for real when your next significant other comes along.

FROM WILD ENERGY TO CLEAR VISION

In this chapter you connected with a major source of your power by awakening the strength of your Wild Self. In doing so, you were able to experience an invigorating, energizing, and healing release of energy. But this wild energy has no direction in itself. It needs to be given a goal, a focus, an intention.

The next chapter shows you how to create a clear vision of your goals, preparing for the moment when you will charge a vision with all your energy resources and channel it up through your body in an alchemical process of refinement and transformation.

Learning how to create such a vision, you start to enter the realm of true magic, penetrating the mysteries of this art through which visions can become realities.

CHAPTER 5

CREATING YOUR MAGIC VISION:

Opening the Door to Sexual Magic

Y ou have empowered yourself as a magician, blessed your body, and awakened your wild self. You are now ready to master another important skill that will help you accomplish your goals: creating and holding a magical vision.

It is your vision that gives focus and direction to your magical powers. You need to see clearly the areas of your life that you wish to transform. You need to identify the personal goals that you wish to attain. And, when you have created a vision of your desire, you need to know how to condense it into a potent magical symbol that can be charged with the power of your sexual energy.

One thousand years ago, in Tibet, it was a vision of revenge against his family's persecutors that drove the legendary yogi Milarepa to study what would now be termed "black magic." Once he had gained mastery over these powers, Milarepa's passionate determination to see his enemies suffer enabled him to create and hold a vision of such strength and clarity that, using occult forces, he succeeded in pulling down houses and devastating whole villages.

Oh, night that guided me,
Oh, night more lovely than
*   the dawn,*
Oh, night, that joined
*   the Beloved with lover,*
Lover transformed
*   in the Beloved!*

—ST. JOHN OF THE CROSS

Later, however, Milarepa was aghast at the destructive nature of his powers and realized that these negative forces would eventually boomerang on their creator. He wisely decided to channel his energy in a positive direction, pursuing a vision of spiritual transformation and eventually becoming an enlightened mystic.

But you do not need to travel backward in time and encounter legendary figures like Milarepa in order to understand the nature of a vision. Creating and holding a vision is one of the most natural things we do in our lives. Consciously or unconsciously, each one of us does it every day.

For example, you're at the office, it's late in the afternoon, and you're starting to get hungry. What do you do? You begin to create a vision about dinner. Sitting at your desk, miles from home, you scan the contents of your refrigerator and kitchen cupboards with your mind's eye and pick out the food you desire to eat that evening.

Then you see yourself dicing mushrooms, onions, peppers, adding them to a spicy sauce for the pasta that is boiling in a big pot on the stove. *Mmm,* smells good! In a flash, you jump to the finished product, seeing, in vivid detail, the pièce de résistance arranged tastefully on a plate, ready to satisfy the hunger that triggered your whole creative process.

Here's another common example. You're about to go for a job interview. It's important, so you're likely to sit down beforehand and envision the whole proceeding: what you are going to wear, what questions you will be asked, what answers you will give, and what issues you will raise yourself. You're likely to plan a certain approach, or strategy, to produce an envisioned result, anticipating how the interviewers will behave and how you're going to deal with the situation. Perhaps you may even envision a party afterwards to celebrate a successful outcome.

This, too, is a form of creating a vision.

Similarly, you may pause before making a long-distance phone call to a friend and ask yourself, "Is this a good time to call?" In doing so, you may hold a vision of the person in your mind's eye, picturing what he or she may be doing, thereby gaining a sense of whether or not to go ahead with the call. This is also a form of vision.

In the sphere of health care, directed visualization is acquiring a reputation as a valuable aid to conventional medicine. Medical doctors specializing in the use of imagery in the treatment of disease, such as Dr. Martin Rossman, author of *Healing Yourself,* cite all kinds of illnesses, ranging from urinary tract blockages to back pain to cancer, that have been alleviated or healed through different types of imagery. Convinced that thoughts can trigger the body's self-healing abilities, Dr. Rossman has successfully developed a wide variety of methods for healing physical illness through imagery and visualization.

When you use vision in magic, you are employing it as a powerful tool to give direction and intent to your magical powers, defining the outcome you desire to manifest. Therefore, your vision needs to be as precisely defined and as clear as possible, for this is the alchemy that will harness all your energies, giving them power and single-pointed direction.

THE MANY DIMENSIONS OF CREATIVE VISION

When I invite people to create a vision in my workshops, they tend to assume that they are being asked to create a picture, or visual image, in the mind. For example, if I suggest that they create a vision of a fulfilled and orgasmic sexual state, the majority of participants will try to "see" a picture of themselves in this state, conjuring up a visual image in which they look happy and sexually satisfied.

Love is Nature's second sun.

—GEORGE CHAPMAN
All Fools

Certainly, this is one way of creating a vision, but there is no need to worry if you are not the visual type. The capacity to think in pictures is just one of several types of imagery available through your imagination. Its imagery can manifest itself as pictures, thoughts, feelings, sounds, tastes, and smells.

For example, the vision that you create may take the form of an affirmation, such as "I relax and open myself to pleasure. I invite the flow of orgasmic pleasure through my body." You may begin a dialogue with yourself, describing your vision aloud, or hear an intuitive voice arising from within, like an inner guide, which may express itself in words, feelings, or impulses.

The physical body has a remarkable capacity to respond to imagery. Try this: Pause for a moment and imagine yourself in your kitchen slicing a lemon, picking up a piece, and sucking the sharp, acidic juice. You will probably feel an immediate flow of saliva in your mouth, especially under the tongue.

Here, a thought or picture is creating a bodily sensation, but you can also do the reverse. By focusing on bodily sensations, you can create an appropriate vision. Simply by lying on your bed, moving your body in a sensual and erotic way, and feeling the touch of your naked skin against the sheets, you can generate a powerful vision of sexual fulfillment.

The link between imagination and sounds and smells is also very strong. The use of incense and bells in religious ceremonies around the world is based on the understanding that these senses can help to conjure up certain spiritual states, such as meditation, devotion, and inner peace. In the more earthly dimensions of life, the smell of freshly baked apple pie or chocolate-chip cookies can trigger a flood of pleasant childhood memories.

Not only do external sounds and smells stimulate internal states and memories, but you may also find that you can *imagine* a sound or smell that gives depth and vibrancy to a vision. In short, you may create a personal vision by using your whole range of sensory perception, as well as words and thoughts. There is no need to limit yourself to a single dimension of imagery.

TWO BASIC TYPES OF VISIONS

There are two basic types of visions: those that we receive as revelation and those that we create with our imagination.

In virtually all spiritual traditions, the idea of receiving revelation through visions is commonplace. Holy men from India and Tibet frequently describe how, during meditation or fasting, a god or "deva" appears and transmits a vital teaching or insight for which they had been questing.

In the Judaic tradition, Moses received the revelation of the Ten Commandments through this kind of vision, while many Christian saints have spoken of divine revelation, seeing the figure of Christ or Mary or hearing a voice or heavenly music.

The Native American tradition of the Vision Quest contains a similar theme of seeking revelation through a vision that is invoked as a rite of passage into maturity—a practice that has been enthusiastically adopted by some modern American seekers.

These are all visions in which the seeker, or quester, is receptive. The manifesting of the vision is left to universal forces that lie beyond ordinary human power and knowledge.

A more intentional type of vision is found in some Indian spiritual

In the realm of magic you also act intentionally, creating a vision of your desired outcome. With magic, you decide what it is that you wish to achieve, then crystallize your desire through visualization and other tech-

Sadhu, or spiritual initiate, receiving divine revelation in a Himalayan cave

traditions, in which the seeker or adept focuses on a particular god or goddess whose divine qualities the adept wishes to attain. The image of the deva is then charged with energy—through chanting sacred mantras, or making special offerings or sacrifices—until the seeker feels that he or she has embodied the desired qualities. In most cases, the seeker is required to hold a vision of the deva constantly in his or her mind until the transmission has been accomplished.

In the realm of magic you also act intentionally, creating a vision of your desired outcome. With magic, you decide what it is that you wish to achieve, then crystallize your desire through visualization and other tech-

The sun, the radiance and power of meditation

niques that are described in this chapter. The more clear, firm, and detailed the vision, the greater the possibility it will manifest itself in your life.

MAGIC, SEX, AND VISIONS

Sexual magic is multidimensional. It has the power to fulfill all kinds of desires, including:

- Personal healing and transformation
- New love relationships
- Greater intimacy and harmony in existing relationships
- Material manifestations such as financial abundance, a new home, or a new job

I recently helped two love partners, Jeffrey and Laura, create a ritual of sexual magic that was designed to bring better employment opportunities for Jeffrey. He had been working for five years on the production team of a well-established Los Angeles film corporation. It was a good job, but it

The face, *The Wildness of Kali*, painted by Mrs. Ajit Mookerjee, a contemporary artist

The yin-yang symbol of balance and harmony, resulting from the idea that opposites such as male and female can be complementary

lacked creative opportunities. Moreover, his love partner, Laura, had just begun to work as an adviser on an exciting new video project with a different company.

"Wouldn't it be wonderful," the lovers dreamed, "if Jeffrey could somehow get a job on the production team that Laura is working for?"

The normal avenue of approaching Laura's employer had produced no results; he said he wasn't interested in hiring Jeffrey.

With my help, they began carefully to create a vision in which Jeffrey was depicted as leaving his old job and joining the other corporation. I encouraged him to make specific conditions for the transfer, such as being hired at a higher salary than previously and obtaining a creative position in which his enthusiasm and talent could find expression.

Once their vision was clearly established, I guided Jeffrey and Laura into the process of creating a Magic Symbol that expressed their vision and charging this symbol with their sexual energy. Then they began to practice sexual magic on a daily basis. After about a week, something totally unexpected occurred: a movie director working for Laura's company approached the boss and talked with him about the advantages of hiring Jeffrey.

Nothing happened immediately, but Laura and Jeffrey felt encouraged and continued to practice sexual magic. One week later, Jeffrey got a phone call—he was hired. Needless to say, both partners were ecstatic.

CONDENSING YOUR VISION INTO A SYMBOL

One of the keys to success in magic is to be able to translate, or condense, the vision of your desired goal into a symbol. Symbols constitute a kind of shorthand that can capture the essence of something more elaborate and complex. As such, they can be tremendously powerful.

Our lives contain many symbols: the cross that signifies Christianity, the flag that symbolizes a certain country . . . Symbols have the capacity to sink deeply into the subconscious mind. They serve as a kind of basic language that can link people and ideas in powerful ways. For example, if you are watching a television news program and you see a crowd of foreigners or protesters burning the flag of your country, you may well feel insulted, enraged, perhaps even violent, even though it is just a piece of colored cloth. On the other hand, if the same flag is raised in a victory celebration because some athlete has just won an Olympic gold medal, you may feel a surge of pride. In both cases it is not the cloth, but what it symbolizes, that has stirred passionate emotions in you.

In esoteric, spiritual, and magical dimensions, symbols are even more widely used, including astrological signs, runes, tarot cards, hexagrams, the yin-yang symbol of Taoism, the chalice of the Holy Grail, the Indian wheel of Life and Death, the teaching wheels of shamanistic rituals.

In magic, one of the most common and potent types of symbol is known as a sigil, which can be defined as the distillation, or essence, of a magical vision that is expressed through words.

For example, if you are dissatisfied with your job, you may want to create a vision of a new, more fulfilling type of employment. Once this vision is clear, you can make a sigil that symbolizes this heartfelt desire. To make the sigil, take a pen and paper and write the statement that expresses your desire:

"I want to create a job in which I feel happy and fulfilled." You may want to experiment with creating a sigil as I explain the procedure. Just pick up a pen and paper and try it yourself.

Now reduce the statement to a simple phrase, preferably no longer than two or three words, such as "I CREATE A GREAT JOB."

Next, you remove any letters that are duplicated in the phrase. In "CREATE A GREAT JOB" you will see that the letters R, E, A, T and E are all duplicated. When the duplicates have been removed, stack the remaining letters together, thus: "GREAT JOB."

Now you can unleash your artistic talents, creating a symbol out of these letters in the same way that a corporation creates a logo. You have complete freedom to create a symbol that feels right for you and that reflects your desire (see illustration page 172).

The letters need not be of equal size; you can make the *o* large and fit all the other letters inside it. You can take the tail of the *g* and run it underneath the whole symbol. The important thing is to create a sigil that you feel happy with, something that captures the feeling or essence of your desire.

Sigils appeal to people with sharp intellects who like to play with words and letters. However, others may feel more inclined toward abstract, intuitive types of symbols.

If this is true for you, there is an alternative and equally effective way to create a magical symbol: you can paint or draw a picture of your desired outcome.

Your picture can be a literal and lifelike representation of the object

God is the lover, the loving, and the beloved, all in one.

—A SUFI SONG

of your desire, or it can be an abstract rendering that conveys feeling instead of form—perhaps no more than an aura of golden light surrounding a warm, pink, glowing center of energy. It doesn't matter if your painting seems meaningless to others. The important thing is that it resonates with your vision.

It can be helpful to include well-known symbols in your painting, such as circles, squares, triangles, moons, and stars. These symbols contain certain elemental meanings that can assist you in expressing your desire. Here are a few common ones:

- Circle: completion, wholeness, life cycles, self-contained
- Square: power, guarded and protected, balanced, structured, potential
- Triangle: ascension of energy, moving from solid foundations to a one-pointed outcome, transformation, alchemy
- Stars: magic, light, goodness, spiritual longing
- Sun: heart, warmth, fire, wealth, expansion, compassion
- Moon: your inner world, mystery, feminine qualities, coolness, deep insights, subconscious urges
- Water: feelings, emotions, depth
- Dolphin: playfulness, happiness, harmony, good luck
- Lion: courage, strength, power
- Dragon: fire, energy, creativity, power
- Snake: wisdom, intelligence, sexual energy
- Eagle: clarity of perception, global vision, freedom, space

A third possibility is to combine a sigil with a painting or picture. You can either create the sigil first and then paint a picture around it, or paint a picture and then add the sigil to it.

Now that we have covered the basic concepts involved in creating a vision and condensing it into a symbol, we can pause to reflect on our reasons for creating a vision in the first place. In fact, at root, there is only one reason: desire.

The Dolphin, symbol of innocent playfulness, the inner child

The Eagle, symbol of the global vision, clarity

The Dragon, symbol of power, courage

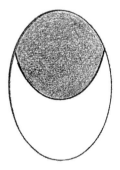

The Moon and Sky, reflecting each other

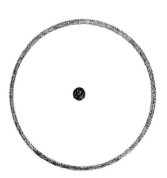

The Sun, symbol of festivity and resilience

The Moon, symbol of receptivity, reflection, gentleness

DESIRE: THE MOTIVATING FORCE OF MAGIC

Desire is the motivating force of magic. The very reason why we seek the aid of magical powers is to fulfill our desires, our heartfelt longings.

But in the history of spirituality, desire has a poor reputation. It is often viewed as an impediment to salvation or enlightenment. Many a would-be saint has lamented over the "desires of the flesh" that keep him tethered to a worldly life, when, according to Scripture, he should be able to renounce such temptations and free himself from earthly bondage.

However, in my experience, there is no virtue in struggling with desires or trying to repress them. Indeed, according to the founder of humanistic psychology Abraham Maslow's celebrated "hierarchy of needs," it is only when our basic, material desires for food and shelter are fulfilled that we become interested in higher matters—intellectual, aesthetic, and spiritual.

Desire is a fact of human life, and even those ascetic souls who desire to renounce life's temptations do so because they are desirous of spiritual rewards. The object of desire may change, but the energy of desire remains. Hence, there is no need to feel guilty about our desires. Each desire can be accepted and enjoyed and, when we grow tired of it, also be left behind.

THREE KINDS OF DESIRE

In the context of making magic, we can distinguish three general kinds of desire:

1. The Desire to Transform Yourself

Here, you are focused on healing negative psychological or emotional states and raising your consciousness, changing your state of being, becoming more loving, sensitive, intelligent, strong, orgasmic.

2. The Desire for Fulfilling Relationships

This includes creating new relationships with people and also enhancing the intimacy, depth, and love of existing relationships.

3. The Desire to Transform Your Environment

This includes a greater sense of financial freedom and material abundance, opportunities for new employment, the fulfilling use of personal skills and talents, the manifestation of such specific material objects such as a home or car.

The simplest introduction to the process of creating a vision is to work with the third category: the desire to transform your environment. The other two types of desire require special considerations that are dealt with later in the chapter.

You may object: "Yes, but the truth is I have no strong desire to change my environment. My primary interest lies in healing and transforming myself, or improving my relationships with others."

This is understandable, especially because over the past two chapters, you have been devoting so much time and energy to healing sexual wounds and awakening your Wild Self. The sudden shift to thinking about material objects may seem strange at first.

However, one of your qualities as a magician is an ability to function on different planes of reality and to shift rapidly between them. As your skill in sexual magic increases, you are going to be asked to become intensely alive in a very physical, sexual way, while at the same time holding before you a clear mental vision of your desires. These two very different dimensions make up the alchemy of sexual magic. So it is good to practice shifting between different aspects of your craft.

AIMING FOR THE POSSIBLE

One obstacle to magic is an underlying sense of unworthiness: on the one hand, we desire beneficial changes in our lives; on the other hand, we don't think we deserve them, and this creates an internal split that divides our energy.

The exercises given in chapter three go a long way to resolving this problem. But there is another, equally effective and simple solution: begin your magical practice with modest desires, aiming at transformations that will not provoke internal division.

For example, in terms of your material desires, instead of creating visions of great wealth, sudden promotion to the head of a company, buying a villa in the South of France, flying your own private jet—things that genies from magic lamps can easily manage but apprentice magicians may not be able to—you will feel more comfortable and integrated if you begin with smaller, more realistic goals such as paying off credit-card bills, finding a new home in a nice neighborhood, taking a vacation in the sun, or getting a useful boost at work.

As these goals are met and you feel strengthened in your abilities as a magician, you will find that you can expand your vision without encountering internal resistance.

The important thing is to begin in a way that will give you the taste of success, for this will open the door to greater and greater achievements.

Now we can proceed with the exercises, in which you will learn to create a clear vision of your desires, translating your vision into a potent symbol for magic.

EXERCISE: CREATING A VISION TO TRANSFORM YOUR ENVIRONMENT

Purpose and benefits

This exercise takes you in careful, detailed steps through the creation of a vision. It then teaches you how to condense your vision into a Magic Symbol that will help you manifest your desire.

With practice, creating a vision for transforming your environment can become a streamlined and speedy affair. In the beginning, however, it is helpful to proceed slowly and carefully, step by step, so that you can build up a sense of trust in your own powers as a magician.

Preparations

- You can do this exercise alone, or with your partner.
- Create your Magic Circle.

≫ Have plenty of drawing paper, pencils, crayons, and paints available. These materials should be new and should not be used for any other purpose. All tools that you use in magical ceremonies or exercises should be kept separate from your normal belongings. This will help you to empower them, giving them energy and significance.

≫ Wear your magician's robes.

≫ Allow one hour for this exercise.

Practice

STAGE 1: CHOOSING YOUR VISION
Enter your Magic Circle.

Sit comfortably, close your eyes, and take a few deep, slow breaths, relaxing your body each time you exhale. Take time to settle yourself.

Begin to reflect on your desires. Ask yourself: "What is it that I need in order to improve my sense of well-being? What is it that I most desire?"

For some people, the answer to this question will come easily. You may have been thinking about a particular goal for some time: a job change, a new skill, a home in a different area, a certain type of computer, car, or sound system.

For others, the question can be a little tricky. After all, we seem to want so many things. How to choose from all our desires? Like a child in a candy store, it can be a confusing task to pick out just one morsel from all the rest.

Here is one way to solve the problem: imagine that you really are a child in a big candy store of desires, or, if you prefer, an adult in a huge, sprawling flea market of desires. Imagine the scene: it's a sunny weekend afternoon; you can relax and wander casually from stall to stall, picking up one kind of desire, putting it down again, picking up another, knowing you have all the time in the world and can come back to reclaim an earlier desire if you wish.

Gradually, as you browse, make a note of the things that attract you most, creating a short list. Write them down on a piece of paper. When you are ready, you can sit down in a quiet corner of the flea market and select the desire you wish to work with. This is the material manifestation that you are going to bring into your life.

STAGE 2: EXPRESSING IT IN A SENTENCE.

State your desire clearly in a positive sentence:

"I, _____ (your name) desire a new job."

Or.

"I, _____ (your name) wish to find a new house."

STAGE 3: DO I DESERVE IT?

Once you have clearly identified your goal, check whether you feel that you deserve to have this desire fulfilled. Ask yourself: "Do I deserve this?" Or, if you prefer: "Am I ready for this?"

If you have difficulty creating a vision of your desire, if the image is blurry and confused, if you find there is a lot of mental chatter surrounding your efforts, or a subtle feeling of pessimism and doubt—"I can't change my life that much"; "I'll never get this desire fulfilled, no matter how hard I try"—this is an indication of resistance in the subconscious part of your mind.

Don't fight these doubts. Simply recognize that you have selected a desire that is creating a split inside you and go back to the flea market for a little more shopping. Continue in this way until you find a desire that feels clear and comfortable.

STAGE 4: CREATING AN ELABORATE VISUALIZATION.

With your imagination, take time to create a detailed picture of the object that you desire. For example, if you desire a new house, create in your mind's eye a picture that represents it. See your house in vivid detail: Is it built on level ground, or on a hillside? Is it surrounded by trees, or is it on a city block? How many floors does it have? Does it have a driveway? Is it made of wood or stone? Take a tour of the interior, as if you were being shown around by a real estate agent. See the whole layout: the living rooms, bedrooms, bathrooms, kitchen, hot tub . . . Don't be in a hurry. Enjoy the tour and take it all in.

Bring in all your senses. Touch the cushions on the sofa, the quilt on the bed, the towel in the bathroom, the wallpaper in the living room; smell the pine-scented air on the back porch. Hear the cosy hum of your computer in the den, or the music that floods through your new sound system.

If your imagination does not respond readily to sensory stimulation, you may prefer to describe, with speech or thoughts, the desired object. For example, "I walk out of my door, into the yard, turn around and see the whole house in front of me. It is made of wood and has two stories . . ."

STAGE 5: "YES! IT HAS HAPPENED!"

Once you have created an elaborate vision, the next step is to feel, as deeply as possible, that it has already happened. This is sometimes called "eliciting the outcome state" and is very important. By feeling that you have already achieved your goal, you are giving reality to your vision. You are creating the emotional state in which your manifestation can be translated into a magical symbol.

Say to yourself, "Yes! It has happened!"

Then you can ask, "How do I feel, now that I have attained what I want?"

Close your eyes and let yourself feel what it is like to have obtained the object of your desire. Naturally, you feel happy, excited, exuberant, fulfilled, grateful. Let these feelings arise in you.

Imagine that you are standing in the kitchen of your new house, picking up the phone, calling a friend and saying "Oh, Hal, the new place is just fantastic! It's everything I've ever wanted . . ." Go on to describe to your friend what it is like to live in your new home.

Or, imagine sitting in the luxurious comfort of your new car and cruising down a favorite street or highway. Feel the pleasure that arises out of this fulfilled desire. Maybe your lover or friend is sitting in the passenger seat and you are talking enthusiastically about the qualities of your new auto: "You know, the way this baby handles the corners is just so smooooth . . ."

Let yourself move deeply into the experience of the outcome state. Gain a feeling of conviction that it has really happened. You are not to be a bystander in this. You need to be a total participant, deeply feeling what it is like to have achieved your goal.

Feel yourself walking through the office, newly promoted to that job you always wanted, receiving the congratulations or envious looks of your colleagues, returning the smile of your assistant with a friendly nod as you glide through the doors of your personal office and walk silently across the thick pile carpet to your desk . . .

Whatever your desire, imagine the pleasure, excitement, and joy you will feel when your vision has become reality, and allow these feelings to be given full expression. Dance around the room, chuckle, smile—enjoy!

When you feel complete in this experience, slowly bring yourself out of the imagined scene. Let your feelings subside. Take a deep breath, relax, and bring yourself back to the reality of the present moment.

Having elicited the outcome, you are ready for the next step: creating a Magic Symbol.

STAGE 6: CREATING A MAGIC SYMBOL

Your Magic Symbol can be a Sigil, a painting, or a combination of the two.

If you decide to create a sigil, write on a piece of paper a statement that clearly expresses your desire. For example, if you have envisioned living in a beautiful house, you can write: "I want to live in a beautiful house."

Having written the statement, reduce it to a simple phrase of no more than two or three words, such as "beautiful house." Write down this phrase.

Next, remove any letters that are duplicated in the phrase. In this case, the letters *e* and *u* are duplicated. Bring the remaining letters together, thus: "beautiflhos."

Create a symbol out of these letters, giving free rein to your talents in graphic design. Remember, some letters can be bigger than others. All kinds of scripts and shapes are allowed. Create a symbol you feel happy with.

If you prefer, make a picture of your vision, using paints or colored crayons. For example, paint a picture of the house in which you desire to live. You may wish to include yourself in the picture, showing how you are enjoying your new home.

You can also create a combination of a sigil and a painting.

STAGE 7: ACCEPTING THE SYMBOL

When you have created a Magic Symbol that represents your vision, check whether you feel happy with it. Stand in the center of your Magic Circle; hold the symbol in both hands and look at it.

Does this symbol feel good to you? Does it represent your desire? If so, you will feel it in your bones, like an affirmation or surge of creative power from an unknown source. You will feel a "yes" inside yourself.

If you are not certain, throw this symbol away and start again, creating a new symbol that feels good to you.

When you have created a symbol that you like, dispose of all the previous writing and drawing that has helped you to arrive at this conclusion.

Stand in the center of your Magic Circle, hold your symbol in both hands, and look at it once more. Then, when you feel ready, hold the symbol aloft and declare aloud: "This is my Magic Symbol. I accept it as the expression of my desire."

If I am not to be for myself, who will be for me? If not now, when?

—FRITZ PERLS

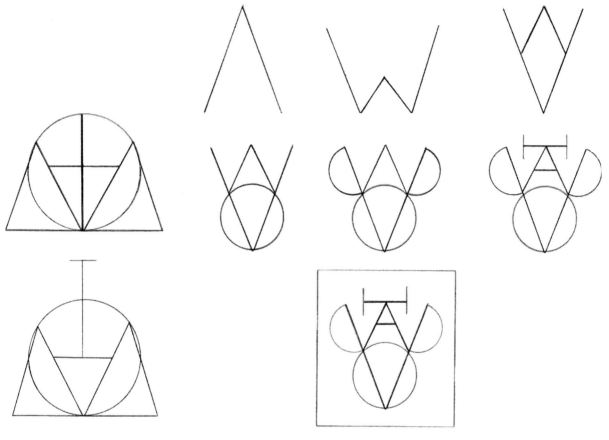

I AM THE MAGICIAN
I AM THE MAGICIAN
MAGI
1. Give the affirmation
2. Cut out the letters and
reduce to magi.
3. Sign

I CREATE AN AWARD-WINNING VIDEO
A WARD WINNIN VIDEO
A WIN VIDEO
A WIN VO

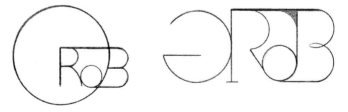

I CREATE A GREAT JOB.
CREATE GREAT JOB
GREATJOB

STAGE 8: IMPRINTING THE SYMBOL

Having accepted your Magic Symbol, you are ready to imprint it in the deeper layers of your mind.

Place the symbol on your altar in a way that allows you to look at it while sitting comfortably in your Magic Circle.

Begin to gaze at your Magic Symbol in a soft, relaxed way, as if you were looking at a friend or object that makes you feel good.

Spend two to three minutes looking this way. It may interest you to know that what you are doing is similar to the Eastern practice of gazing at tankas, mandalas, and other spiritual designs that create imprints in the deepest layers of the human psyche.

Now close your eyes and imagine that your Magic Symbol is becoming steadily bigger and bigger. Continue until the symbol is larger than your own body.

Imagine yourself floating, or walking, forwards until you find yourself inside your Magic Symbol. Rest in the symbol. Feel at ease with it. Relax in this new relationship with the symbol of your desire.

This is a powerful way to embody your Magic Symbol, allowing it to become part of you. You are creating within yourself a blueprint for something new to happen, some outcome that is going to be manifest in your life.

When you are ready, walk out of your symbol and allow it to become smaller and smaller, shrinking to a tiny point that soon disappears altogether.

End with a Heart Salutation, bowing toward your Magic Symbol.

Pointers

It may take several sessions for you to feel completely satisfied with your symbol. Take your time, be patient, continuing to experiment with new drawings until you are sure that your Magic Symbol expresses the essential spirit of your vision.

You may find that you want to begin by creating a very basic symbol, then steadily adding new features every day until it feels complete.

Remember: Keep it simple so you can hold the visualization easily inside your mind's eye.

DUPLICATING YOUR MAGIC SYMBOL

To absorb further the imprint of your Magic Symbol, you may want to make several copies of it and place them at strategic points in your home: by your bed, in the bathroom, in the kitchen.

Look at it frequently. Your general attitude toward the symbol should be one of friendly acceptance and mutual cooperation.

Each day, spend a few minutes visualizing the symbol on various objects that lie at some distance from yourself. For example, as you sit on your back porch, imagine the symbol imprinted on a tree trunk at the end of your yard, or on a distant hillside, or on a white, puffy cloud.

Each time you see the symbol, or visualize it, you will be imprinting it deeper in your mind, giving it greater significance and energy. This process of imprinting will be of immense help when you begin to fuse your Magic Symbol with your orgasmic, sexual energy.

CANCELING A SYMBOL

Your Magic Symbol is canceled when you burn it. With this fiery act, the power of the symbol is destroyed and the spell is over.

This burning should be done in the same deliberate, ritualistic manner that you used to create the symbol.

Prepare a special metal bowl or fireplace for this purpose, either inside or outside your house. Create a Magic Circle around it.

Place your Magic Symbol in the receptacle. Light the symbol, step back, raise your arms to the sky, and say, "I now declare the power invested in this symbol to be dissolved."

In addition, the power of a Magic Symbol tends to cease automatically once the object of your desire has been manifested.

ACCEPTING A DIFFERENT OUTCOME

When creating a vision of your desire, it is important to go into elaborate detail. But you also need to be open to the possibility that your manifestation, when it occurs, is going to look different from the vision you created.

This may seem paradoxical. You may ask, "Well, what's the point of going into such detail with my visualization if the reality is going to be different?"

To which I can only reply: that's the way magic happens. Your energy needs to be totally focused on creating your vision, and your vision needs to be as clear and as crystallized as possible. This will result in a very potent symbol for practicing sexual magic.

But at the same time, you need to remain flexible. Rigid attitudes can crush the spirit of creativity with which you are working. The essence of magic is transformation, the possibility of creative change, which may happen spontaneously and unexpectedly. So it is important, in the service of magic, to remain open and flexible, avoiding the seductive but wrong idea that you can control all outcomes at all times. The universe may have a delightful surprise in store for you—be prepared to accept it.

Now that you have learned the knack of creating a vision to transform your environment, you are ready to explore a deeper, more internal type of desire: the desire to transform yourself.

EXERCISE: CREATING A VISION TO TRANSFORM YOURSELF

Purpose and benefits

This exercise will enable you to transform yourself in whatever way you desire, such as rising in consciousness, acquiring greater self-understanding and wisdom, becoming more loving, more orgasmic.

The desire to transform yourself can be described as a "state of self-healing" because the very fact that you want to be more loving, more courageous, more orgasmic indicates that these qualities are lacking in your life right now. In other words, there is a negative state that needs to be healed so that a more positive and fulfilling one can manifest itself.

For example, if you desire to be more orgasmic, your negative state may be expressed as "I don't feel my body very much when I make love," or "I don't experience orgasm very often," or "I don't seem to be able to relax into the pleasure that I know is inside me."

Healing the negative state and anchoring the positive state are important steps in magical self-transformation.

In this practice you will also reconnect with your Inner Magician, whom you met in chapter 2, and enlist his or her cooperation.

Your Inner Magician will speak on behalf of all those hidden parts of yourself—your hidden demons, your wounded child, the deepest layers of your subconscious mind—so that they can be included in your desire for transformation. This is a powerful way to integrate your energies.

Preparation

- You can do this exercise alone or with your partner.
- Create your Magic Circle.
- You will need a pencil and paper.
- Wear your magician's robes.
- Allow one hour for the exercise.

Practice

STAGE 1: CHOOSING A STATE OF HEALING
Enter your Magic Circle.

Sit comfortably, close your eyes, and take a few deep breaths.

Bring yourself to this moment, now, letting go of any mental preoccupations or daily concerns.

When you feel ready, begin to identify your desires, your personal goals, relating to your transformation. Who are you? What qualities do you wish to improve in yourself? To be more loving? To be more sensual and sexually alive? To be happy? To be more confident and powerful? To be more understanding with the people nearest and dearest to you? To access higher, more blissful states of consciousness?

Take time to review your desires, writing them down on a piece of paper. After a few minutes, when you have made a short list, select one desire with which you would like to work. Write it down separately, on a fresh piece of paper.

Now see if you can identify the negative state that corresponds to this desire.

For example, if you want to experience more love in your life, the negative expression of this state may be "I don't feel very lovable," or "I don't feel capable of giving and receiving love."

If you want to be more capable and confident, the negative state may be "I don't feel adequate to meet life's challenges."

Write the negative expression on your piece of paper.

STAGE 2: TALKING TO YOUR INNER MAGICIAN

Now you are going to connect with your Inner Magician.

Close your eyes and recall the moment in your initiation ceremony as a magician when you stood before the gate of your Inner Sanctuary. See yourself again opening the gate and walking through the beautiful garden to the small clearing where two chairs are located (you can refresh your memory by rereading the initiation ceremony in chapter 2).

Sit in one of the chairs and silently invite your Inner Magician to come to you. Feel the Inner Magician's approaching presence, hear the rustle of robes as he or she sits in the other chair, and allow the image of your Inner Magician to appear in your mind's eye. He or she is now sitting before you.

Feel the strong bond of love and trust that exists between you.

Ask your Inner Magician, "Are you willing to speak for all those hidden parts of myself—my hidden demons, my wounded child, the deepest layers of my subconscious mind? I need their full cooperation in creating a clear vision of transformation."

Most probably your Inner Magician will immediately agree to your request. Or, he or she may ask a few questions, seeking a deeper understanding of your desire. Take time to explain fully the aspect of yourself you want to transform.

If your Inner Magician says no to your request for assistance, take this as a sign that you are not being sincere. Check and see what is going on inside yourself. Perhaps you are in a hurry to get on with the exercise. Perhaps you are preoccupied with something else, not really focused on the practice.

Stand up, take a few deep breaths, shake your body, clear your head of any preoccupations, then sit down, close your eyes, go back to your Sanctuary, and ask again. If you are sincere, you are sure to get a yes from your Inner Magician.

STAGE 3: LEARNING THE POSITIVE INTENT

When you have obtained the cooperation of your Inner Magician, show him or her the piece of paper on which you have written your desire and

If you observe well, your own heart will answer.

—DE LUBIEZ

your negative state. Ask your Inner Magician to shed light on your negative state.

Your negative states have a certain function of which you may not be aware. You created them with a positive intention, as a form of protection or survival, probably during early childhood, when you were vulnerable and helpless.

Ask your Inner Magician, "What is the positive intention behind this negative state?"

Listen carefully to his or her reply. It may come in the form of words; it may come as a feeling, a silent transmission, or your Inner Magician may take you back to your childhood years so that you can reexperience how this negative state was created.

For example, if your negative pattern is a lack of sensitivity and feeling in lovemaking, your Inner Magician may reply, "When you were very young your feelings gave you much pleasure, but they also brought you much pain. You decided that it is better not to be hurt, so you learned not to feel so deeply. Now you are afraid really to let go in lovemaking. You think you'd become too vulnerable. You think you'd get hurt again. You're still trying to protect yourself."

Recognizing the positive intention that created your negative state is a major step toward healing and transformation. Listen carefully as your Inner Magician explains the reasons why you created this particular negative state.

When your Inner Magician has finished, you can ask: "You speak for those hidden parts of myself that I sometimes have difficulty connecting with. You speak for my child within; you speak for my demons, for my subconscious mind. Is it okay with them if I begin to explore new, alternative behaviors, new solutions? Can I count on their cooperation?"

Again, if you are sincere, you will receive a yes from your Inner Magician.

STAGE 4: CONJURING UP AN EMPOWERED STATE
The next step is to create a vision of the desire that you wish to see manifested in your life.

In magic, this is known as "conjuring up an empowered state."

Close your eyes and begin to breathe slowly and deeply.

Describe aloud, to yourself, the transformed state that you wish to achieve. For example, you may declare, "I want to be more loving," or "I want to be more orgasmic in lovemaking."

Ask your Inner Magician to show you a time in your life when you experienced this state. This memory can be a valuable resource and a key to self-healing.

If you have no previous experience of the state that you desire, ask your Inner Magician to show you a time when you experienced something very similar.

Allow yourself to bathe in the memory of that moment when, for example, you felt orgasmic in lovemaking, or you felt love radiating from your heart.

Use all your senses to submerge yourself in the experience. Let it become your present reality. Let it take you over—just as in chapter 3, when you learned how to anchor a magical state.

If it was a moment of lovemaking or pleasure, let your body move in accordance with your memory of what happened. Deepen your breathing. Use your voice to make sighs. Perhaps there are certain smells associated with this memory, or certain sounds you made when you felt orgasmic. Evoke the sensations associated with that precious moment.

When you feel that you are reaching the peak of this experience, touch your body in a way that feels comfortable and appropriate, in a friendly place where you can feel grounded and centered. You may find

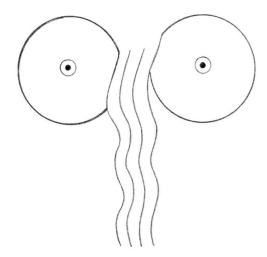

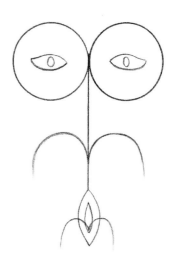

I AM AN ORGASMIC WOMAN   I AM AN ORGASMIC WOMAN

Two different ways of symbolizing an affirmation

179

yourself placing a hand on your heart or abdomen, or you may gently touch the back of one hand with your fingers.

With this touch, you anchor the experience.

Make an affirmation, a positive statement, such as "I am feeling relaxed and orgasmic in my body," or "I am being flooded with love."

STAGE 5: CREATING A SYMBOL OF TRANSFORMATION

When you have anchored the positive state, you are ready to translate it into a Magic Symbol. For this, it is important to have the continued cooperation of your Inner Magician.

Close your eyes and ask your Inner Magician for a symbol that represents the positive state you have just experienced and that you wish to be manifested in your life.

Wait quietly, passively, innocently. See what images your Inner Magician will cause to appear in your mind's eye. Remember, your Inner Magician is speaking for your subconscious mind, so these images will come from the depths of your psyche.

The symbol could be an animal, such as a deer or dolphin. It could be a shining sun, a radiant silver moon, a flower, or a cornfield swept by the wind. It could be something abstract, like a certain pattern or color, or a mysterious symbol or sigil that arises out of nowhere. Or it could be something mundane, like a telephone or change purse. Resist the temptation to censor or dismiss the images that arise, for they are keys to hidden power.

As you receive the symbol, or symbols, gather your drawing and painting materials and begin to express the images on paper. Give them concrete reality. This may happen all at once, in the form of a sudden revelation. Or it may happen in stages: you may draw a certain basic shape or pattern, then close your eyes again, connect with your Inner Magician, and receive more details.

Keep going until you feel the symbol resonating with your desire, capturing the spirit, the feeling, the vibe of your transformation.

When your symbol is finished, your Inner Magician's role in this exercise is also complete.

Thank him or her, enjoy a Melting Hug, then say good-bye.

STAGE 6: ACCEPTING AND IMPRINTING YOUR SYMBOL

Hold your finished symbol in both hands, stand in the center of your Magic Circle, raise your symbol to the skies, and declare aloud: "This is my Magic Symbol. I accept it as the expression of my transformation."

Now you can begin the process of imprinting your Magic Symbol on your mind. Place the symbol on your altar, sit comfortably a short distance away, and gaze at the symbol in a soft, relaxed way, as if looking at a friend.

After two or three minutes, imagine that the symbol is growing bigger and bigger until you are able to walk into it.

Rest in your symbol for two or three minutes, acknowledging that it is now part of you.

Bring the exercise to a close by walking out of your symbol and allowing it to become smaller and smaller, until it shrinks to a tiny point and disappears.

End the exercise with a Heart Salutation and bow toward your Magic Symbol.

Pointers

These symbols have tremendous power. I am reminded of Rachel, who, working with her husband in one of my training sessions, complained that she had a tendency to block her orgasm during lovemaking. This blocking was usually accompanied by a sharp pain or cramping feeling in her vagina.

I asked Rachel to recall the last time she felt this pain and guided her into a reexperience of it. After a while, she was able to connect with the pain; then I asked her if any kind of symbol—an animal, an object, a word—appeared in her mind as she experienced this painful state.

Immediately, she received a vivid symbol of a roaring lion. I said, "That's good! Use the power of the lion, the courage and strength of the lion, to express how you're feeling right now."

Immediately she started to roar like an angry lion, while looking directly into her husband's eyes—they were sitting opposite each other—while he, supporting the process, roared back. They continued in this way for about twenty minutes, while Rachel moved her pelvis backward and forward, focusing on the feelings in her vagina.

Afterward, Rachel reported that the pain in her vagina had disappeared and that her lovemaking had been magically transformed. The symbol of the lion had given her the strength she needed to show and release the pent-up rage that was causing her pain.

Symbols are mysterious. We don't know where they come from, or why they come when they do. But in magic they have tremendous significance, for they speak in a language that is far more ancient than words, far more powerful than any statement made by the rational, intellectual part of our minds.

Now we come to the third type of desire for which you can create a magical vision: the desire to connect deeply with another person. This desire is dealt with in two exercises: the first envisions a new love relationship, a new love affair; the second, the enhancement of an already existing relationship.

EXERCISE: CREATING A VISION FOR A NEW RELATIONSHIP

Purpose and benefits

By creating a vision of a new love partner or intimate friend, you are preparing to manifest a relationship that will be lasting, enriching, and fulfilling.

You will be following the same procedure outlined in the previous exercises: first, you create a detailed vision of your desire; then you condense it into a magical symbol.

However, the desire to create a new love relationship is more subtle and complex because it involves another person. The main point to remember here is that your efforts to attract a new relationship should be spread as widely as possible and not confined to a person whom you already know.

In this way, you avoid the trap of making your happiness dependent on a specific person—on whether he or she decides to love you or not. You will not be dependent on that person's moods, attitudes, and reactions, and you will not get involved in the unpleasant business of trying to manipulate another person to conform to your will.

Instead, your desire for a new beloved needs to be addressed to the spirit of love that resides in every human heart, and to be broadcast to the four corners of the earth, reaching out across time and space to the unknown partner who is already waiting for you. Then all the possibilities are open and the magic can unfold in its own mysterious and unpredictable way.

Glorious is the moment we sit
in the palace, you and I,
Two forms, two faces, but a single
soul, you and I;
And the flowers will blaze, and
the birds will cry and
shower us with immortality
The moment we enter
the garden, you and I.
What a miracle, you and I,
One love, one lover, one fire,
you and I.

—RUMI

Preparations

- ☙ Create your Magic Circle.

- ☙ Have a pen and paper nearby.

- ☙ Prepare your drawing and painting materials.

- ☙ Wear your magician's robes.

- ☙ Allow one hour for this exercise.

Practice

STAGE 1: DESCRIBING YOUR NEW LOVER
Enter your Magic Circle.

Sit comfortably, close your eyes, and take a few moments to bring your attention here, now, in the present moment.

Focus your attention on your breathing, watching the in-breath and the out-breath. This is a good way to stop any mental chatter that may be distracting you.

When you feel ready, pick up your pen and paper and begin to write about the person whom you are attracting into your life. For example, you may write, "I am attracting a mature man, forty to fifty years old, good-looking, passionate, financially secure, in good health, a nonsmoker, who is looking for intimacy and depth in a relationship, who has the courage to be open and honest, who likes to hike, go out to dinner, go to concerts, the theater, movies . . ."

In a way, it is rather like writing an advertisement for the personal columns in a local newspaper.

Take your time, be thorough, and enjoy this creative act. It is just like creating a character for a fictional story—a fiction that may soon become reality. However, try to avoid giving your new lover a specific physical description, as this may inhibit the range and scope of your magical invocation.

STAGE 2: SYMBOLIZING YOUR NEW BELOVED
When you have written down the qualities of your lover, you can begin to create a symbol or painting that represents this person.

This can be done in several ways:

Picture the love you want.

1. You can create a sigil, using a suitable phrase such as "new lover" or "new relationship."

2. You can create a painting that symbolizes your new lover. Here again I advise you not to create a detailed, lifelike portrait. It is better to paint in an abstract way that indicates your feelings about this per-

184

son—a shining star, a beautiful bird, a phallic symbol, a rose lying on a moonlit pathway, or a sports car with a coffee mug sitting on the hood.

3. You can create a combination, incorporating the sigil as part of the painting.

Make sure the feeling and promise of your desired relationship is captured in your symbol. Don't be afraid to throw away unsatisfactory efforts and start afresh.

The happier you are with your symbol, the easier it will be to attract a new beloved.

STAGE 3: SENDING YOUR MESSAGE TO THE FOUR DIRECTIONS

When you feel your symbol is complete, hold it in both hands, raise it to the skies, and declare: "I accept this symbol as the expression of my desire for a new love partner."

Offer your symbol in a special ritual. Stand in the center of your Magic Circle and turn to face each of the four directions: north, south, east, west.

As you face each direction, imagine that the energy of your symbol is radiating out in that direction. By the time you have finished, you will have sent your message of love to the four corners of the earth.

Place your symbol on your altar, sit where you can look at it comfortably, and begin to imprint it on your mind. Gaze at your symbol in a soft, loving way—the way you would look at your beloved.

Close your eyes and imagine your symbol growing bigger and bigger, until you can easily walk inside it and rest there. In a poetic way, you are already inside your beloved. The bond has been established.

After a few minutes, leave your symbol and let it become smaller and smaller, until it vanishes into a dot.

End with a Heart Salutation and bow toward your Magic Symbol.

Pointers

It is important that you complete the written description of your desired beloved before you proceed to create a sigil out of phrases like "new lover" or "new relationship," and before creating a painting.

I have already talked about the importance of creating a clear vision, and in this case it is your written description of your new beloved that gives clarity and potency to your symbol.

If you choose to paint or draw, be sure to include a little book or notepad in the painting that symbolizes all that you have written about this person.

Be prepared for a surprise when this person becomes manifest in your life. He or she may look very different from how you imagined, while still being exactly right for you.

EXERCISE: CREATING A SHARED LOVE VISION TO ENHANCE YOUR RELATIONSHIP

Purpose and benefits

The creation of a Magic Symbol to fulfill a shared vision of greater love and intimacy with your beloved is perhaps the sweetest and most potent way to bring sexual magic into your life. Working together with a shared vision, you and your love partner are harnessing the power of sexual magic in a very unique way: you are applying Tantra to Tantra.

Sexual magic works on the principle of blending male and female energies. So does a loving relationship. The two dimensions run on parallel lines, embracing the alchemical union of the male and the female.

This generates a positive and nourishing cycle: the more you apply sexual magic to your relationship, the better your relationship becomes, and the better your relationship becomes, the more energy you have for sexual magic. It can be an ever-climbing spiral of pleasure and joy, lifting you far beyond any old difficulties or negative habits concerning intimacy and lovemaking.

Preparations

- Make an agreement with your partner that you will each spend fifteen to twenty minutes alone, in separate rooms, during the first stage of this exercise, and then come together for the second stage.

- Prepare your drawing and painting materials.

- Before beginning the exercise, take time to shower, anoint your body with your favorite oils or scents, and wear your magician's robes.

- Create a romantic atmosphere in the room where you will come together. Light candles, burn incense, play soft music.

- Allow one hour for this exercise.

- You may also wish to make additional time available after the exercise so that you can move into lovemaking.

Practice

STAGE 1: VISUALIZING YOUR DESIRE

Create your Magic Circle, while your partner does the same in another location.

Sit comfortably in the center of your Magic Circle, close your eyes, and take a few deep breaths, relaxing your body as you exhale.

In your mind's eye, begin to create a vision of the kind of love relationship that you would like to experience with your partner. Use your senses and your voice to express the qualities that you want.

For example, you may say, "I want us to open new doors of pleasure together, so that we can set each other aflame with passion and orgasmic delight." You may see a vision of yourself aglow with sexual pleasure, your skin warm and flushed with arousal, a deep feeling of contentment in your abdomen, like a cat that just lapped up a bowl of cream.

Or perhaps you want to bring more heart into your relationship, saying "I want to feel more tenderness and sensitivity in our relating and our lovemaking. I want us to be warm and cuddly together, nourishing each other, taking care of each other."

Or it may be that you want greater intimacy in the form of more open communication, saying "I want more sharing of feelings, greater understanding of each other. I want us to feel so in tune that even when we aren't talking I still feel connected with you, my beloved."

STAGE 2: SHARING YOUR VISION

When your desire is clear in your mind, come together with your partner in your Magic Circle.

Sit facing each other.

Choose who is partner A and who is partner B.

Partner A asks partner B, "What vision do you bring to our relationship? What is it that you long for?"

Partner B, share your vision. You may say, "I bring a vision of healing and nourishment that can help us move beyond our problems and remember our ecstasy."

Take time to explain your vision fully.

Partner A, listen in an open-minded, receptive way.

When Partner B is finished, change roles.

Partner B asks the question "What vision do you bring to our relationship?"

Partner A responds.

You may find that your visions are similar, in which case you can move to stage three of the exercise and begin to create a Magic Symbol together.

A couple creating a shared vision of love and abundance. The cup and heart represent love; the circle is the sun, or passion. The two birds represent freedom and love; the water flowing in the cup represents abundance.

However, you may find that your visions are different. One partner may have a strong desire for more sex, while the other may have a vision of greater intimacy in nonsexual areas.

If the two visions are acceptable to both of you, you can agree to create two Magic Symbols, or combine both visions in a single symbol.

If you cannot agree to one or both visions, then you need to continue exploring together until you find a common ground—visions that are mutually acceptable.

Be generous and supportive with each other. Help each other find visions that will fulfill your desires and allow you to move together toward higher and higher peaks of pleasure and harmony.

STAGE 3: CREATING YOUR SHARED SYMBOL

Begin to paint or draw the Magic Symbol that represents your vision, your desire.

If you share a single vision, paint it together on one sheet of paper. Taking turns to add creative touches to the same symbol can be great fun. Or one partner may prefer to create a sigil while the other makes a painting. See how you can best work together to express your shared desire as a Magic Symbol.

If you have different desires, create two Magic Symbols on separate pieces of paper. When you have both finished, show each other your symbols, explaining what they represent.

In my workshops, many couples like to incorporate their hopes and aspirations in a single Magic Symbol. For example, Nick and Marissa, two enthusiastic newcomers to sexual magic, had different visions. Nick wanted more intensity, heat, and passion in their relationship, while Marissa wanted both of them to honor and respect each other's freedom.

They created a beautiful Magic Symbol together, painting a large, ornate silver cup, with fountains of water pouring into it and overflowing. They decorated the sides of the cup with their astrological signs and painted a red heart at the base. Above the cup they painted a yellow sun with two birds flying across it.

"The cup symbolized our love and the water pouring into it showed our willingness to receive more love, more energy, more abundance," Marissa explained. "The birds symbolized our freedom and the sun expressed our desire for passion. When our symbol was complete we both felt that we had accomplished something very special. We couldn't wait to start working with it."

STAGE 4: IMPRINTING YOUR SHARED SYMBOL

Take time to create a Magic Symbol you are both happy with. Don't hesitate to start again if you are not satisfied with the results of your first efforts.

When you have finished, stand together in the center of your Magic Circle, hold your shared symbol aloft, and declare, "This is our Magic Symbol. We accept it as the expression of our vision."

Place your shared symbol on your altar and sit together, a short distance away, gazing softly at the symbol, allowing the image to be imprinted on your minds.

If you have created two symbols, perform the ceremony of acceptance separately, then place both symbols on the altar and gaze at them softly, imprinting the images on your minds. For the first few minutes, gaze at your own symbol. Then look at your partner's symbol. Allow both symbols to be absorbed into your heart, into your mind.

End with a Heart Salutation and bow toward your symbols.

Pointers

You may also wish to experiment with creating a jointly held vision for a single session of lovemaking. By deciding together, in advance, the goal to which you are dedicating this particular sexual union—such as greater sensitivity toward each other's needs, or prolonged sensual foreplay, or a certain style of sexual loving—you will find that you can greatly enhance your sexual intimacy and pleasure. Your energy will be more focused, your sensations will be more intense, and old, habitual ways of lovemaking will be replaced by new, fresh responses. Try it and see.

EXERCISE: MAKING LOVE WITH YOUR MAGIC SYMBOL

Purpose and Benefits

In this chapter you have learned how to create Magic Symbols for every aspect of your life: for transforming yourself, your relationships, and your environment.

Now you can begin to employ these symbols in the alchemy of sexual magic. You can make your Magic Symbol an integral part of your lovemaking—a living force that can dance and weave its way through the passion and pleasure of your sexual union, adding spice, magic, and mystery to this most intimate act.

This is the way to empower your Magic Symbol and to charge it with sexual energy, including your final orgasmic climax. In this way, you move strongly and purposefully in the direction of creating the new reality that you desire to manifest.

You are acting very much like a gardener, showering the plant of your desire with the nourishing juice of sexual energy. You are helping your symbol to travel through your veins, muscles, organs, brain, through every cell of your body. You are charging it with the very ecstasy and fluids of your love.

You can do this while making love with a partner, or, if you are alone, while giving sexual pleasure to yourself.

Preparation

- ❧ Create your Magic Circle.

- ❧ Conjure up a romantic, sensual atmosphere, using soft lighting, mood music, incense.

- ❧ Create a comfortably, luxurious area within your Magic Circle on which you can make love. It may be your bed. It may be a comfortable rug or mattress on the floor. It may be a natural, outdoor setting such as a garden or forest.

- ❧ Select the Magic Symbol with which you want to work with your partner, or by yourself.

- ❧ Wear your magical robes and costumes.

Practice

STAGE 1: CONNECTING WITH YOUR MAGIC SYMBOL
Enter your Magic Circle with your partner.

Stand in the center of the circle, facing each other.

Close your eyes for a moment and take a few slow, deep breaths, bringing your attention to the present moment. Shake your body a little, loosening and relaxing your muscles.

When you feel centered, present, open your eyes and gaze lovingly at your partner.

Make a Heart Salutation and bow toward each other, then enjoy a long Melting Hug.

Bring the Magic Symbol you have selected and place it in the center of the circle, between you.

Sit facing each other, on either side of the symbol.

For this exercise it is good to sit on a cushion, to be close to the earth, to be able to move your body easily from a sitting position to lying or rolling around on the carpet with your partner.

Spend two to three minutes gazing at your symbol together.

Close your eyes. For an additional two to three minutes, see the symbol on the screen of your mind, as if you are looking at a movie screen with your inner eye.

Open your eyes and communicate with each other about the way you resonate with the symbol: whether you see it as a picture or feel it somewhere in your body, or think about it in words or hear it as a sound or mantra.

STAGE 2: MOVING INTO LOVEMAKING
Put the symbol to one side and move closer to each other.

Begin to move gently into lovemaking, opening each other's robes, lightly caressing each other's bodies, turning each other on, choosing any style that is enjoyable and feels good to you.

As your sexual energy awakens, allow yourself to become absorbed in these pleasurable feelings. Do not try to remember your Magic Symbol. Let your sexual energy build to a level where it is flowing strongly between you.

When you are both immersed in an enjoyable flow of lovemaking, stop. Pause for a moment. Gaze together at your symbol in a relaxed way. There is no need to try to do anything. Just look at it.

After a few moments, close your eyes and see the symbol inside yourself. Then let go of the symbol's image and once again move into the pleasure of your lovemaking.

Repeat this pattern several times—making love, stopping, gazing at your Magic Symbol, making love again—until you both feel that you have embodied the symbol and can summon it easily inside.

STAGE 3: BLENDING THE SYMBOL WITH YOUR SEXUAL ENERGY
Now, as you make love, imagine that you are drawing the symbol into your sexual center. Feel or see the symbol in your genitals, whirling and churning inside you, empowered by the dance of your sexual energies as they

penetrate and mingle with each other. You are showering your symbol with the streaming energies of your sexual juices.

You may wish to communicate in words what is happening. For example, the woman may say, *"Mmm,* yes, I see our symbol in my Yoni [vagina] being charged with the energy of your Vajra [penis]." The man may reply, "I can feel the heat of our lovemaking pouring into the symbol." It is important to let your voices play their part in intensifying your energies.

If you forget your Magic Symbol at times, this is perfectly okay and natural. Enjoy the gap, knowing that the symbol is firmly imprinted on your subconscious mind. It is still working, even when you are not consciously thinking about it.

Blending the symbol with your sexual energy. This is the symbol of yoni containing sun and moon. Creating the magic blending of amrita: male and female energies.

STAGE 4: TAKING YOUR SYMBOL INTO ORGASM

Decide together when you want to move into the final intensity of orgasmic release. Communicate this clearly, when you both feel ready. Maybe one of you will say, "Shall we go for it now?" The other may reply, "Wait. I'm not quite ready. Let's relax for a moment. I need more sexual stimulation before the final letting go."

When you are ready, take a last peek at the Magic Symbol, then close your eyes and draw the symbol into the sexual center once more. As you move to your climax and your energy is released, feel that the symbol is exploding into a million pieces, flying out into the universe, carried by the explosive power of your orgasmic release.

As your orgasm fades, let any traces of the symbol also fade, dissolving into the universe, sending out the message of your desire.

End the exercise with a Heart Salutation and bow toward each other.

Congratulations! You have just had your first experience of sexual magic.

Loving people are happy, and happy people are loving.

—KEN KEYES

Pointers

If you are alone, you can follow the same steps, integrating your Magic Symbol with your sexual pleasure. Even if you are with a partner, you may want to practice alone at times, turning yourself on while looking at your Magic Symbol, then visualizing the symbol inside your sexual organ.

During lovemaking there is no need to think about what the symbol means. All that is required is for you to retain the image of your Magic Symbol and allow it to be charged with your sexual energy.

CHANNELING YOUR SEXUAL ENERGY

Having mastered the art of creating a Magic Symbol, you will learn in the next chapter how to channel your sexual power. Soon you will be able to blend your Magic Symbol with this powerful energy and bring it up through your body, passing through the seven energy centers on its way to the Astral Network.

In preparation for this exciting step into the alchemy of magic, it will be helpful for you to select a Magic Symbol with which you would like to experiment. Choose from any of the symbols that you have created in this chapter.

Perhaps there is one symbol that stands out in your mind as especially potent or significant. If so, you may decide now that you and your beloved will work with this particular Magic Symbol through all the remaining exercises in this training. Working with the same symbol makes it easy to hold the image in your mind, and this in turn will make each new practice easier to grasp.

SEXUAL ALCHEMY:
Charging Your Magic Symbol

Now it is time to generate an alchemical fusion between your sexual energy and the magical vision you created in the previous chapter. The methods used during this stage of sexual magic comprise a dynamic, modern approach based on the ancient science of Tantra.

First, you will learn how to awaken your body's seven energy centers, or chakras, and to circulate sexual energy so that you can experience a full body orgasm. Then, you will learn how to use your sexual energy to carry your Magic Symbol through your chakras, charging it with seven exquisitely different energies. Finally, you will send your highly charged Magic Symbol to the Astral Network, the vast, intangible, vibrating force-field through which desires can be channeled into manifestation.

The three exercises in this chapter—the Chakra Rub, Chakra Breathing, and the Chakra Wave—are powerful teachers. When you have practiced these exercises you will:

- ❧ Gain a clear perception and experience of each of your chakras
- ❧ Awaken your sexual fire

- Harmonize your body's rhythms and your breathing

- Enhance enjoyment and aliveness

- Open your inner energy channel

- Connect your root chakra, or sex center, to your crown chakra, or ecstasy center

- Use visualization to bring your Magic Symbol through the seven chakras

- Experience the Astral Network

- Learn how to work with a partner, being receptive to each other, guiding and taking initiative, giving love to each other, supporting each other in an ecstatic climax

If you are more kinesthetic and auditory, then feel and listen for images of the Beloved. You may find yourself hearing words or music, or you may be drawn into a dance.

—JEAN HOUSTON

These exercises introduce you to completely new orgasmic sensations. In fact, when sexual energy is channeled through your chakras, you are bound to experience radically new types of orgasmic feelings that expand your range as a lover and transform lovemaking into an art.

The knowledge of how to transform your sexual energy through the chakras can truly change your life. Incredibly, 99 percent of what most people know as love is centered in the lowest three chakras. We rarely move beyond these limited dimensions into the realm of spiritual transformation.

For example, usually we experience genital orgasm as an explosive, lustful energy, pulsating through our sexual organs, driven by our longing for fullness and release. This desire is often associated with the urge to possess the other, to be taken, to let go into the wild animal aspect of our nature, to "fuck" in the most earthy, primordial sense.

This passion encompasses some familiar pitfalls that the sexual magician must recognize and transcend. We tend to believe that "you are mine and cannot belong to anybody else," or "I cannot live without you," or "I need you," or "if you love me, you cannot love anyone else."

In other words, the energy of lovemaking is often mixed with feelings of possessiveness and jealousy, which have their origin in our first three chakras. It is here that we become trapped in a complex sexual interplay between desire and power, need and scarcity, self-esteem and dependency.

But this need not happen. When you learn how to channel your orgasmic energy to the fourth chakra, for example, you can experience an "orgasm of the heart." Here, the influx of pulsating, highly aroused energy may give you a sensation comparable to jumping out of a plane with a parachute: letting go, opening, falling deeper and deeper into the realm of acceptance, relaxing into feelings of love, joy, tears, and laughter. In this state there is no sense of possessing the other, because whatever is needed is found within oneself. There is a sense of fullness, of love overflowing, of a merging and melting in which no distinction can be found between the lover and the beloved.

With such exquisite experiences available in just one of the higher chakras, it is not difficult to imagine the delight of charging your Magic Symbol with the qualities of all the chakras as you take it through your body.

At first, the process of opening inner pathways and channeling sexual energy may seem strange or difficult. This is not really surprising, because most people today are unfamiliar with such Tantric practices. However, it is actually quite straightforward—the more so because you will be using very powerful and effective exercises. With practice, you will soon find that channeling energy from your sex center up through your body is no more difficult than, say, learning to ride a bicycle.

*Love and the self are one,
and the discovery of either is
the realization of both.*

—HINDU SAYING

BILL AND JUDY:
SURRENDERING TO PLEASURE

These experiences are not limited to skilled *Tantrikas* who have practiced for years and years. They are available to everyone. Take the example of Bill, who came to me for a private consultation with his love partner, Judy. They were very interested in learning the art of sexual magic, but, as is frequently the case, it soon became apparent that they needed to resolve some sexual problems first.

Bill was worried that his sexual energy was stuck, as his interest in lovemaking had decreased markedly over the past two months. As we talked, it became apparent that Bill was in a double bind: he was tired of being the "captain of the ship," in command of their lovemaking, responsible for Judy's orgasms, and yet he was afraid to lose control and surrender to her.

I sensed that Bill's real difficulty was not with Judy but with himself. He was longing for, and at the same time resisting, his own desire to relax and allow sexual pleasure to happen *to* him rather than *doing* it every time as a sexual performer.

Over a series of sessions I took them through the exercises in this chapter, culminating in the Chakra Wave. In this exercise, Bill sat on the floor with his legs crossed, while Judy sat behind him so that he could relax and rest his back on her chest. Under my guidance, Judy rested one hand on Bill's Vajra (penis) and the other on his lower belly. I then led Bill into the technique for awakening his sexual energy and drawing it up through his chakras, while Judy supported him, breathing in harmony and giving gentle impulses to his Vajra to stimulate his sexual energy.

Bill continues:

> Each time we inhaled together, I felt the impulse given by Judy's hand on my penis like a very agreeable, erotic tickle that kept stimulating me like the regular beat of a drum. A feeling of warm pleasure began to spread through my pelvis that I hadn't experienced before. Normally, when I make love, I focus entirely on the sensations in my penis.
>
> I didn't know much about the chakras, but Margo guided Judy's hand first to my belly, then to my solar plexus, and soon I felt my sexual energy spreading upward through my body. It was wonderful to give myself permission to relax and feel what was happening, rather than creating everything myself.
>
> When Margo placed Judy's hand on my solar plexus, there was an initial feeling of tightness and I felt that I wanted to scream. I heard Margo say, "Let out your power." I breathed deeply into my chest and started shouting—I don't know what—and suddenly it was as if the sun exploded inside my solar plexus.
>
> There was a radiance, an expansion, which felt very male and assertive, and yet I wasn't doing anything. It was just happening to me. I felt powerful in a new way, and I felt this energy traveling down to my penis, which stood erect in my pants. This suddenly seemed very funny to me, because this was the male kind of sexuality that I'd always wanted. So I was laughing and shouting "Aha!" and making all kinds of movements with my arms. Judy was laughing, too, and it was as if we were making love in a totally new way. It was just beautiful.
>
> Margo guided me through all the chakras and then Judy and I lay on the floor together for a long time, enjoying what had happened between us, feeling very soft and peaceful.

This was a new beginning for Bill's style of lovemaking. From then on, he was able both to give and receive, to allow sexual sensations to arise spontaneously as well as to strive for orgasmic release in himself and his partner. This new dimension also opened the way for their initiation into sexual magic, which they now practice regularly, with impressive results.

The exercises in this chapter initially require a certain amount of physical effort, breathing and movement. They are a kind of sexual aerobics. But once you have learned the knack, no effort is required. It is enough to visualize your inner channel opening—either when you are alone or when making love—and energy will begin to flow. Your practice becomes an effortless meditation.

PLAYING YOUR INNER FLUTE: OPENING THE ENERGY CHANNEL

It is well known in many cultures that the physical body has meridians or grids along which energy flows. For example, in acupuncture an intricate web of meridians links essential organs, such as the kidneys and lungs, which are seen as vital sources of energy for the whole body. When needles are inserted into these meridians at key points, the energy of the organs is stimulated and released, flooding the network and restoring any imbalances that may exist. In this way, good health is maintained throughout your physical body.

Similarly, there are subtle meridians that channel sexual energy through your body. The main meridian is a vertical channel that begins at your perineum, the point between your genitals and your anus, and rises through the center of your body, up through the middle of your head to the crown at the top of your skull. I have given this channel the name "Inner Flute" because, when you know how to play with this instrument, you can create the most beautiful orgasmic "music," giving yourself exquisitely pleasurable experiences.

There are seven centers, or fueling stations, along this inner highway that transform and boost your sexual energy, helping it to continue its upward movement. In traditional Hindu and Buddhist terminology the word *chakra* means "wheel" or "vortex," because of the way energy gathers and spins at these strategic points. The chakras also correspond to more recent discoveries such as the body segment system developed by pioneering psychotherapist Wilhelm Reich.

In my workshops, when I introduce the idea of moving sexual energy through the seven chakras, I sometimes ask participants to imagine that

Now if a thousand perfect men were to appear, it would not amaze me.
Now if a thousand beautiful forms of women appear'd, it would not astonish me.
Now I see the secret of the making of the best persons:
it is to grow in the open air and to eat and sleep with the earth.

—WALT WHITMAN
Song of the Open Road

201

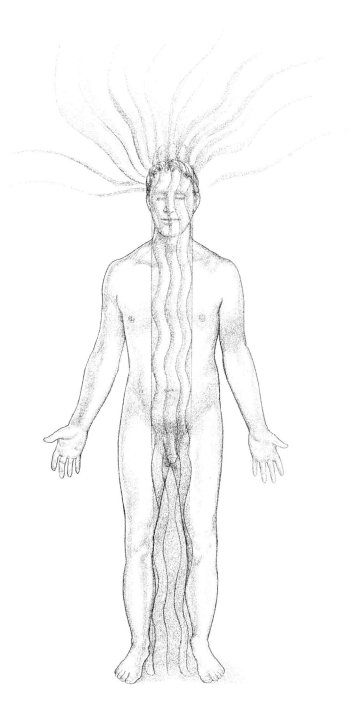

The Inner Flute

they are on a seven-day honeymoon trip with their sweethearts, journeying by car from Paris to Rome. Each day takes them through different landscapes and, because their journey has a magical quality, they find that the outer landscape reflects their inner moods.

On the first day, they stop to walk in a forest and spontaneously become playful animals, chasing each other through the trees, making love fiercely and hungrily on beds of fern and moss. On the second day they wander through an old town and their mood becomes mellow, warm, and cozy, as if they were sipping vintage red wine. On the third day, they reach the Mediterranean and feel exhilarated and expanded, reveling in the sea and sunshine. On the fourth day, they visit a restaurant where a violinist plays romantic tunes, and their hearts are filled with love, tinged with sadness for lovers that have gone before them. On the fifth day, they enjoy singing together in their car as they speed along the *auto route*. On the sixth, they climb a mountain in the French Alps and their love is carried aloft to new heights, becoming pure and clear. As they reach the peak, they enjoy a panoramic vision. On the seventh day they drive to Rome, feeling that they have arrived home, that the journey is complete and they are fulfilled.

I use this story to illustrate a certain truth about the flow of sexual energy through the seven chakras, a journey that can be even more exciting than the one I have just described. By traveling this inner route, you will come to know how sex energy transforms itself at each chakra. Each staging post will provide a unique experience, a different flavor of orgasmic pleasure.

Moreover, you will be learning how to move your energy in a powerful, wavelike motion to maximize orgasmic sensations and prepare the way for sexual magic. When you master this skill, your Magic Symbol will ride a wave of orgasmic energy from your sex center all the way to the top of your head and beyond into the cosmos.

Having achieved this goal, you will be in a position to broadcast your magical vision through the vibrating force fields that I refer to as the Astral Network. In view of the mysterious nature of this network, it may be more helpful if I explain its function now, and then backtrack to describe each of the chakras.

THE ASTRAL NETWORK

The Astral Network is the final destination of all that wonderful orgasmic energy that, together with your Magic Symbol, you will send rushing through your body as you practice sexual magic.

This network can be examined from different angles. For example, the pioneering psychologist C. G. Jung coined the term *synchronicity* to indicate a meaningful coincidence of two apparently unconnected events, where something more than probability or chance is involved in their occurrence.

In his notes, Jung gives many examples of synchronicity, including the experience of an Englishman, J. W. Dunne, who, while serving in the Boer War in South Africa in 1902, dreamed that he was standing on a volcano threatened by catastrophic eruption. In his dream, he desperately tried to get French officials, stationed on a nearby island, to mount a rescue operation that would save thousands of lives. A few days later, Dunne received a copy of a newspaper with the shocking headline: "Volcanic Disaster in Martinique: Town Swept Away in Avalanche of Flame, 40,000 Lives Lost." Obviously, there was a meaningful but inexplicable connection between the man's dream and the actual eruption.

Experiments with group telepathy, astrology, and extrasensory perception convinced Jung that Synchronicity exists as a powerful universal force, serving not only as a link between individuals and natural events like the disaster in Martinique, but also as a psychic communication network between human beings.

The concept of synchronicity conjures up strong images of a hidden force-field that permeates the visible and invisible universe, connecting us to a vast, highly sensitive, and responsive network about which we know little. In this way, Jung's idea supports my approach to magic, for if an individual can receive a vision of an event through this network, the same individual may be able to create a vision that influences events through the same network. In other words, if an event can cause a vision, a vision can cause an event.

When I introduced the idea of an Astral Network in chapter 1 I mentioned Rupert Sheldrake's work with morphic fields, which asserts that every human experience, when repeated over time, establishes an energy imprint, or morphic field, within the vibrating web of electromagnetic fields that comprise the fabric of the universe. An individual who knows how to create visions that resonate with these morphic fields can, in my view, reproduce any experience that he or she desires.

I also mentioned Deepak Chopra's worldview in which human bodies are seen not as solid, separate objects but as extensions of "infinite fields of energy and information spanning the universe." Potentially, we should be able to access the infinite fields of energy and information which are an integral part, thereby harnessing powerful universal forces and shaping events according to our vision.

Opening to accessing the eighth chakra in the astral network

The best proof of the existence of the Astral Network lies in your own experience. The real understanding arises when you practice sexual magic, create a vision that resonates with the Astral Network, and receive the appropriate response. A single personal experience of this kind is more valuable than a thousand theoretical arguments.

From a practical perspective, the most important thing to know about the Astral Network is that it can be accessed by creating a potent, condensed vision of your desire, such as the Magic Symbol that you created in the previous chapter.

Blending your Magic Symbol with your sexual energy initiates a process of alchemical transformation, which continues as you bring your symbol up your Inner Flute, passing through the seven energy centers where it becomes steadily more refined—just like refining crude oil into high-octane fuel—before your symbol is released through the crown of your head, the seventh chakra.

It is at the seventh chakra, the last energy center in the body, that your individual consciousness meets, melts, and merges with the universe; so this is a natural connection point with a universal force-field like the Astral Network. In fact, the best place to access the Astral Network is in the space directly above your head, which I sometimes refer to as the "eighth chakra."

Your symbol, your vision, the blueprint of your desire, is going to be felt as a strong imprint, or resonance, on the Astral Network. It is going to have an impact on everyone and everything around you.

When your Magic Symbol reaches the Astral Network you probably won't hear any sounds, even though this network is in constant use. It is rather like walking into a highly sophisticated telephone exchange and hearing nothing of the hundreds of conversations buzzing through it. At the most, you may hear a gentle hum, or a single, vibrating note. More likely, you will experience it as an empty, quiet space, as if you had entered a deep, silent cave.

Having described, as well as I can, the destination of your Magic Symbol, I will now take an elevator back down the Inner Flute and, beginning in the genitals, explain the transformative function of your seven energy centers.

God respects me when I work, but loves me when I sing.

—RABINDRANATH TAGORE

THE ENERGY CENTERS: LEARNING THE NOTES ON YOUR INNER FLUTE

When you practice magic you do not remain on the physical plane, the plane of material objects. You reach out into other dimensions, following invisible pathways, tapping hidden currents of bioenergy in order to influence the relationship between yourself and the world around you. You are using unseen forces to create outcomes that you desire. You are an alchemist, playing with subtle energies in many dimensions.

Seen from this perspective, the ability to channel energy up through your Inner Flute is of great value, because this is how your energy is refined, becoming less raw, less physical, more subtle, more exquisite. The higher you go, the more subtle your energy becomes. As a magician, it is important for you to experience these subtle transformations so that you can learn to work with energy in a multidimensional way.

As the energy moves through your chakras, you will be flushing out energetic and emotional blocks that have prevented you from living to your full potential. To illustrate these blocks, we need look no further than society's attitude toward sex. During the last few thousand years of social evolution, we have made a collective decision to reject the sexual energy of the first chakra. Innocent, animalistic, natural sex has been heavily condemned, especially by organized religion, as something lower than the lofty ideals to which all civilized men and women should aspire. The "sins of the flesh" work against the spiritual purification needed for our salvation.

But, try as we may, we have not been able to move sex energy beyond the third chakra which, as you will see, is strongly associated with personal power issues. As a result, sex today tends to be heavily polluted with power struggles, ranging from the struggle for domination in bed between a wife and her husband—"Not tonight, dear. I have a headache"—to a mounting toll of sexual abuse, sexual harassment, and rape.

The turning point will come when we can move sexual energy to the fourth chakra, the heart center, whose fundamental quality is love. From this vantage point of wider understanding we can reembrace the first chakra in all its natural beauty without being trapped in the passions that normally rule our basic sexual instincts.

You are likely to experience energy blocks in several of your chakras, while other chakras will feel free and clear. As the blocks are understood

207

The seven chakras. The first symbolizes survival, balance, and grounding; the second (navel), flow and equilibrium; the third, radiance and expansion; the fourth, love and compassion; the fifth, communication, the expression of truth; the sixth, creation; the seventh (crown), transcendence.

and released, all your chakras will begin to function in a harmonious and vital way, allowing your energy to move upward.

The color sequence of the chakras is: first, red; second, orange; third, yellow; fourth, green; fifth, blue; sixth, purple; seventh, white.

Here, then, is a description of the qualities of each of the seven chakras, or energy centers:

1. Sex Center

This chakra is located in the genitals but includes the pelvis, legs, and feet. It is referred to by Reich as the "pelvic segment." At the sex chakra we experience our connection to the earth, our sense of grounding and our

208

sexuality. Here, too, is the source of our vital energy and physical well-being.

NEGATIVE STATE When the sex chakra is blocked, we live in a state of chronic, underlying fear of survival. We worry that we do not have enough, that we need more, whether it is sex, food, or money. We tend to be distrustful and hold back our energy. We may also try to hide our bodies and feel shameful about our genitals and sexual desires.

POSITIVE STATE When the sex chakra is open and the imprint of traumatic sexual memories is healed, we transcend our fears and become orgasmic. We receive what we need from life and are fulfilled by it. We feel that we can be alive, sexy, outgoing and seductive without embarrassment or shame.

The color associated with this chakra is dark red.

2. Hara Center

This chakra is located in the lower belly, three finger widths below the navel. Reich calls this the "abdominal segment." Through this chakra we are connected with our feelings, a sense of physical balance, and grace of movement. This area is the body's furnace. On a physical level, the belly absorbs and burns fuel, but this area also governs our emotional "digestion," regulating our feelings and what emotions we express.

NEGATIVE STATE When this chakra is blocked, we tend to be afraid of showing emotions, especially anger and fear. The natural ease and balance of the body is lost, and we may feel awkward in terms of how we move through the world.

POSITIVE STATE When this chakra opens there is usually a catharsis as held-back emotions are released through screaming, shouting, growling, and so on. There is a renewed fluidity and natural grace to the way we move and a sense of energy streaming freely through the body. Lovemaking becomes a dance between two bodies that move and flow naturally together.

Associated color: orange.

3. Solar Plexus Center

Located in the central hollow beneath the rib cage, this center is referred to by Reich as the "diaphragm segment." The third chakra is associated with breathing, expansion, energy, and power. It determines how much power we allow ourselves, how much we radiate in the presence of others, and the sense of "who I am."

NEGATIVE STATE When this chakra is blocked, access to a natural state of personal power is restricted and there is a tendency to manipulate others in an effort to feel powerful and dominant. There is an underlying feeling that "I don't have what it takes to make it by myself," including low self-esteem and a constant need for attention. A blocked third chakra makes it difficult to relax and trust our sexual energy. As a result, men tend to have difficulty maintaining an erection, while women tend to fake orgasm.

POSITIVE STATE When sexual energy floods this chakra there is an immediate sense of self-affirmation and self-confidence. Suddenly, there is no fear of expressing who we are, what we think and feel. There is no need to manipulate or depend on other people. It's "okay to be who I am." Connecting sexuality and power in a healthy way gives us permission to show our wild power and make love as equals.

Associated color: yellow.

4. Heart Center

Located at the midpoint of the chest and termed the "thoracic segment" by Reich, the heart chakra functions as the body's alchemical transformer. This is the turning point for the ascent of energy, because there are three chakras below and three above. Below the heart, sexual energy is fettered by a gravitational pull, a tendency to move downward into ejaculation rather than upward into bliss. At the heart, the energy is freed and can easily ascend through the remaining three chakras.

The heart is associated with love, compassion, trust, care, and nurturing. Many of these qualities are developed through our connection as young children with our mothers. As adults, they are rekindled in us through a childlike state of playfulness, vulnerability, and innocence, specially in lovemaking.

NEGATIVE STATE When this chakra is closed there is a sense of sadness, loss, and longing, especially in terms of broken relationships and former love partners. There is often a feeling of loneliness and "nobody cares about me." Sex becomes mechanical and tends to feel rather flat.

POSITIVE STATE When sexual energy opens the fourth chakra there is often a release of sadness through tears, together with an accompanying sense of relief. This is followed by expansive feelings of laughter and joy, opening the doors for understanding, compassion, self-appreciation, wholeness, and gratitude. In lovemaking, a strong connection is felt between sex and love, and a sense of dissolving any boundaries between two lovers.

Associated color: green.

5. The Throat Center

Located in the midpoint of the throat, this center is called the "throat segment" by Reich and includes the jaws, mouth, and lower face. Here, our energy is given tone and color as it is expressed and communicated to others through the voice. The fifth chakra is also the springboard to creativity and higher dimensions of soul or spirit.

NEGATIVE STATE When this chakra is closed, we tend continuously to swallow our authenticity out of a desire to conform to what others say and want. This is the chakra where, as children, we learned to muffle self-expression in accordance with our parents' wishes.

POSITIVE STATE When sexual energy opens the throat chakra, all kinds of vocal expressions are released. You can say what you need, what you like, how you want things to be, especially in lovemaking and intimate relating. Joy in sex is expressed through singing, shouting, moaning, giggling, or speaking nonsense or baby talk. There is a very strong connection between your sexuality and your voice, as if you can have an orgasm in your throat by making sounds. The whole jaw area loosens up and there is a desire to make faces, stretching the face muscles.

Associated color: blue.

6. Third-Eye Center

The sixth chakra, or third eye, is located at the midpoint between the eyebrows and is referred to by Reich as the "ocular segment." This is your personal movie theater, where imagination, intuition, and perception determine how you see yourself and the world around you. Here, visions and symbols are imprinted on your subconscious mind, while sudden insights can arise unbidden, seemingly out of nowhere. This is also the center for deep, nonverbal communication through the eyes, the "windows of the soul."

NEGATIVE STATE When this chakra is closed we tend to hide ourselves, not wishing to look into the eyes of other people or expose our innermost being. There is a tired, dead look about the eyes, reflecting a loss of inner perspective—not knowing where we are going and what we want from life. In this state, our sexuality lacks a sense of the sacred.

POSITIVE STATE When sex energy opens the sixth chakra there is often a feeling of expansion inside the head, as if the skull had suddenly become very large and spacious. States of meditation, peace, and silence are easily accessed. The physical eyes gain new clarity and vitality, while the inner eye may perceive light and colors. In lovemaking, there is a sense of great freedom, moving beyond the boundaries of the body. You also find that you can look deeply into each other's eyes, opening the door to true intimacy and mutual understanding.

Associated color: purple.

7. Crown Center

The seventh center is located at the top of the head. Referred to by Reich as the "brow segment," this chakra is the seat of the soul and the doorway to the universe. As such, it is the meeting point of matter and spirit, earth and heaven. It is the door through which we receive higher energies, such as transmissions from enlightened beings, teachers, and guides, and access states of deep trance. It is also the doorway to the Astral Network.

NEGATIVE STATE When the seventh chakra is closed there is no sense of being an essential part of an organic, cosmic whole. There is an inability to trust that life will give us what we need, a feeling of being cut off and isolated in a hostile universe.

POSITIVE STATE When sex energy opens the seventh chakra, there is an ecstatic communion with the whole of existence—an experience that can also be described as a "cosmic orgasm." Boundaries of self dissolve, and there is a blissful feeling of merging and melting into oneness with everything.

Associated color: white.

WORKING WITH CHAKRAS

The chakras form a fascinating and ever-changing energy map that you can work with in many ways. Some of the ancient Indian and Tibetan practices used to awaken the seven chakras are extremely complex, involving labyrinthine patterns, secret mantras, elaborate rituals, and invocation of deities. In another system, which works with chakra polarities, each chakra holds a positive or negative charge, and the adept learns how to regulate the flow of energy among them.

However, for the purposes of developing skills in sexual magic, I use a simple and powerful method of awakening the chakras that is available to all aspiring magicians.

By way of encouragement, I will tell you the story of Celeste, a French-born woman living in New Mexico, who was practicing the Chakra Wave—a method you will learn in this chapter—in one of my workshops. After a few days, she began to feel frustrated. Nothing seemed to be happening and, worse still, she felt that she did not really understand the chakra map with which she was working. Nevertheless, she persisted in her practice.

She was sitting on a rug, eyes closed, rocking her pelvis and breathing strongly in an effort to circulate energy from her sex center to her crown chakra, trying to overcome what she felt to be a block in the movement of her energy.

She continues:

> I had almost convinced myself that I was wasting my time when, all of a sudden, I felt a snakelike energy uncoil from the base of my spine and go whooshing through my body. It moved at light speed, like liquid

When you understand one thing through and through, you understand everything.

—ZEN SAYING

fire, shooting straight up through my throat and out of my head like a laser beam.

I could hear strange, amazing sounds coming out of my throat, but I was somewhere apart from it, as if watching with an inner eye that I had never been aware of. Then my body began to heat up. A swelling wave of energy was enveloping me. I had energy glowing from the tips of my fingers to the top of my hair. As I was filled with this energy, my body seemed to be made of light rather than physical substance.

Then I saw my chakras. They were concave, like the lens of a magnifying glass, each one bigger than a hand, made up of some thick but translucent material, and they were spinning like airplane propellers. I saw colors, too, like the green and gold sparkles dancing in my heart. I felt a tremendous urge to love and accept myself, and to remind myself that this experience is not an illusion but something wonderful, real, and precious.

After this, I moved into a timeless space of complete serenity, peace, oneness, as if I had become part of the whole universe. When I came back into my body, I immediately began wondering if I had dreamed it all but discovered that I could still focus on the chakras with my inner vision and see the spinning colors of their discs.

Such experiences are more common than you may think. Even though they happen spontaneously, unexpectedly, they come as a result of solid groundwork and careful preparation. Celeste's experience is an encouragement to all those logical, rational thinkers among us who secretly wish to be transported into mystical states of consciousness but who think, "Well, anyway, even if it does happen to some people, it probably won't happen to me."

It can and it will, providing you are willing to practice the exercises that are presented here. Moreover, I would like to emphasize that there is no need to try to recreate Celeste's experience. You may not "see" your chakras the way she did. You may have very different kinds of experiences. You may be flooded with strong, wonderful feelings that change as the energy rises from chakra to chakra. You may hear beautiful sounds or music, like those created by Tibetan monks who use a complete system of "healing bells" for the seven chakras. You may have profound insights into the meaning of your life. You may feel a state of blissful contentment and well-being, as if you have arrived home after a long journey. Nobody can predict the experiences that will occur when you begin to channel your sexual energy.

What can be predicted, however, is that if you practice the techniques for opening your energy channels you will be able to send orgasmic energy

The nature of life is passion. Passion is the total sense of being alive in every fiber of your being, a heightened awareness, and the ability to feel at peace and intense at the same time. A sense of your self as a rhythmic flow in harmony with the flow of the universe.

—AZUL

to your crown chakra and beyond into the Astral Network, regardless of what may occur as the energy passes through a particular chakra.

Now you are invited to explore a sequence of exercises that will give you direct experience of moving your sexual energy and your symbol through the seven chakras. These exercises are easy to understand but involve a number of steps. It is important to proceed slowly, mastering each step in turn.

I also wish to stress that these exercises are of great benefit to your physical body and mental health. They tone up your muscles, oxygenate your brain, revitalize your endocrine system, expand your capacity for orgasmic pleasure, and help you to celebrate the wonder of being in an alive, pulsing body. They are also great fun to do, especially when working with a partner.

EXERCISE: THE CHAKRA RUB

Purpose and Benefits

The Chakra Rub is a very pleasurable massage that will energize your seven chakras, opening the way for sexual magic. In this exercise, you will be using one of the Magic Symbols that you created in the previous chapter.

During the Chakra Rub, you imprint your Magic Symbol on each chakra in turn, increasing and refining the symbol's power as it rises toward the Astral Network.

Preparations

- This exercise is done with a partner.

  Create your Magic Circle.

- You need a massage table or, if you prefer, you can use a mattress on the floor. The massage table or mattress should be located within your Magic Circle and covered with a clean sheet.

- You need two pillows, one large and one small, to help you feel comfortable while you are being massaged.

- You also need massage oil. There are specific oils that correspond to each chakra (see appendix) and these can be helpful in giving a chakra rub, but a good-quality, all-purpose massage oil is also okay.

- The room should be warm enough so that you can be naked.

- Bring your Magic Symbol to this exercise.

- Take time to create a magical and sensuous atmosphere in the room. Light a candle, burn incense, put on soft music, wear fresh, silky clothes that feel good on your skin. Allow the whole massage to have a sensuous, erotic, and playful quality.

- Allow about forty minutes for each partner.

Practice

STAGE 1: SENSUAL AWAKENING

Choose who is Partner A (receiver) and who is Partner B (giver). You will reverse roles later.

Sit on cushions, facing each other. Place the Magic Symbol of Partner A, the one who is going to receive the massage, on the floor between you. Close your eyes. Take time to become centered and relaxed, breathing slowly and deeply.

At a prearranged signal, perhaps a light touch on the knee, open your eyes and together gaze at the symbol that is lying between you.

Look with receptive eyes, allowing the symbol to be absorbed into your bodies through your eyes and through your breathing.

After a few moments, raise your eyes from the symbol and gaze into each other's eyes. Allow a feeling of trust and love to arise between you. Together, you are going to create sexual magic.

Partner A, receiver, stand up and slowly slip out of any clothing that you are wearing, enjoying the sensual pleasure of exposing your naked body while your partner is watching. Then, with your eyes closed, slowly and erotically caress your body, appreciating its sensitivity.

Partner B, giver, look at Partner A's body. See the hidden sources of sensual, sexual energy that can be awakened in this beautiful instrument for alchemy and magic. You are going to play on it like a skilled musician, awakening hidden harmonies.

STAGE 2: TUNING IN

Partner A, receiver, when you are ready, lie facedown on the massage table or mattress. Your body, neck, and head need to be in a straight line so that your energy can flow easily. Make sure you are comfortable. Place a large

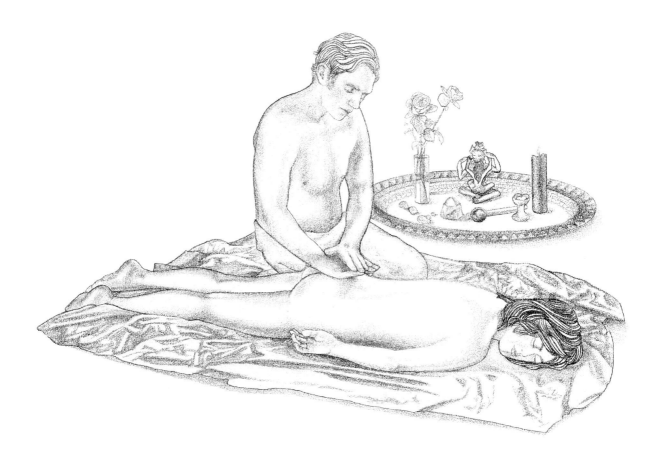

The Chakra Rub: energizing the chakras

cushion under your upper chest and a smaller cushion under your forehead.

Partner B, giver, if you are working on a massage table, stand on your
partner's left side. If you are working on a mattress, sit on the left side. Place
your right hand on Partner A's sacrum, at the point where the spine meets
the buttocks. Place your left hand in the middle of the upper back, directly
behind the heart chakra.

Partner A, receiver, begin to breathe slowly and deeply through your
mouth, staying relaxed and receptive.

Partner B, giver, take time to tune in to the rhythm of your partner's
breathing, inhaling and exhaling through your mouth. Close your eyes and
sink into a feeling of deep synchronicity with your partner. Gently rock the

217

pelvic area and then trace both your hands lightly over the entire body in a sensuous massaging movement. Enjoy the pleasure that you are giving to your beloved.

STAGE 3: ENERGIZING THE CHAKRAS

When you are ready, bring both hands to the sacrum, at the base of the spine, just between the buttocks. You are about to energize your partner's first chakra.

Using plenty of oil, begin to massage the sacral area with small circular movements, one hand placed on top of the other. Use both hands to massage in either a clockwise or counterclockwise direction. As you massage, breathe deeply through your mouth, keeping the same rhythm as your partner. Take time to establish a comfortable rhythm of massaging and breathing.

Partner B, giver, when you feel ready, visualize a dark red color flowing out of your hands and spreading through your partner's first chakra. See red spreading through the sacrum, the buttocks, the genitals, and the pelvis as you massage this area. Communicate to your partner: "See the color red flowing from my hands into your first chakra."

Partner A, receiver, visualize a dark red color flooding this entire area of your body, bringing aliveness and healing to your sex center.

Continue until both partners feel comfortable with the visualization.

Partner B, giver, when you feel ready to move to the next step, visualize your partner's Magic Symbol and imagine that you are massaging it into his or her first chakra. Visualize the symbol floating in the red energy that is moving within this chakra. Communicate this to your partner: "I see your symbol floating in your sex center."

Partner A, see your symbol floating and swirling in your genitals, pelvic area, and lower back, mixing with the dark red energy that is awakened there. Continue with this visualization while your first chakra is being massaged.

Partner B, giver, after two or three minutes, stop the massaging movement. Be still for a moment, with both your hands resting on the sacrum.

Both partners, tune into the first chakra and feel what is happening there. Perhaps there is a sensation of warmth, or a glow of red light. You may see the symbol floating in a pool of energy. You may have a sensation of light or darkness, or of energy moving in a spiral, or flowing between the back and front of the body. Simply observe whatever is happening.

Partner B, slowly slide your hands up Partner A's back, imagining as you do so that you are bringing your partner's symbol to his or her second chakra. This chakra is located in the small of the back, opposite the navel. Tell your partner that this is happening.

Partner A, receiver, as you feel the hands move up your back, visualize your symbol rising from your first chakra to your second.

Partner B, rest your hands on your partner's second chakra for a few moments. Tune in to your partner's breathing, make sure you are breathing together in harmony, and then slowly begin to massage.

Begin to massage the lower back with small, circular movements, in quick, dynamic rhythms.

Visualize the color orange flowing out of your hands and spreading through this area, flooding your partner's second chakra, filling it with vitality and strength, coloring the symbol that is floating there. Communicate with your partner that this is happening so you can share this visualization.

Repeat these steps at each of your partner's chakras, bringing the symbol to each chakra in turn, flooding the area with the appropriate color, imprinting the symbol in each energy center.

Move slowly and carefully, enjoying the massage and breathing deeply through the mouth.

Only the lovers can get through the fire of the ring of the mandala. Open your heart. God is searching God in this creation.

—SUFI SAYING

STAGE 4: CONNECTING WITH THE ASTRAL NETWORK

Partner B, giver, when you come to the seventh chakra, use only your fingertips to massage your partner's crown with a light, feathery, circular motion. When you have finished, stop, and rest your fingertips lightly on the crown for a few moments.

Partner B, close your eyes. Slowly lift your fingertips off your partner's head and visualize the symbol rising out of your partner's crown chakra. Communicate to your partner that this is happening.

Partner A, receiver, inhale deeply and visualize your symbol rising out through your crown chakra, floating in the space just above your head. Hold your breath for a few moments as you see the symbol shining brightly and clearly, energized and purified by its journey through your chakras. This is the area of the "eighth chakra," the place where you can connect with the Astral Network.

Relax and breathe normally.

Both partners, continue to visualize the Magic Symbol in the eighth chakra position for a few moments.

STAGE 5: GROUNDING THE ENERGY

Partner B, giver, when you are ready, move to a position near your partner's feet. Gently grasp the feet, one in each hand, squeezing and massaging them in a firm manner. Do this for a few minutes. This will ground the energy that has moved upward through the body.

Partner A, receiver, take a deep breath and exhale, visualizing your energy moving down through your body, all the way from your head to your feet.

Partner B, when you have finished, sit quietly by Partner A's side for a few moments, allowing time for both of you to integrate this powerful experience.

When you are ready, sit opposite each other and share your experiences.

Partner A, thank Partner B for giving you this pleasurable experience. End with a Melting Hug and Heart Salutation.

Reverse roles. Partner B is now the receptive partner, while Partner A gives the massage. Take time to start at the very beginning of the exercise, sitting opposite each other with the symbol lying between you. Then proceed through all the stages.

Pointers

It is quite common for both partners to feel sexually stimulated during the chakra rub, especially when the first two chakras are being massaged. This is perfectly okay. Welcome these sexual feelings. They will help you to stimulate the chakras and enhance the flow of energy.

When you are the receiver, you may feel some of your chakras more strongly than others. This is natural, especially in the beginning. Take time to give energy and support to those chakras that feel weak or not very sensitive.

When you are the giver, use your whole body in the massage, not just your hands and arms. Move from your belly, rotating your hips in time to the circular movement of your hands.

There are several elements in the chakra rub: breathing, massaging, and visualization of colors and the symbol. For both partners, it is easy to lose track of one or more element while focusing on another aspect.

If you realize that you have forgotten to breathe deeply or to visualize your symbol or a particular color, there is no need to feel you have made a mistake. Come back to your breathing. Let this be the source to which you return in moments of uncertainty. Breathing deeply, welcome the sensations created by the massage, visualize the appropriate color for the chakra, then introduce the symbol.

Now that you have sensitized each energy center with the Chakra Rub, you are ready to move into a more powerful chakra exercise.

EXERCISE: CHAKRA BREATHING

Purpose and Benefits

In this exercise you continue to energize the seven chakra points, opening your Inner Flute so that your sexual energy and your Magic Symbol can rise together through the seven energy centers, on their way to the Astral Network.

This practice is especially suited to the use of the Three Keys— breathing, movement, and sound—which I introduced in chapter three. As you will see, these keys are invaluable aids to awakening your energy and opening pathways for it to move.

Preparations

- This exercise can be done alone or with your partner.

- Create your Magic Circle.

- Rhythmic music can be helpful to this exercise. A special chakra-breathing audiocassette is available for this purpose (see Resources: Music List on p. 372). It is also possible to work without music.

- You will combine breathing, movement, and visualization as you focus on each of the seven chakras in succession. You will spend two to three minutes focusing on each chakra, so it may be helpful to have a clock where you can see it.

- You will be using your Magic Symbol.

- Your body will get hot during this exercise, so it is good to be naked or to wear light, loose clothing.

- It is good to work on an empty stomach, or at least one hour after eating. In fact, the best time is before breakfast.

- You may want to make noise, so be sure that you are in a place where you will neither disturb others nor be disturbed by them. It is important to be able to complete the whole exercise in a single session without interruption from telephone calls, doorbells, or questions from curious onlookers.

🕉 This exercise requires intense physical activity. Even though, to any observer, it would certainly look strange, put any self-conscious thoughts aside and give it all you've got. Use your whole body. If it helps, think of yourself as participating in some form of breath therapy, such as a rebirthing session, or perhaps as a primitive warrior engaged in a tribal war dance.

🕉 This exercise is usually done standing, but people who get easily tired or who have lower-back problems can do it lying on their backs, knees raised, feet flat on the floor.

🕉 You will be breathing strongly through your mouth and may get a dry throat, so it is a good idea to have a glass of water handy.

🕉 Allow one hour for this exercise.

Practice

STAGE 1: WARM-UPS WITH THE PC PUMP

Stand in the middle of your Magic Circle. Your feet are shoulder-width apart, with the soles of your feet flat on the floor and your knees slightly bent, arms hanging loosely by your sides. It is preferable to close your eyes, because you are going to focus on awakening the inner sensations in your body.

Take a few deep breaths, relax your body, and focus your attention on your genital area, particularly on the large muscle located between your anus and your genitals that connects these two areas with your pelvis. I call this the PC muscle, after its technical name—pubococcygeus. See if you can tighten and relax your PC muscle. It feels like a valve, opening and closing around the genitals. This is the muscle you clamp down when you want to stop the flow of urine.

Take a few moments to tighten and relax your PC muscle in a series of brief, squeezing reflexes. In *The Art of Sexual Ecstasy,* I termed this squeezing reflex the "PC Pump."

Do the PC Pump ten times. This pumping action stimulates your sexual energy and helps to focus your attention in your genital area.

Rest for a moment, then start another series of ten pumps, this time rocking your pelvis up and back as you do so and arching your lower back

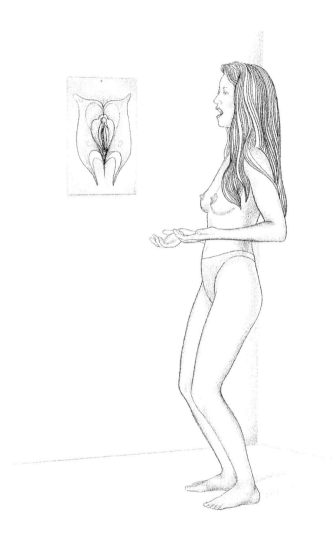

Chakra breathing and
integrating the magic symbol
into the chakras.

slightly. Squeeze your PC muscle and rock back. Relax your PC muscle,
letting your pelvis drop down and forward. You will find that these movements go together easily and naturally (see illustration).

After a short rest, begin a third series of ten PC pumps, this time
adding your breath to the movements. Inhale strongly through your mouth
as you squeeze the PC muscle and rock back with your hips. Exhale as you
relax the PC muscle and push your pelvis forward.

Practice this combination of PC pump, pelvic rocking, and breathing.
It all goes together easily. Let your whole body become involved, bending

forward at the knees as you push forward with your pelvis, moving your arms in time to your breathing. As you breathe out, let your voice participate, making a sound like *"Hoo!" "Ugh!"* or *"Huh!"* Feel the sound vibrate in your first chakra.

When you have gotten the knack, you are ready to begin the full exercise.

STAGE 2: CHAKRA BREATHING WITH YOUR MAGIC SYMBOL
Put on music if you wish.

Bring your Magic Symbol into the circle and place it on the floor or on the wall in front of you.

Stand over your symbol so that it lies between your legs.

Resume your earlier posture, feet flat on the floor, knees slightly bent, arms hanging loosely by your sides.

Breathe in deeply, squeezing your PC muscle and rocking back with your pelvis.

Exhale strongly, making a sound, relaxing your PC muscle and pushing your pelvis forward.

Continue breathing and moving in a strong rhythm. The more total you can be in these first few minutes, the more sexual energy you will awaken and the stronger the effect will be. Make a sound that vibrates in your sex center, your genitals.

Feel tingling sensations, warmth and energy spreading through your pelvis, bringing aliveness to your sex center. Visualize this energy as a dark red color.

When you feel that your first chakra is awake and energized, look at the Magic Symbol between your legs or on the wall in front of you.

Inhale, imagining that you are sucking your Magic Symbol up into your body, into your sex center.

Visualize your symbol inside your genitals. Feel the symbol becoming charged with sexual energy, soaked with the color red. Squeeze your PC muscle. Move your hips.

Take time to anchor your symbol firmly in your sex center. Usually, this takes two to three minutes per chakra, but you may need more time in the first chakra, because this is the starting point.

When you feel that your Magic Symbol is charged with sexual energy, focus your attention on your second chakra, located below the navel. This is your hara center, the balance point in martial arts.

Make a sound that vibrates in your belly. Play with the pitch of the sound until you feel it resonating in your second chakra. See the color orange spreading through your belly. Feel the fluidity, the graceful body movements, that originate in your hara.

When you are ready, visualize your Magic Symbol rising up through your body from your genitals to your lower belly, where it can be charged with the energy you are generating.

As you do so, breathe vigorously through your mouth, do the PC pump, and rock your pelvis. (Throughout this exercise, you need to keep your foot on the gas pedal!) Keep infusing your symbol with orange-colored energy as it floats inside your second chakra.

After two or three minutes, bring your awareness to your solar plexus. This is your power center, so here is an opportunity to enhance your sense of power. Expand your chest, breathe strongly, move your body, raise the pitch of your sound to vibrate your third chakra. Here, your sound may be more of a *"Ho!"* than a *"Huh!"* Choose a sound that feels right for you. See the color yellow radiating through your chest.

When you are ready, visualize your symbol rising through your body from your belly to your solar plexus. Charge your symbol with the yellow-colored power you are generating here. Inhale and exhale strongly through your mouth as you focus on your solar plexus.

After two or three minutes, focus your attention on your heart center, your fourth chakra. Alter the pitch of your voice to vibrate this chakra, located in the midpoint of your chest. The sound may be an explosive *"Ah!"* almost as if you are surprised by the feeling of sex energy reaching your heart. Move your shoulders and arms, stretching your chest as you inhale and exhale, flooding your heart center with green-colored energy. Then bring your symbol up to this chakra so that it can be charged with the qualities of the heart.

Notice if the rate of your breathing and movement is quickening as you rise through the chakras. This is perfectly okay, but be sure to keep breathing deeply through your mouth as you focus on each chakra.

After two or three minutes, bring your awareness to your throat, your fifth chakra. See the color blue spreading through your throat area.

Keep your throat relaxed and your mouth wide open as you breathe vigorously. The more you energize your throat center, the more you can open your sex center. There is a deep connection between the two.

Bring your symbol up to your throat chakra, soaking it in the color blue. As you inhale, feel that you are sucking in life with great gulps, expressing your desire to be fully alive.

After two to three minutes, focus your attention at the point between your eyebrows, your sixth chakra or "third eye" center. Raise the pitch of your sound so that it vibrates behind your forehead. Breathe vigorously. See the color purple flooding your sixth chakra.

Bring your Magic Symbol to the middle of your head. Make sure that your eyes are closed and your attention is directed inward. Your physical eyes may roll gently upward behind the lids. You may see purple light surrounding your symbol, or see it floating in space, or experience a tingling sensation behind your forehead. You may receive new insights about your symbol. Allow this to happen as you breathe and move.

After two to three minutes, focus your attention on the crown of your head, your seventh chakra. Raise the pitch of your sound so that it seems to resonate against the crown of your skull from the inside. Bring your symbol up to this point. You may see white light. You may lose a sense of boundary between your head and the space that surrounds it. You may feel that your physical form is only part of an expanded sense of self that seems to have no limits. Enjoy these sensations of diffusing and dissolving, while continuing to breathe and move.

After two to three minutes, breathe in deeply, and in so doing shoot your Magic Symbol out of the top of your head and allow it to float freely in space. Hold your breath for a few seconds, as you see your symbol hovering above your head, shining, brilliant, energized and clear, connecting through invisible wavelengths to the Astral Network.

As soon as you feel that your Magic Symbol is floating freely above your head, breathe normally and relax. Stop all movement. Let this moment be timeless. Simply remain aware of your Magic Symbol floating above your head and resonating with the Astral Network.

After a pause, let your symbol move away from your head, like a bird flying off to a faraway tree, growing smaller and smaller. See it shrink to a tiny dot, far away, then disappear completely.

Inhale deeply.

Exhaling slowly, allow your energy to sink down through your head and into your body. Watch your energy fall down through your throat chakra, your heart, solar plexus, hara, and sex center. Watch it move slowly down your legs, into your feet, and down into the earth. Feel that your energy is soaking into the earth, leaving you clear and empty.

Rest for a few moments, then repeat the entire exercise twice more, always making sure that, after you reach the Astral Network above your head, you bring your energy back down through your body into the earth. The whole process of three rounds of chakra breathing takes about an hour.

Pointers

Some people ask, "What happens if I don't see anything inside as I do this exercise?"

Remember, you can experience energy in many ways: as colors, sounds, bodily feelings, images, shapes, messages, words, even tastes and smells. There is no need to try to make everything happen at once. Begin by focusing your attention on the Three Keys—breathing, movement, and sound—then let the experience unfold in whatever way it may.

It is important to keep breathing actively and deeply through your mouth during the whole exercise. This will give you the energy charge you need to enter into expanded states of consciousness as you connect with each chakra.

A few people have reported that they tend to get cramps in their lower rib cage or belly during the exercise. If this happens, slow down, relax the area that has become tense, and then build up again once the cramp has passed.

As with any exercise that moves energy up through your body, it is important to end by grounding the energy into the earth. If you bring energy to your third eye or crown without grounding it afterward, you may begin to feel light-headed or dizzy or have a headache. It may also be difficult to concentrate on ordinary daily tasks.

Although it is better to do the chakra breathing exercise three times in a single session, if you do not have much time, you can do it once.

If you like, you can piece together seven different moods of music on a single tape, choosing one type for each chakra, to play while you do the exercise. Each section should last two to three minutes. The pace of your breathing tends to speed up as you move upward through the chakras, and the pitch of your sounds will become higher. The rhythm of your music needs to reflect this trend, quickening with each new piece.

EXERCISE: THE CHAKRA WAVE

Purpose and Benefits

A beautiful practice to do with your beloved, the Chakra Wave crowns the experiences of the previous two exercises. It teaches you how to channel sexual energy through your chakras, how to develop and circulate orgasmic

The Chakra Wave Exercise: creating circles of energy between the sexual center root chakras and each chakra.

energy, and how to help each other bring a Magical Symbol through the seven chakras to the Astral Network. It also helps partners to tune into each other's rhythms and harmonize their energies. This is a major step in your mastery of sexual magic.

Preparations

- ⚘ This exercise is done with a partner.

- ⚘ You can be naked or clothed. If you are dressed, be sure to wear loose clothes that do not constrict your waist. If you are naked, make sure the room is warm and the space comfortable.

- ⚘ You will need to sit on a thick carpet, mattress, or futon, and have pillows available.

- ⚘ Also, make sure you have massage oil or a water-based sexual lubricant, in case they are needed during sexual stimulation.

- ⚘ Music is important in this practice. My favorite pieces are listed in the appendix. You may choose to play one piece all the way through or create a prerecorded sequence of different music for each chakra.

- ⚘ You will be using your Magic Symbol.

- ⚘ Allow one hour for this exercise.

Practice

STAGE 1: FINDING THE CHAKRA WAVE POSITION
Enter your Magic Circle together.

Stand in the center of the circle, facing each other.

Greet each other with a Heart Salutation, followed by a Melting Hug, and feel the love and trust that flows between you as you enter into this exciting exercise.

Choose who is Partner A and who is Partner B.

Partner A, you are the leader, moving through the Chakra Wave first. Partner B, your role in this exercise is one of support, sensitivity, and encouragement.

Partner B, as the supporter, sit on the floor with your legs crossed in the semi-lotus position (see illustration). You may wish to lean your back against a wall, or have some solid support for your lower back.

229

Partner A, as the leader, sit in front of your partner with your back against his or her chest and your buttocks between his or her thighs (see illustration). Do not lean too heavily against your supporting partner. Keep your spine straight, but without tension.

Partner B, you may want to place a small pillow in front of your genitals, to cushion them from your partner's lower back, as this exercise can get quite wild. You may also prefer to spread your legs wide apart, with your partner sitting between them.

Both partners, take time to make yourselves comfortable.

Place your Magic Symbol on the floor in front of you.

Partner A, leader, when you are ready, take your partner's left hand and place it on your genital area. Choose a place where you feel a tingle of sexual excitement, like the first impulse when you move into lovemaking. If you are a woman, the best position is with his fingertips lightly touching your clitoris, or "cleo" as I call it. If this feels too invasive, then allow his hand to rest on your "mound of Venus," your pubic bone, just above the cleo.

If you are a man, the best position is with her fingertips pressing against the perineum, halfway between the testicles and the anus. If this is not comfortable, let her hand hold your penis, or rest above your penis on the pubic bone. Enjoy this delightful sensation, the first sexual stirrings, the promise of pleasure.

Now take your partner's right hand and place it on your lower abdomen, just below your navel. When you are both comfortable, you are ready to begin the Chakra Wave.

STAGE 2: AWAKENING SEXUAL FIRE

Partner A, leader, close your eyes, relax and begin to take slow, deep breaths through your mouth. As you inhale, feel that your breath is flowing all the way down to your sex center.

Partner B, you are in a support role, so it is important that you follow your partner's lead. Close your eyes and tune in to your partner's breathing. This practice offers a wonderful opportunity for you to be completely receptive, putting your own will aside. Breathing at the same pace as your partner, begin gently to stimulate his or her genital area by pressing and caressing with the fingers of your left hand. Be guided by Partner A as to the most pleasurable way to do this.

Both partners, take time to establish a harmonious rhythm of breathing and gentle impulses on the genitals.

Partner B, avoid strong stimulation as this will lead to a striving for sexual release, and then it will be difficult for Partner A to channel the energy upward. Just a small impulse on the woman's clitoris or on the man's penis is needed to awaken sexual energy. Do it lightly.

Partner A, leader, you are awakening a sexual fire in your first chakra. Breathe strongly through your mouth. Inhale, squeezing your PC muscle, rocking your pelvis back slightly, drawing energy into your first chakra. Exhale, relaxing your PC muscle and pelvis. Do this until it feels tingly, warm, alive.

STAGE 3: MOVING THROUGH THE CHAKRAS

First Chakra   Partner A, when you feel that your first chakra is awake, visualize the vital strength of the color red filling your pelvis with life and power. Feel that you are generating fire, warmth, lust, excitement in your sexual center. Make sounds, moans, murmurs, growls, whatever expresses your feelings. Take time to generate a strong charge of sexual energy that fills your first chakra.

When you are ready, open your eyes and look at your Magic Symbol on the floor in front of you. Inhale strongly through your mouth, feeling that you are sucking the symbol into your first chakra, imprinting it on the fiery red energy.

Partner B, supporter, you can help by visualizing the color red spreading beneath your hands, filling your partner's sexual center. Continue to give stimulating impulses to your partner's sexual organ with your left hand.

Both partners, continue to breathe strongly together.

Partner A, leader, close your eyes and anchor the image of your symbol firmly in your first chakra. Breathe, do the PC pump, move your hips, moan, as you charge your symbol with the warm red energy.

Second Chakra   Partner A, when you are ready, focus your awareness on your belly, your second chakra, where your partner's right hand is resting.

Inhale, drawing your sexual energy up into your belly. As you do so, visualize the color of this energy changing from red to orange. Feel the burning orange color spreading fire through your belly, stirring your deepest emotions. Exhale, letting the sexual energy flow back to your sex center.

As you inhale and exhale, feel your sexual energy circling between your first and second chakras. Inhale, drawing the energy up into your belly. Exhale, letting the energy flow down to your sex center.

Life is celebration! Celebrate life in all its forms. Let the river flow in you, trust in life. Accept yourself as you are and the river will reach to the ocean of its own accord.

—OSHO

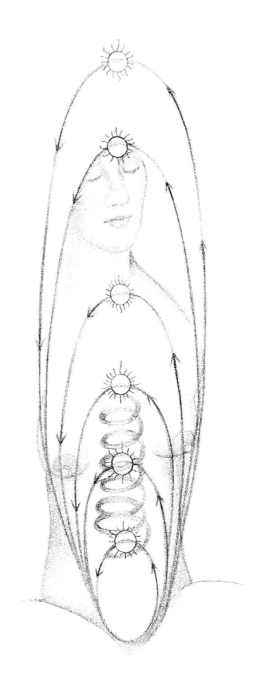

Circulating energy from the
first to the seventh chakras.

When you feel that your belly is charged with warmth and energy, visualize your Magic Symbol rising through your body and resting in your second chakra. Let your symbol be drenched in the color orange.

Keep your eyes closed. Stay focused on yourself, your genital sensations, arousing yourself through the PC pump, body movement, deep breathing, and visualization, combining all these instruments of sexual magic in your own private orchestra. This is how to make music in your chakras.

You will know that your first two chakras are connected when you feel a fire burning in your belly. It may be a cool fire, it may be hot, but either way you are stoking the flames, the cauldron is bubbling, energies are being released and transformed. You are reaching to the wild woman or man inside you, to the primordial energies of life and love.

As your second chakra awakens, its unique qualities will be released. You may feel like a wild animal growling, or experience a sudden surge of pent-up emotion, or feel a fluid movement radiating from your hara center and capturing your body in an exotic dance.

Let your whole body be involved. Rotate your hips, move your torso, draw circles in the air with your hands to stimulate your visualization and help the energy circulate. Build up the charge in your second chakra until your belly feels warm and vibrant. See your symbol burning with orange fire in your second chakra.

Partner B, supporter, stay in tune with your partner's breathing, continuing to stimulate Partner A's sexual organ lightly with your left hand.

Third Chakra   Partner A, leader, when you feel that your belly is filled with energy, take your partner's right hand and move it to your solar plexus, your third chakra, your power center. Inhale deeply through your mouth, visualizing your sex energy rising from your first to your third chakra. As the energy reaches your solar plexus, visualize a bright yellow color spreading through this area.

Now your energy is making a bigger loop, circling between your first and third chakras. Inhale, pulling the energy up your spine. Exhale, letting the energy flow down the front of your body. In this way, make big circles with your energy. When the circle is established, visualize your Magic Symbol rising up through your body and resting in your third chakra. See it glowing in your solar plexus like a bright yellow sun.

Your sexual energy is rising to the challenge of awakening your power center, awakening your sense of "I am!" as a radiant expression of self. Feel your strength. Connect with your inner power. Feel a growing sense of trust in yourself. Let this sensation build into a joyful shout, an exclamation of "Yes! I am me, and I love it!"

If feelings of inadequacy are triggered, these may manifest themselves in the form of a constriction or blockage in the third chakra. Give yourself permission to growl or a shout, using sound to push through the constriction and release the powerful energy bottled up there.

Fourth Chakra   Partner A, when you can feel the strength, the radiance filling your solar plexus, take your partner's right hand and place it on your heart center, in the middle of your chest. As your partner continues to give frequent impulses to your genitals, inhale deeply, picking up the sensation with your breath, bringing it from your genitals to your heart.

As the energy reaches your heart center, visualize a beautiful green color flooding through your chest. Feel the healing, the love, the sense of hope and renewal that this color awakens here. Let the energy circle between your first and fourth chakras. When you feel ready, bring your Magic Symbol up to the midpoint of your chest, infusing it with green.

Breathe deeply and strongly, opening up your chest. Let your hands and arms make circles, emphasizing the movement of energy and the rhythm of your breathing.

Often, the energy expanding in your chest will trigger feelings of sadness or longing. Tears may arise. Let them flow freely. Let them release the tension and heal old wounds, so that tears of sadness can turn to tears of gratitude for being able to open so deeply. As your heart center opens, you may connect with the child within you—the innocence, playfulness, and laughter. Let this also be expressed. Hold nothing back.

Fifth Chakra   Partner A, take your partner's hand and place it on your throat chakra. Inhale, drawing sexual energy from your first chakra up to your throat. As the energy reaches here, see your throat being bathed in a deep blue color. Circle the energy between your first and fifth chakras and, when you are ready, bring your Magic Symbol up from your chest and place it in your throat, infusing it with a radiant blue light.

Opening the throat chakra releases your true voice, your vocal expression of who you really are, long held back by parental warnings to "be quiet." Now is the time to express it, sing it, share it. Express whatever comes. Perhaps there is a choking sensation as your energy struggles to free itself. Help to release this energy through sounds. Speak nonsense, gibber-

Magic is self-seeking. Mysticism is self-surrendering..
   —The Book of Magic

234

ish. Feel the joy of expressing who you are, in an orgasm of the throat, healing all the times you held yourself back.

Sixth Chakra   Partner A, take your partner's hand and let the fingertips lightly touch your third eye. Just the tip of the middle finger will do. Inhale, drawing sexual energy to your third eye and, as the energy reaches this center, visualize the color purple expanding through your head. Breathe deeply, circle the energy between your first chakra and your third eye. The energy has a long way to travel now, so stay connected with your sex center by moving your body, doing the PC Pump, making circles with your hands and arms as you inhale and exhale.

When you are ready, raise your symbol to the center of your head, so that it floats amid a sea of purple. As your third eye awakens there is a sense of spaciousness, freedom, and global vision, like an eagle soaring high above the earth. Everything is more peaceful, more expanded. Problems seem far away, as if you have risen above the clouds into a clear and endless sky.

Seventh Chakra   Partner A, place your partner's hand on your crown chakra, very delicately, with only the fingertips touching the top of your head. Inhale, drawing sex energy up through your body and, as it touches your crown, see the top of your head shining with white light. Feel the lightness, the purity of this color. Feel its wholeness, embracing all the colors of the rainbow.

Circle your energy between your first chakra and your seventh, breathing deeply and strongly. When you are ready, bring your Magic Symbol to the crown of your head. Visualize it shining brilliantly with white light.

Now there is boundless silence and peace. Sexual energy is transformed into timeless ecstasy. You are connected with the whole universe, as if everything that has ever been created is now part of you, as if every cell in your body is a reflection of the cosmic dance that surrounds you.

Astral Network   From this space, you are going to send your Magic Symbol into the Astral Network. Tighten your PC muscle and inhale deeply, propelling your Magic Symbol out through the crown of your head into the space above it. Hold your breath for a few moments as you see your symbol floating just above your head, shining with white light.

Relax and breathe normally, supported by your partner. Now your work is done. Your symbol has all the energy it needs to imprint itself on the vast energy field of the Astral Network and dissolve into this multidimensional, telepathic web of communication that links you with the whole universe. You can trust that your message is being received, your call is being heard, and in due course it will be answered.

Remain in this deep, relaxed, trancelike state for several minutes, continuing to visualize your symbol floating just above your head.

When you are ready, visualize your Magic Symbol floating slowly away from your head. Watch it move farther and farther away, growing smaller and smaller until it becomes just a tiny dot, far away, then vanishes into space.

STAGE 4: GROUNDING THE ENERGY

Take a deep breath and, as you slowly exhale, bring your sexual energy back down through your body. See the energy sink down through your crown, your third eye, your throat chakra, chest, belly, and pelvis. Let it travel down your legs, into your feet, and down into the earth.

When you feel grounded, slowly move away from your partner. Both partners should now lie down on the floor and relax, doing nothing, for about ten minutes. This will give you time to integrate the experience.

When you are ready, sit up and share your experiences.

End with a Melting Hug and Heart Salutation.

Before changing roles it is good to take a break, have a shower, and freshen up the room, to be ready for a totally new experience.

Pointers

The Chakra Wave is advanced energy work. As such, it cannot be confined to a rigid system, because energy often takes unexpected twists and turns, revealing aspects of yourself that you never knew existed.

For example, you may begin with the intention of moving sexual energy all the way through your chakras to the Astral Network, but you may suddenly experience such an exquisite, overwhelming, orgasmic sensation in your heart or throat that this becomes the whole experience. Allow this to happen. Move spontaneously and naturally with the energy. The instructions in this exercise are simply guidelines to help you discover your own potential, your own ecstasy.

You may lose track of your Magic Symbol during such experiences, because it has already been deeply imprinted on your subconscious mind. It will continue to do its job. Human beings are broadcasting along telepathic wavelengths all the time, and the fact that you have created a

We must remember that magic is basically the development of a psychic faculty which enables a person to see below the surface of normal reality.

—COLIN WILSON

236

symbol and infused it with sexual energy ensures that a strong message will go out—especially if it dissolves during an orgasm in one of your chakras.

You will find that each time you do the Chakra Wave you will have different experiences, but they can all be used in the service of sexual magic. There need be no contradiction between your pleasure, your ecstasy, and your desire to create magic.

Partner B, as the giver, you need to focus on being supportive, harmonizing your bodily movements with those of your partner. Take care not to adopt a posture or sitting position that makes your partner uncomfortable. You can help your partner to breathe deeply and rhythmically throughout the exercise by breathing in the same rhythm, close to partner A's ear.

Expanding Sexual Orgasm

Now that you have discovered the basic steps of sexual alchemy—moving sexual energy through your body's seven chakras, harmonizing your breath with movement and visualization—you are ready to enhance your sexual power source further. In the next two chapters, you will learn how to expand your orgasmic potential, generating strong charges for sexual magic. You are on your way to becoming a skilled sexual magician.

SHAKTI'S MAGIC:
The Alchemy of Female Orgasm

Every woman knows that she holds inside herself a tremendous capacity for love. This love can take many forms—from the nurturing mother to the devoted partner in a committed relationship to the wild and ecstatic lover. For a woman to open herself to this love, to expand into it, to be fulfilled by it, is perhaps the greatest magic that she can accomplish.

The key to opening the door of love is expanded sexual orgasm. This is the root of the woman's tree of love, her earthly base, her dark, fertile, hidden source of vital energy out of which her tree can grow to great heights, blossoming in spectacular abundance with the wonderful, fragrant flowers of love.

At the risk of making the rest of this book seem almost redundant, I have to say that a truly orgasmic woman needs no other tools for magic. Her radiance, her bubbling energy, her sexual vitality, her overflowing heart, make her so magnetically attractive that she naturally and effortlessly draws to herself everything that she needs.

But how many women can claim to know this magical state, which is both our potential and our birthright? Even today, in a relatively liberal culture that has become aware of the repression of women and is beginning to undo the damage inflicted by centuries of male domination, the art of attaining fully satisfying orgasmic states remains frustratingly elusive for the vast majority of women.

In this chapter, women learn the secrets of how to experience intense, prolonged, and ecstatic orgasms, while their male partners learn the delicate art of giving this ultimate pleasure to their beloved. And, should this task seem too one-sided, men can take comfort in the knowledge that in the following chapter they will learn the secrets of expanding male orgasm. For just as most women have been denied their potential for orgasmic pleasure, so the majority of men have settled for something less than true sexual fulfillment, contenting themselves with a local, genital, ejaculatory release instead of bathing in the exquisite sensations of total orgasm.

Both women and men can direct their expanded orgasmic energy into the practice of sexual magic. In the Chakra Wave exercise in the previous chapter, you learned how to stimulate sexual energy and channel it through the seven chakras. But this is just the beginning. Having opened

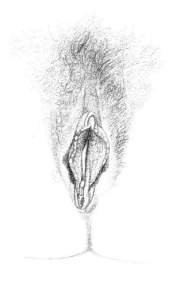

Yoni "au naturel"

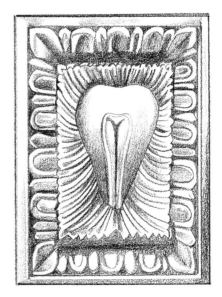

Icon of the yoni emanating rays of energy. From a South Indian wood carving of the nineteenth century.

the inner pathway, you are now ready to generate the maximum amount of orgasmic power as an alchemical fuel for your transformation, using the full spectrum of your orgasmic sensations to change your vision and give it tremendous potency.

Without this incredibly powerful energy, the ceremony and ritual of magic look rather like a beautiful automobile that has no engine. Its appearance is magnificent, your neighbors can admire it, but it cannot go anywhere. Sexual orgasm provides the engine, the horsepower, the pulsing, dynamic force that drives the vehicle of your magic to the destination you have chosen.

In this chapter you will be focusing on the fundamentals of expanding orgasm. You will not be asked to work with your Magic Symbol or the seven energy centers, because learning to create orgasmic states is a sufficient challenge in itself. It requires your total attention. Later, when you have mastered this essential skill, it will be easy to add the remaining steps of sexual magic.

You will also discover that, in the process of increasing your orgasmic potential, a profound healing will take place in your capacity to relate intimately with your beloved. As you will see, when two love partners move through the delicate stages that lead to expanded orgasm, and through the equally important steps of helping each other attain this experience, they learn every element needed for an intense and fulfilling relationship, including deep communication, courage, honesty, sensitivity, and trust.

Venus yields to caresses, not to compulsion.

—PUBLILIUS
Moral Sayings

HEALING THE PAST

Today, women's psyches are still influenced by centuries of patriarchal repression. This means that, until recently, we were programmed by a male-dominated society to believe that our main purpose in life was to service the needs and pleasures of the man, particularly in regard to sex. His pleasure was paramount, both in terms of his immediate sexual gratification and his goal of creating male heirs to inherit his name, his property, and his social status. If women got any sexual pleasure at all, it was in the form of crumbs that fell from the man's plate while he was eating.

During this time, most women had no idea that such a thing as female orgasm existed and, if they did, they were usually intelligent enough to keep quiet about it. The last thing men wanted to know was that their "inferior" partners were capable of experiencing more sexual pleasure than they permitted themselves.

All this has been well documented, and there is no need for me to cover this sad and painful story again. However, in terms of fulfilling orgasmic potential, it is important for women to understand that they still carry the legacy of this conditioning, especially in the delicate area of sexual satisfaction.

Eros is the force that draws a child to lie in its mother's lap, that evokes magical passion between lovers of all ages, the force that in its higher manifestation attracts souls to love. Eros is the power of the shakti. Eros is the child of Aphrodite.

—ANDREW HARVEY

This legacy has its origins in our religious roots, in the historical shift that occurred when patriarchal religions like Judaism, Christianity and Islam succeeded in wiping out all forms of worship devoted to a female or mother goddess. As part of this victory, female sexuality was condemned. It had to be, because the very essence of the religion of the mother goddess was fertility and the renewal of life through sexual union. Through the goddess, sexuality had a natural, sacred role to play in religion and therefore in society.

To a significant extent, the annihilation of the mother goddess depended on the ability of the patriarchal priesthood to condemn sex and make people feel guilty about their natural sexual feelings. And, in a cunning strategy that has to be admired for its enduring impact, the priests and prophets succeeded in creating a powerful myth that made women responsible for our sexual shame, thus further eradicating the influence of the mother goddess in religious practice.

Through propagating the myth of Adam and Eve, the priests showed how the first woman tempted the first man to commit the original sin. It was Eve who encouraged Adam to disobey Jehovah and eat from the Tree of Knowledge.

And what was the first dawning of their knowledge? Not a sudden understanding of the laws of nature, such as how to create fire or shape a wheel. Not the discovery of music, poetry, dance, or painting. No, the first "knowledge" that came to Adam and Eve was the discovery that they were naked. In other words, that they were sexual beings. They had genitals, sexual organs, a vagina or a penis, and these they shamefully covered with fig leaves. But concealment proved useless in the face of an all-knowing, unforgiving tyrant, and Adam and Eve were thrown out of the Garden of Eden. All because of the woman.

This legacy of shame, of condemnation, lives on in the subconscious minds of all women. Even today, when asserting their equality with men, there is a strong tendency for women to prove their worth by imitating men and competing with them for success in a patriarchal society, rather than through acknowledging and reembracing their truly female qualities.

Sexually, this tendency manifests itself as an effort to meet the man in a contest of sexual athletics, with both partners focusing on performance and achievement, striving for excitement and release. The woman may succeed in having an orgasm, but through this approach it usually remains superficial. It does not go deep. It does not flood her very being with the ecstasy of which she is capable.

Beneath a surface layer of liberated attitudes, women still carry a deep wound around their sexuality. All kinds of deep-seated beliefs and fears inhibit the natural flow of their orgasmic energy. Beliefs such as "I can't ask for what I want because I don't deserve it," or "I shouldn't be feeling this pleasure," or "It's the man's role to give me pleasure, and I must settle for what he gives me," and fears such as "If I really let go into my orgasmic energy, he'll think I'm too much."

In my work with women during the past fifteen years I have discovered that this is their constantly recurring dark secret: the belief that they are not worthy of receiving pleasure and, since they are not important, they can gain value only by serving and pleasing the man. It is time to remedy this imbalanced state of affairs. It is time for women to experience true liberation as female sexual beings.

THE HEALING ALCHEMY OF ORGASM

The damage caused to human society by the condemnation of sex is incalculable. Instead of accepting sexual union of women and men as a natural, healthy, and blissful act, we have turned sex into a furtive, guilt-ridden affair. Instead of celebrating sex as the creative, fertile life force that it really is, we have tried to hide it behind locked doors and even to pretend that it does not exist.

The effects of this misguided attitude stretch far beyond lovemaking and even beyond the flood tide of pornography, prostitution, rape, sexual abuse, and sexual harassment that our society is currently experiencing. It influences our entire worldview.

For example, these days, a tremendous amount of well-intentioned effort is being made to heal the global environment, to stop the destruction of our planetary biosphere, to bring peace to warring ethnic, national, and religious factions.

Yet how can any of this happen when the very source of human love is poisoned? How can love for the planet and love for each other flourish and prosper when the basic teaching of organized religion is that the sexual life force itself is evil, that our flesh is corrupted, that a vast and unbridgeable gap exists between the world of spirit and the world of earthly pleasure?

Intellectually, we may feel that we have discarded damaging myths such as Eve's original sin, but we need only look at the wounded state of human sexual behavior to realize that this ancient propaganda still lives in the subconscious part of our minds. The old paradigm has not yet been replaced. We have not yet stepped out of the prison of patriarchal history.

Fortunately there are effective and simple ways to free ourselves from this primitive programming. For woman, the road to true sexual liberation consists of walking the sacred path that begins with the first stirrings of sexual pleasure in her genitals and ends in a prolonged and thoroughly fulfilling orgasm. With this creative act of cherishing her body, encouraging her own ecstasy, the woman can reconnect with the goddess within, not as some mythical deity but as the living principle of female wholeness.

The reemergence of the sacred feminine principle goes hand in hand with the rebirth of the feminine pleasure principle, and with the balancing of male and female prerogatives to the experience of sexual pleasure.

The sexual ecstasy of a woman has a very high value. It is a magical, healing force. When she has been well loved, sexually fulfilled, she herself becomes a goddess with magical powers—radiating love, devotion, caring, gratitude, happiness. She has the capacity to restore the life force of sex to its rightful place in the temple of human understanding, opening the way for planetary healing and transformation.

An important part of this healing is the recognition that the male and female principles are not opposites, locked in an endless struggle for domination, but complementaries whose destiny is to unite in a Tantric dance of energy, flooding both partners with orgasmic joy.

Healing also comes in the form of a deep understanding between man and woman. In the following exercises, both partners learn new forms of communication. The woman, especially, learns to ask for what she wants, teaching her partner how to give her pleasure. She will be defining her sensations, recognizing any resistance that may surface as she rises to heightened states of orgasmic pleasure, learning the art of surrender and letting go into ecstasy.

The man learns how to caress and stimulate his love partner's sexual organ, taking her to new peaks of excitement. In doing so, he will experience the immense satisfaction that comes from voluntarily and gladly serving the other, gaining a deep appreciation of the interdependence that exists between a man and a woman when they move into lovemaking as true equals.

Only out of such equality can both partners experience their complementary roles as co-creators of ecstasy.

ANATOMY OF FEMALE ORGASM: THE CLITORIS AND THE G-SPOT

Before introducing the alchemy designed to enhance a woman's experience of orgasm, I would like to describe the physical anatomy of the female sexual organ. As I explained in *The Art of Sexual Ecstasy,* a sound working knowledge of the genitals is essential for those who wish to expand their orgasmic potential.

You will be exploring two orgasmic trigger points in the female sexual organ: the clitoris, which is the source of external or clitoral orgasm, and the so-called G-Spot, which is the source of a deeper, vaginal orgasm. You will be learning how to stimulate these points, first separately, then together in a blended orgasm that can fill the whole pelvic area and even your entire body.

Female readers are invited to treat the following description as an exercise by sitting down in front of a mirror and exploring the vagina as I describe it. Men can study the vagina of their partners, who may want to recline comfortably on cushions and open their legs, inviting the man to explore this normally invisible area of female sexuality.

The vagina is surrounded and protected by soft folds of skin called the labia. When these are spread back, you can see the mouth of the vagina, which leads into the vaginal canal (see illustration, page 246). Above the mouth of the vagina, at the point where the labia meet, or sometimes a little higher, is the clitoris.

The clitoris looks like a small round pearl or button. It is covered by a hood of skin which, when pulled back, reveals the tip of this delicate mechanism. There is a shaft, just below the tip, that divides into leglike parts that run on either side of the vaginal canal. Although you can see only the tip, you can feel the shaft just beneath the surface of the skin.

Thinking always of the Goddess, one is transformed into an image of the Goddess.

—HINDU TANTRA

245

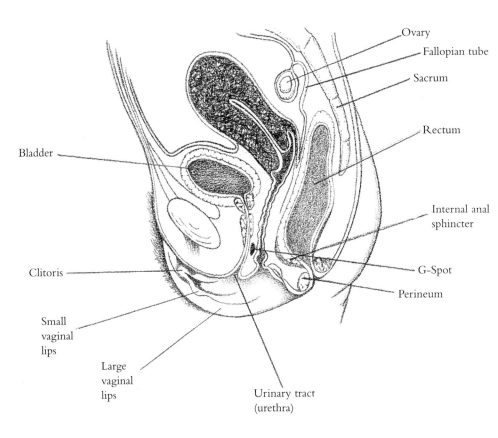

Ovary

Fallopian tube

Sacrum

Rectum

Internal anal
sphincter

G-Spot

Perineum

Bladder

Clitoris

Small
vaginal
lips

Large
vaginal
lips

Urinary tract
(urethra)

Female sexual anatomy

According to well-established research, a large majority of women who experience orgasm do so through manual stimulation of the clitoris, either by themselves or by a partner. Only a small minority of women experience clitoral orgasm during penetration by the penis, and even fewer experience a deeper orgasm inside the vagina. That is why it is so important to know how to stimulate the clitoris before sexual penetration.

As you can easily discover by gently touching its tip, the clitoris is quite mobile. It can and does move around during lovemaking, sliding in and out of the vaginal opening. When a woman becomes sexually aroused the clitoris enlarges to approximately double its size, but when she gets really excited and approaches sexual climax the clitoris tends to retract until hidden once more under the clitoral hood. If the woman becomes less excited, but still aroused, the clitoris will reappear.

The anatomy of a woman's clitoris can vary greatly. In her book *Sex for One,* Betty Dodson relates that when a group of women gathered to view and compare their sexual organs they discovered that "when the hood was pulled back and each clitoris appeared, the variations were astounding, ranging from tiny little seed pearls, to rather large and protruding jewels."

Members of Dodson's group found no relationship between the size of the clitoris and the degree of pleasure of which it was capable. It was not a question of the bigger the clitoris, the better the orgasm. All sizes seemed to perform well, when correctly pleasured.

The most remarkable thing about the clitoris, as many women know, is its incredible sensitivity. As you will discover in the first exercise of this

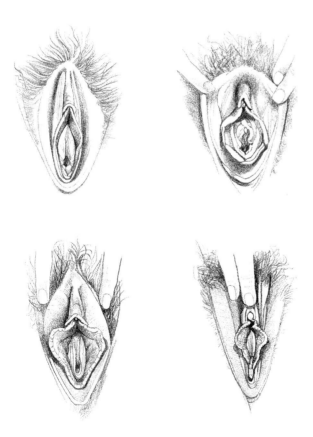

Different types of Yonis showing how varied female sexual anatomy can be, after Betty Dodson's drawings from *Sex for One*

chapter, the more this pleasure trigger is stimulated the more responsive and sensitive it becomes.

The second orgasmic trigger point in a woman's sexual organ is the G-Spot, named after Ernst von Grafenberg, the German physician who discovered it. The G-Spot lies inside the vagina, behind the pubic bone, on the roof of the vaginal canal.

The best way to locate the G-Spot is to rest a finger on the tip of the clitoris, then trace the finger slowly down, entering the mouth of the vagina at the top of the opening, then moving the finger inside for a distance of about one and a half to two inches, staying on the roof of the vaginal canal. The telltale mark of the G-Spot is that the tissue here feels ribbed or rigid, like a small button with tiny bumps on it, whereas the rest of the vaginal walls are smooth. The best time to feel the G-Spot is soon after a woman has experienced orgasm, when it becomes somewhat enlarged and more sensitive.

There are several theories about why the G-Spot is sensitive, the most interesting being that the nerves that provide pleasure at the clitoris pass through this area on their way to the spine. There is also a nerve connection between the G-spot and the bladder, resulting in an illusory impression that you need to urinate when this area is stimulated.

The G-Spot is surrounded by spongy tissue known as the "glands of Bartholin" which, when stimulated, may release prostatic-type fluids in the form of female ejaculation.

Attaining sexual arousal and orgasm through massaging the G-Spot is a delicate art which I will describe in the second exercise of this chapter. Having mastered the art of stimulating both the clitoris and the G-Spot you will be ready to explore a blended, expanded orgasm created by pleasuring both spots simultaneously.

In this way, the practice of expanded orgasm is given in three steps:

1. Clitoral stimulation and clitoral orgasm

2. G-Spot stimulation and vaginal orgasm

3. Simultaneous stimulation of clitoris and G-Spot leading to an expanded or blended orgasm

Once you have acquired the necessary skills, you can do all three steps in a single session.

OVERCOMING INITIAL EMBARRASSMENT

It can be quite scary for a woman to open her legs and allow a man to examine her Yoni, her vagina. There is something about the delicate act of exposing the genitals to detailed inspection that triggers feelings of insecurity, vulnerability, and embarrassment.

In normal lovemaking, the woman is filled with reassuring sensations as she is taken by the man and held in close body contact while he caresses her Yoni and penetrates with his Vajra. But in this exercise both the man and the woman are adopting an approach that is almost scientific. It is rather like taking a magnifying glass and holding it in front of the genitals, revealing not only the physical anatomy but also any attitudes you may carry about your sexual organ and your right to sexual pleasure—whether you deserve it, whether you can allow it and surrender to it.

In spite of these doubts, you are going to give yourself permission to lie back and receive, allowing a man to pleasure you for as long as it takes to feel totally orgasmic. You deserve this moment. You have waited patiently for it long enough.

And the beauty of it is that, although you are vulnerable and receptive during this exercise, you, the woman, are in charge. You are the one who is going to discover how and where you like to be touched, exploring and bringing awareness to every millimeter of your sexual organ, teaching your beloved exactly how to caress each pleasure point.

Knowing that you are in charge will give you courage to move through any resistances that you encounter during clitoral stimulation, knowing that you can at any time stop or change the nature of the caresses that are being given to you.

One more thing: Many women experience that massaging the clitoris and the vagina heals and sensitizes scar tissue in the area, such as may be caused by a difficult childbirth. However, if you have an ongoing history of vaginal infection or other medical problems relating to your sexual organ, you should not do this massage unless you receive permission from your doctor.

Look upon a woman as a Goddess, whose special energy she is, and honor her in that state of Goddess.

—UTARA TANTRA

EXERCISE: PLEASURING THE CLITORIS

Purpose and Benefits

As the receiver in this exercise, you, the woman, are about to experience one of the most challenging and ecstatic pleasuring sessions of your life. For centuries the clitoris has been a hidden part of our sexual anatomy, often disregarded as an unimportant, incomplete appendage. It has been our guilty secret, a place that only we know how to pleasure fully.

The majority of women do not realize that it is possible to teach a man how to pleasure this secret part skillfully and masterfully.

This exercise gives you full permission to enjoy and celebrate the sexual pleasure that arises from your clitoris, thereby healing any negative beliefs that you may have regarding your sexual organs.

As a woman, and as a magician, you are about to enter a new era that will enhance your self-esteem and embrace the alchemy of your orgasmic power. In this session, let the goddess of love blossom within you. You are worth it!

Know that the key for moving from good sex to great sex is to allow yourself to fully receive this gift while you encourage your man to give you exactly what you like. This, in turn, will validate his skills as a great lover.

This exercise will:

- Provide detailed knowledge of the female sexual organs.
- Bring new awareness to the areas where sexual pleasure is available and to ways of caressing these areas.
- Open the way for ecstatic states of sexual orgasm
- Reveal and dissolve any psychological or emotional blocks that may inhibit the flow of orgasmic energy.
- Enhance communication between love partners, deepening their sense of intimacy.
- Teach you, the woman, how to take responsibility for your sexual well-being.
- Help you, the woman, to learn the art of trust.
- Teach you, the man, how to bring a woman to orgasmic ecstasy.
- Help you, the man, to feel validated as giver, supporter, and expert lover.

Preparations and Practice

- In this exercise you will be addressing each other by your magical names. Here, I will continue to use the names Shakti and Shiva, the deities of Tantric union.

- It can be fun and helpful to create an atmosphere of sexual anticipation before the exercise, as if preparing for a special date. Earlier in the day, Shiva can call Shakti on the phone and say whatever words may turn her on, like "I want you, I want your pleasure trickling down my fingers, I want your wetness, I want you to be totally open to me . . ."

- Shiva, you may want to buy Shakti some sexy underwear, to be worn at the appointed hour of the exercise. Or perhaps you may decide to take her out to a restaurant and flirt under the table, reaching with your hands to forbidden places. Find ways to generate an aura of sexual, erotic excitement between you and your partner. Be creative.

- Shiva, you are also the one who creates the Magic Circle, taking time to make the space beautiful, adorning it with things that Shakti loves. Bring colorful cushions, a nice sheet for her to lie on, some flowers, incense, and candles, put on soft, nonintrusive music in the background. You can also bring objects that will give your woman reassurance, such as a favorite teddy bear or certain tarot cards and, of course, her Magic Symbol. You can enhance your woman's sense of self-esteem and her love for you, when she sees how much care you have taken to create a safe and sacred environment to support her pleasure.

- Shakti, while Shiva is preparing the Magic Circle, take a relaxed shower or bath, caress your body with oil, put on a touch of perfume, give yourself the feeling that you deserve luxury and care, as if you are the most important person in the world. Wear something soft and silky, like a kimono-style gown that opens in front.

- Shiva and Shakti: proceed at your own pace through the exercise, mastering each stage in turn.

- It is a good idea to have a jug of water or fruit juice handy, as this can be thirsty work.

- The room needs to be warm enough to work without much clothing.

- There needs to be plenty of lubricant available. For massaging the clitoris, an oil-based lubricant like Vaseline will be best because you may be stimulating this area for quite a long time and water-based lubricants tend to dry up too quickly.

- Shiva, check that your fingernails are trimmed and smooth.

- Shakti, make sure that your bladder is empty.

- Allow sixty to ninety minutes for this exercise and be sure that you will not be interrupted.

STAGE 1: SENSUAL FOREPLAY

Shiva, when the room is prepared, bring Shakti into the Magic Circle. Be gracious, playful, reassuring. This is a good time to dance together for a few minutes, shaking off any nervousness or tension.

Greet each other with a Heart Salutation.

Have a long Melting Hug, breathing deeply, in synchronicity together.

Shiva, gently remove Shakti's gown and invite her to lie on the cushions. Or, if she wishes, let her keep the gown on, parting it to reveal her thighs and pelvis.

Sit cross-legged on her left side, close to her body, and take a few minutes to create a position that will be comfortable for both of you. In my experience, the best position for the exercise is as follows:

Shakti, open your legs, resting your left leg on a pillow that is placed on Shiva's left knee.

Shiva, rest your left elbow and forearm on the same pillow.

Shakti, rest your right knee on another pillow so that your legs are spread comfortably apart and your knees slightly bent.

Shiva, place a pillow on your right thigh, which will support your right forearm.

Shiva, ask Shakti, "Are you comfortable?" If not, experiment with other positions, adjusting the cushions, until both of you are comfortable.

Be sure that your lubricant is nearby, so that you can reach it easily later in the exercise.

Shiva and Shakti, close your eyes for a few moments and breathe deeply into your abdomens. Take time to become centered and focused on what is about to happen.

Shiva, tune into your partner. Rest your left hand gently on Shakti's Yoni and your right hand on her heart chakra in the middle of her chest.

Oh, recluse, if you aspire to paradise, go fast to that place where dwells the woman of lust.

—KUTTNI MAHA TYAN
TANTRA

252

Gaze softly into her eyes and begin to breathe in harmony. Feel the love in your heart for this beloved friend who is making herself vulnerable to you.

Shiva, when you feel ready, begin to stroke and caress Shakti's whole body very lightly, either with your fingertips or with feathers. As you do so, encourage her to breathe deeply through her mouth while staying relaxed and receptive. Talk to her gently, reassuringly, whispering "Just relax, beloved, and receive this gift that I am bringing to you. There is nothing to do, no goal to reach . . . All is for your pleasure."

With light fingers, caress every part of Shakti's body. Touch her lips, her neck, her nipples, belly, pubic mound, tugging gently at her pubic hair, caress her thighs, her feet, making sure that you touch every part of her body, bringing love and reassurance to each area. There is no hurry.

Shakti, this is your opportunity to relax more deeply into a mood of receptivity, giving yourself permission to enjoy what is being showered on you, letting go of the feeling that you have to do anything or please anyone.

STAGE 2: TIMING YOUR APPROACH

Shiva, watch Shakti's body language, which will indicate when she is ready for you to begin massaging her sexual organ directly. Through your gentle caresses, she is becoming sexually awakened. Her thighs are likely to open even farther, exposing her Yoni, while her pelvis may begin to push up slightly, raising her hips off the sheet as she invites you to explore her genitals.

If you are not sure, ask Shakti, "Is this a good time, beloved?" She may nod, or give a little sigh of agreement, or perhaps say, "No, please, spend a little more time caressing around my neck and shoulders, that feels so good."

Shiva, remember that you are in a response mode, listening to Shakti's guidance, learning how to caress her in ways that bring the maximum amount of pleasure.

Shakti, you are receiving pleasure, guiding your partner as to how to touch you, where to touch you. Don't be afraid to say exactly what you want. This is the time to give yourself everything.

STAGE 3: TEASING THE CLITORIS

Shiva, cover the fingers of your right hand with plenty of lubricant. Begin to stroke Shakti's genitals lightly, caressing the surface of her Yoni, touching the upper ridges of the lips, very delicately, like a feather. Gently tug on the pubic hair. Place your hand so that it covers the whole Yoni and gently vibrate the hand.

Take the lips of the Yoni and spread them apart like the wings of a butterfly so that the Yoni is completely open, then pass your lubricated fingers around the inside of the lips, near the entrance of the vagina itself, and all around the clitoris, then softly blow warm air from your mouth on the open lips.

Close the lips of the Yoni, pressing them gently together and massaging the outside of the lips, from the bottom up toward the clitoris. Continue to massage inside the lips of the Yoni, lightly sliding up toward the pubic mound, then down toward the anus, using lots of lubricant.

Shiva, tease Shakti's cleo, her clitoris, with an occasional touch, a tickle or caress, giving her a suggestion of more, then move to some other area of the Yoni, as if to say "I promise you pleasure. With this touch, light as the wings of a bird in flight, I honor your tenderness, your sensitivity. With this touch I show you that I can be sensitive and caring, in tune with you, listening, calling forth your pleasure."

Using a lot of lubricant is very pleasurable for Shakti. When your fingers are dry, they tend to pull and drag the surface of her Yoni in an uncomfortable way.

STAGE 4: STIMULATING THE CLITORIS
Shiva, now you can begin to rub Shakti's cleo lightly, allowing it to remain covered by the folds of its hood. Begin softly, caressingly, then start to explore the following massage strokes that can bring so much sexual pleasure to a woman.

The Two-Finger Basic Stroke   Begin with the two-finger basic stroke. Your thumb and index finger rest at the point where the clitoris goes inside the body and is no longer visible, that is to say, just below the tip, where the shaft disappears beneath the skin.

In this position, you are holding the shaft between your thumb and index finger and can roll it lightly between them. Experiment until you find this point and then slowly begin to massage evenly, rubbing up and down on either side of the shaft, finding a comfortable rhythm. For many women, the best timing is one stroke per second.

This movement has been called the "bread and butter stroke" because it is the easiest and simplest way of giving pleasure to a woman through her cleo.

Ask Shakti, "How does this feel?" Encourage her to give feedback, to tell you what kind of touch brings her the most pleasure.

The Double Stroke   After a while, try another stroke.

Rub up and down one side of the shaft with your thumb, while your index finger makes light circular motions on the other side.

The Rooted Stroke   Rest your thumb motionless on one side of the clitoral shaft and, using your index finger, caress the other side with small circular motions, moving from the root to the tip.

The Top Rub   Hold the shaft of the cleo with your thumb and middle finger, and use your index finger to massage the tip of the cleo very lightly, still with the hood covering the tip.

The Three-Finger Tickle Stroke   Use your thumb and middle finger to hold the root of the cleo, leaving the index finger free to massage the tip of the cleo.

Directly Stimulating the Cleo   When Shakti is strongly aroused, pull back the hood of the cleo with your thumb and middle finger and directly stimulate the tip of the clitoris with your index finger, rubbing lightly and consistently.

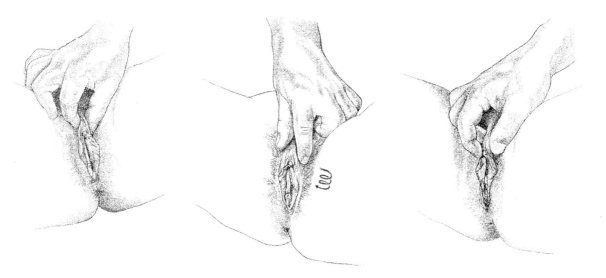

Pleasuring the clitoris   The two-finger basic stroke   The rooted stroke

Ask Shakti, "How does this feel? Do you want it stronger or lighter?" Remember, you can do this only when Shakti has become aroused and her cleo is engorged, otherwise direct contact on the tip is likely to be too strong to be really pleasurable.

When Shakti is aroused, the shaft and tip of the cleo become stiff and swollen, like a little mound that sticks out of the surrounding flesh. Using the same basic grip, you can make vertical strokes up and down the sides of this mound, almost as if you were stimulating an erect penis. Or you can pulse, squeezing rapidly, or use circular motions.

Using two or three fingers, you can achieve a surprising variety of movements.

Making an Inventory Take time to explore all the variations available, giving each other continuous feedback.

Shakti, it is tempting to get lost in the pleasure you are receiving. You may find it difficult to speak, or lack words to communicate with Shiva. But it is important for you to stay aware of each sensation, expressing how you feel, what you like, what you want to change. Communication is very important here.

Shiva's finger moves around the vaginal labia, making tiny circular motions from the cleo (twelve o'clock) down toward the perineum (six o'clock).

Six-o'clock position

This is a work of great art. You are teaching Shiva the delicate skills of generating orgasmic arousal on a tremendously sensitive but small part of your body.

Give feedback on each stroke or caress you receive. If this is difficult, ask Shiva to repeat one stroke for about a minute, staying on the same point with the same rhythm while you find words to describe how this feels. When you are ready, move to another stroke, proceeding systematically as if learning a type of massage.

Shakti, you are looking for a point that can be very tiny, where the most pleasurable sensations arise. It can be a little circular motion on the right side of the clitoris shaft, or a thumb and index finger moving up and down the shaft on both sides.

Take time to make an inventory of strokes and rhythms that are pleasurable.

The Pleasure Clock   Going "around the clock" while caressing the Yoni can be a very helpful image in locating areas that are especially pleasurable on or near the cleo.

Shiva, with your mind's eye, imagine that a clock dial surrounds Shakti's cleo, so that the highest point, nearest her pubic mound, is the twelve o'clock position and the lowest point, nearest her vaginal opening, is the six o'clock position.

Move around the clock with your fingers, exploring each point. Make tiny circular motions with your index finger. When Shakti moans with pleasure, let her know "This is at three o'clock," or "This is at nine o'clock."

STAGE 5: BUILDING AROUSAL IN STEPS

Shiva, when you feel that you have mastered the various strokes for massaging Shakti's cleo, choose one and stay with this stroke for several minutes. Now you can explore your ability to raise Shakti's level of sexual excitement steadily.

Bring Shakti toward a peak of excitement with a slow, steady rhythm of about one stroke per second. Then, when she is on the edge of orgasm, slow down so that she has time to relax and absorb this energy.

Shakti, you can help Shiva know when to slow down by saying "I'm very close now."

Shiva, when Shakti is ready, increase stimulation again to help her move to an even higher level of pleasure, then slow down again. This is like helping Shakti to walk up a series of orgasmic steps, each one more pleasurable than the last.

The Pleasure Rating System

Shakti, one way to let Shiva know your level of arousal is to communicate via a zero-to-ten pleasure rating system.

For example, if you say "three," this tells Shiva that you are mildly aroused. If you say "six," this lets him know that you are getting really turned on, and a "nine" warns him that you are very close to orgasm. A "ten" means that you have gone over the orgasmic edge.

Shiva, watch carefully so that you can learn how to "read" Shakti's level of arousal. As she gets more and more excited, watch for the following signs:

1. Nipples becoming stiffer and darker
2. Pushing down and out with her pelvis
3. Arching her back
4. Flexing her toes and fingers
5. Vaginal opening becomes dark and engorged with blood
6. Vaginal canal becomes more visible
7. Clitoris becomes more stiff and exposed

Spreading Orgasmic Energy

Shiva, when Shakti's sexual excitement gets very strong, spread the sexual energy by moving your fingers down the outer lips of the vagina, stroking to the base near the anus, caressing up and down in this manner.

Shakti, you can also help to spread your orgasmic energy. Breathe deeply, letting each exhalation go down all the way to your Yoni. Caress your belly, your breasts, your shoulders. You will find that there is a sexual connection between your nipples and your cleo, and you may like to caress and squeeze them.

Stay relaxed and receptive. When you feel really aroused you may be tempted to strive for orgasmic release, but see if you can relax into this energy that is awakening in you, letting it spread through your pelvis, rather than tensing up and striving for the explosive orgasm of release.

If you feel your sensations are becoming too intense, ask Shiva to slow the rhythm of his massage, change the stroke, or move his fingers to some

The woman you love, you must not possess.

—AZUL

other part of your Yoni. If it feels just right, say "Yes, yes!" or make pleasurable sounds. Vocalizing helps to increase your arousal level and conveys a message of encouragement to your partner.

STAGE 6: ORGASM OF THE CLITORIS

Shakti, you will know that you are approaching orgasm when you feel a tingling, buzz, or current of excitement coming from deep inside, at the root of your clitoris, rising steadily toward the surface. Welcome this sensation with your total attention. Communicate to Shiva, "Yes, now, I'm coming!"

Shiva, watch carefully so you can learn the signs of a woman's sexual climax. For example, just before orgasm, Shakti's breathing may become shallow and her body may become very still, as if she is listening, waiting for the ultimate sensation to arise in her. This is because the sensations in her cleo become so pleasurable that chaotic bodily movements would distract her from experiencing their intensity. Or, alternatively, she may tense her thigh and leg muscles, raising her feet off the mattress.

As Shakti moves into orgasm, you will feel her cleo and vagina pulsing with a series of contractions. Her cleo will become so sensitive that it can be stimulated only very lightly or perhaps not at all.

After orgasm there will be a period, lasting anywhere from three to thirty minutes, when Shakti may not want you to touch this delicate trigger point.

Shiva, stay in communication with Shakti. After a few minutes have passed, ask her whether you can continue the massage. Sometimes, a woman's orgasm is composed of many miniorgasms that build on top of one another. The woman's first reaction may be "Okay, that's it, I've had my orgasm," but, with a little stimulation, she quickly realizes that she is ready to go on, opening herself to even more excitement.

STAGE 7: CLOSING THE SESSION GRACEFULLY

For both Shiva and Shakti, it is important to close a session in a tender and sensitive way. You have both participated in a deeply moving experience. Any abrupt movement, cutting the flow of energy between you, could be disruptive and emotionally painful.

Shiva and Shakti, when either of you feels that the session is complete, gently ask your partner, "Is this a good time to make a pause?" or "I feel satisfied. Is it okay to stop?"

Phrase your suggestion as a question so that your partner feels included and respected. There has to be mutual agreement that it's time to close the session.

There is a simple ritual for ending the session that I call "closing the door."

Shiva, place your right hand on Shakti's heart center. Rest the palm of your left hand on Shakti's mound of Venus, with your fingers covering the lips of her Yoni, pressing slightly, helping Shakti's sexual energy flow back inside herself.

Look into each other's eyes for a few moments, then close your eyes, feeling how the energy that was focused on Shakti's cleo is now diffusing through both your bodies.

Five Basic Points of Clitoral Stimulation

Here are five basic points to remember for clitoral stimulation:

1. Erotic foreplay
2. Mastering the strokes
3. Rhythmic stimulation
4. Building arousal in steps
5. Eliciting full orgasm

Pointers

ACKNOWLEDGING SHIVA

Shakti, at the end of the session it's very important that you acknowledge Shiva and reward him for having done such a good job. Show him your gratitude and appreciation. Shower him with compliments, hugs, and, if it feels right, honor him with the ultimate reward of making love.

Remember, in this exercise, the man often becomes as vulnerable as the woman. He is like a new musician, learning to play Shakti's erotic instrument, discovering how to bring forth the right notes of orgasmic pleasure. He will want to be reassured that his audience has appreciated the concert.

PERSISTENCE PAYS OFF

Shiva, exploring all the strokes available for clitoral stimulation may take up to three sessions, so don't be in a hurry to "get it." Acquiring this new skill is bound to take time.

In the beginning, a certain patience and stamina is required. You must be prepared to "be in it for the long haul," giving pleasure to Shakti in a steady, supportive way so that she can relax, trust, move through any resistance, and reach a point where she can fully enjoy her orgasmic pleasure.

Shakti, you are the one who decides how long you want the stimulation to continue. You know when Shiva has attained mastery when he is as skillful at giving you a clitoral orgasm as you are at giving one to yourself. At this stage, you can totally relax into his expert hands.

Shiva, when you stimulate Shakti's cleo you may feel that your fingers are becoming delicate antennae that not only give but also receive pleasure. You may feel Shakti's warm, fiery energy flowing into you, turning you on, giving you an erection. This can be a very beautiful experience.

However, giving a clitoral massage can also be a bit of a technical task for you, so be patient and your persistence will pay off.

STAYING PRESENT TO PLEASURE

Shakti, there are times when communicating with Shiva will be difficult. This can happen when you get lost in pleasure, when you are experiencing resistance, or when a particular thought or idea captures your attention and distracts you from the exercise.

Shiva, you can learn how to "read" Shakti, noticing when she becomes silent, when she no longer seems to be present, or when her pelvis becomes still or starts to pull way from your fingers.

If Shakti doesn't say anything, gently ask her a question, such as "How does this feel?"

Use as few words as possible. Getting into a conversation may distract both of you from the exercise, cutting the flow of sexual energy. For example, a question like "What's going on?" invites a long explanation. It is better to ask simple, specific questions like "Does this feel good?" "Do you want more?" "Shall I press more firmly?"

Shakti, the key to good sexual communication is always to address what you like first, before you ask for a change. For example, "This is good, but now I'd like to try . . ." rather than saying "Hey, this doesn't feel good." In this way you acknowledge that Shiva is open and available to you and that critical feedback is likely to discourage him. By staying positive, his willingness to give is respected.

Watch how the mind takes you away from ecstasy. For example, you're feeling relaxed, enjoying the stimulation, and then suddenly you're thinking of the kids at school or the groceries to buy for supper . . . Before you

The eternal feminine draws us upward.

—GOETHE

know it, you're not feeling anything. You have detached yourself from your sensations.

Catch yourself when this happens and come back to the present. Here's a great tip: exhale all the way out, bringing your attention fully to your Yoni as you do so, holding a vivid picture of it in your mind (as described in chapter 3), visualizing that you are pushing all your energy down into your Yoni, seeing your blood flowing into your cleo and your vaginal lips. Immediately you will start to feel more. This is a real key for enhancing female pleasure.

BEGINNER'S MIND: EMPTY CUP

Shiva, be careful not to enter a session with preconceived ideas about what Shakti wants, how she will behave, what goal has to be attained, or that you have to deliver the ultimate cosmic orgasm in the next thirty minutes. Shakti, the same applies to you.

In my experience, people often come to this exercise with all kinds of expectations, and this results in unnecessary disappointment when something entirely different occurs.

Come to each session with a fresh mind, like a beginner, like an empty cup that is about to be filled with unknown things. There is no need to know what is going to happen. There is no need to perform. Be open to whatever sensations and experiences arise. The more relaxed and easy you are, the better it gets.

CONTAINING SEXUAL AROUSAL

Shakti, once you have the ability to move easily into orgasm, a new and exciting dimension can be added to the exercise. Now you can allow Shiva to determine the length of the session, stopping when he feels tired or no longer comfortable.

This creates a challenge for you, because you may be left in a condition of strong sexual arousal without orgasmic release, feeling very turned on, wanting more yet not receiving it.

Your challenge is to relax into your sexual energy, allowing it to be absorbed in your body. This is not easy but is an important stage in building a strong orgasmic charge for sexual magic. It can also be a delightful sensation in itself.

Two partners in sexual magic, Laura and Ted, describe the difficulties and rewards of this stage. They had been practicing clitoral stimulation for about two weeks, with many sessions ending in full clitoral orgasm. Then, as Laura recalls:

One night, Ted stopped about fifteen minutes after we had started, saying he was feeling tired and didn't have energy to go on. It was at a point when I was really getting into it, when my excitement was rising toward my first strong peak.

Even though we'd agreed that Ted could determine the timing, I had a strong impulse to say "No, wait, you can't do this. You can't leave me like this." But then I thought, "Well, why not just follow the exercise and see what happens?"

As I got up from the couch, I could feel my pussy pulsing with energy, with desire. Ted headed for the bathroom to have a shower and prepare for bed, but I found myself walking restlessly around the house in this stage of great sexual excitement. I felt more horny than at any time in my life, because for two weeks we'd been practicing this massage and I'd been having a great time.

After a while, I figured I'd just go to Ted and ask him to finish me off, but then I started feeling awkward, almost like some sort of cheap slut who has to beg for sex, so I didn't. Instead, I started feeling angry with him, thinking "what kind of uncaring creep leaves a woman like this?"

Then I started laughing, because suddenly I knew how guys must feel when they are all charged up with excitement, ready to burst, and the girlfriend just kisses them on the cheek and says good night. My clitoris was aching at that moment, just wanting release in sexual climax.

I thought about pleasuring myself, but I wanted to see where the energy would go if I just stayed with the feeling, not doing anything about it. I heard Ted get into bed, and then there was silence in the house.

I turned off the downstairs lights and slid out of my bathrobe, then opened the curtains so I could see the city lights. After a while, I started wandering slowly from room to room, with no clothes on, softly touching my body now and then. As much as I could, I relaxed into the throbbing feelings in my sex. I gave in to the situation, giving myself permission to be this way.

"Gradually, I noticed a kind of sensuousness spreading through my body, a delicious, silky feeling that wasn't localized in my pussy but all over me. I picked up a silk scarf and began to play with it, slowly drawing it across my body, around my neck, down my legs. It felt cool and soft on my skin. I was being filled with pleasure in a different way, not so direct, more exquisite. Everything I touched had a sensual quality to it, the smoothness of the tabletop, the fine lace of the curtains, the softness of the carpet . . .

"After a while, I no longer wanted sexual release. I still felt sexual—extremely sexual, very erotic—but I didn't want to do anything about it. I was really enjoying this new feeling. This went on for a couple of hours, then I began to feel tired and went to bed. When I saw Ted lying there, curled up,

Feminine wisdom accords with no abstract, unrelated code of law by which dead stars or atoms circulate in empty space. It is a wisdom that is bound and stays to the earth,
to organic growth. Matriarchal consciousness is the wisdom of the earth.

—ERICH NEUMANN

fast asleep, I felt grateful to him, that he'd been too tired to go on, otherwise I wouldn't have had this extraordinary experience. I went to sleep feeling very happy and content.

Laura's experience is indicative of the way sexual energy can be transformed. The clitoris is the most *yang* part of the female organ. In other words, it has male qualities. When aroused, it can be very demanding, pulling you toward climax with the feeling "I've got to do something about this right now!"

Women, this is how men usually feel when sexually aroused, so enjoy this opportunity of deepening your understanding of your partner's biological urges. In this stage of the exercise, the trick is to stay on the edge of your desire without wanting to get anywhere. Then the energy can move in a totally new direction.

OVERCOMING SEXUAL SABOTAGE

As I already mentioned, when it comes to allowing ourselves sexual pleasure, a surprising number of us women don't believe we deserve it.

In the theater of our childhood years, many of us were trained to follow a script in which Daddy played the leading role and our parts were "walk-ons" as supporting cast. We always had to do something, give something, serve someone in order to value our role in the drama. Hence, we have difficulty in feeling that we deserve pleasure, that we can just lie down and receive.

In addition, many women today have cultivated a dynamic male aspect to their personalities in order to compete as men's equals in a world that is still essentially patriarchal. This can make it difficult for us to switch gears, to become soft, open, vulnerable, and receptive.

These difficulties often manifest themselves in a variety of strategies designed to sabotage those situations in which we receive sexual satisfaction.

For example, Renee, an educational therapist in her mid-thirties and a student of sexual magic, had no difficulty learning the practices outlined in earlier chapters of this book. But when she began to receive clitoral stimulation from her partner, everything changed.

Renee explains:

I had a lot of trouble keeping my agreement with Mike, my partner, that I would receive a "do" once a day between two to three in the afternoon. That was the time that worked best for us, but, even though I'm self-employed

We are bearers of magic and our circle of support is a circle of mystical power.
It is a woman's prerogative to know of magic and to practice and to use her knowledge to help the world.

—MARIANNE WILLIAMSON

and schedule my own hours, I felt guilty about leaving work to go lie down and prepare for orgasm.

One way or another, I ended up not arriving on time, or found myself talking on the phone until the last minute before joining Mike so that I wasn't really in the mood, or I'd try to pick a fight just before the session, or I'd have a headache, until Mike finally sat me down and said, "Renee, what's going on here? It's like you're doing me a big favor by coming to these sessions, but you're the one who's receiving!"

At first, I tried to deny what was going on, but Mike just kept pointing out what was happening and pretty soon I had to admit that it was true. After that, I paid more attention to the things I did before a session, and even though I still went through feelings of guilt, or worrying that I couldn't spare the time, I made sure that I arrived at the sessions on time and gave myself fully to the experience.

Even so, I still noticed a moment of discomfort, right when I had to lie down and spread my legs. It was like giving up control over my most private part. I also noticed feelings of shame, feeling somehow cheap that I could just walk in, take off my clothes, and lie down, exposing myself like this. But then I would say to myself, "The hell with it. This is for me. I don't care if it's ladylike or not—it feels great!"

An hour and a half later I would go back to my office, orgasmic, and happy, seeing everything with fresh eyes. It was clear that the work issues I'd been worrying about were no big deal. I'd exaggerated them to justify not giving myself the sessions. Moreover, some of my clients started commenting on how good I looked, and from then on I could keep a more relaxed attitude.

I remember one session, particularly, that was a breakthrough for me. We'd spent a long time finding a stroke I really liked and then Mike settled into a steady rhythm that seemed to go on forever. During this time, I went through so many fears, like "This is not for me; I'll never manage; I can't do it; I'm not really an orgasmic person; I'm taking too long; he's getting bored . . ."

But Mike just stayed with the massage in a steady, relaxed way, giving me reassurance until, in the end, I finally let go and had the most extraordinary orgasm of my life. It was a real teaching in how not to sell myself short and also gave me a tremendous trust in Mike, my partner.

After becoming familiar with the various ways of inducing a clitoral orgasm, the next step is to explore the G-Spot.

EXERCISE: PLEASURING THE GODDESS SPOT (THE G-SPOT)

Purpose and benefits

Through this exercise, you will discover the pleasure available to Shakti through massaging and stimulating her G-Spot. Massage of the G-Spot will heal any negative or painful sensations that may be connected to this part of the Yoni, allowing Shakti to broaden her spectrum of sexual pleasure and facilitate her experience of vaginal orgasm.

This session can be done as a continuation of the previous exercise, or separately.

Preparations

- Shiva also creates the Magic Circle to welcome Shakti in an atmosphere of sensuality and security.
- Shakti pampers herself in readiness to relax and enjoy.
- Remember to have some water or fruit juice handy to quench your thirst, and be sure that the room is warm enough to work comfortably without clothing.
- As with the clitoral massage, Shiva listens and supports, while Shakti guides and receives.
- The best lubricants for massaging inside the vagina are water based, such as Astroglide or K-Y Jelly. Oil-based lubricants tend to clog the pores of the vaginal canal, preventing natural lubrication.
- Shiva, remember to have clean, trim, smooth nails.
- Shakti, make sure your bladder is empty.
- Allow sixty to ninety minutes for this exercise.

Practice

STAGE 1: SENSUAL FOREPLAY WITH THE CLITORIS

Shiva, invite Shakti into the Magic Circle. Help her to lie in the same basic posture that was described for clitoral massage.

For the massage of Shakti's G-Spot you may wish to sit directly between her legs, or you may prefer the position you used for clitoral stimulation. Experience will show you which is best.

Make sure that you have enough pillows under your forearms to support their weight so that your hands don't get tired. Have both kinds of lubricant near at hand, the oil-based lubricant for Shakti's cleo and the water based for her Goddess Spot.

Tune in to your partner. Put one hand on Shakti's heart center and the other on her Yoni. Synchronize your breathing. Look into her eyes, feeling the bond of love, acceptance, and compassion that connects you in this sacred experiment. Let everything except this precious moment fall away from your mind; forget any preoccupations or concerns.

Shiva, caress Shakti's body, taking plenty of time. The more Shakti is aroused through this delicate foreplay, the easier it will be for her to receive pleasure.

Using plenty of lubricant, caress Shakti's Yoni, beginning with the outer lips, then spreading the lips apart and circling the vaginal canal. When you feel Shakti is ready, focus on her clitoris, playing with a variety of strokes, then settling into a slow, steady, rhythmic stroke that gives her pleasure.

STAGE 2: APPROACHING THE GODDESS SPOT

Shiva, as you stimulate the cleo, let your free hand slide between her legs, under her sacrum, with your thumb pressed lightly against the opening of her vaginal canal.

Take time to bring Shakti to a level of strong clitoral excitement. As she becomes more and more aroused, your thumb will be gradually sucked inside by a series of pulsations, or contractions of her Yoni. Shakti's Yoni is welcoming your thumb like a penis.

The connection between your thumb and Shakti's Yoni can help you "read" her level of excitement. When the tissues around her vagina become engorged and swollen, when she is lubricating, when her pelvis pushes forward as if wanting to swallow your thumb, she is ready for you to begin stimulating her G-Spot.

Ask Shakti, "May I visit you?" If her answer is "yes," gently and slowly slide your thumb out of Shakti's Yoni. Now you are going to penetrate with the index and middle finger of the same hand.

The palm of your hand is facing upward and your two fingers are slightly curved, or crooked, so that, once inside, they can press against the roof of Shakti's Yoni at the "twelve o'clock" position.

Be sure that your fingers are well lubricated with a water-based lubricant before entering.

As you penetrate Shakti's Yoni, continue to massage her cleo lightly with your other hand.

How to enter into the vagina
and find the Goddess spot

STAGE 3: FINDING THE GODDESS SPOT

The G-Spot is felt as a bumplike place, the size of a pea, on the roof of the vaginal canal, beneath the pubic bone. Here, the tissues have a raspy quality, rather like the tongue of a cat, differing from the smoothness of the surrounding vaginal wall. You will need to probe the area, pressing fairly strongly, until Shakti experiences a specifically sensitive point.

Shakti, if you have never been stimulated in this area before, pressure from Shiva's fingers may manifest itself as a feeling of burning or a sharp nerve reaction like a "zing" that passes through the area of your Yoni. In other words, you may not feel pleasant sensations the first few times your G-Spot is touched. On the other hand, you may immediately feel a warm glow of pleasure, or you may feel nothing special.

If you feel the need to urinate, remember that this is probably an illusion caused by the nerve connection with your bladder, which you emptied before this exercise. If possible, stay with the session rather than breaking off to go to the bathroom.

It's important not to get discouraged by feelings of discomfort in your G-Spot. Like any part of your body that hasn't been touched for a long time, there are likely to be a few aches and pains as tensions start to release.

Shiva, when you have found the G-Spot, remove your other hand from Shakti's cleo and rest it on her belly. She needs to be able to experience her G-Spot free from other stimulation.

Shakti, it is usually helpful for you to move while Shiva is stimulating your G-Spot. Rock your pelvis, do the PC Pump, breathe strongly, and use your voice to sigh and moan, relaxing your throat and neck.

Remember: The Three Keys to enhancing your feelings and physical sensations are breathing, movement, and sound.

STAGE 4: STROKES FOR PLEASURING THE GODDESS SPOT

Shiva, you may have to press quite deeply, more deeply than you would expect, before your partner feels something. There are three basic strokes for G-Spot stimulation, using the two fingers that are inside Shakti's Yoni. Begin to experiment, checking which gives her most pleasure.

1. Massage in a zigzag pattern, moving crossways over the whole area. This will relax the G-Spot and the surrounding tissues.

2. Massage in and out, your fingers running over the roof of Shakti's vagina from the opening to the cervix. This way, your fingers pass over the G-Spot without staying on it.

3. Place two fingers directly on the G-Spot and begin to pulsate, pressing strongly in this area.

Shakti, the degree of pressure is up to you. You are the guide. Make sure you give Shiva plenty of feedback.

Shiva, try different strokes and pressures. Circle around the G-Spot. Pulse on the same spot. Stroke in and out.

STAGE 5: GENERATING AROUSAL

Shiva, you know you have found the right stroke and rhythm when Shakti gets the glorious feeling that she is making love with your fingers. Her pelvis will lift up and she will get into a rhythmic movement with her hips, as if she is being penetrated by your penis.

Shakti, communicate what you really want. You can say things like "Yes, yes, that's it, keep going," or "Oh yes, this is good, do it to me, give it to me!" It can be very enjoyable to call for your pleasure in this uninhibited way.

Shiva, this is a signal for you to stroke Shakti's G-Spot in a rhythmic way, helping her climb toward new heights of sexual pleasure. However, be prepared for unexpected changes. On the G-Spot, a certain stroke can provide great pleasure one moment and the next moment can suddenly cease to be stimulating.

Shakti, if this happens, don't hesitate to request a change. Shiva, follow your partner's guidance.

Shiva, use your free hand to press on the G-Spot from outside the Yoni, on Shakti's lower belly. This is a good way to enhance G-Spot sensation. Another way is to rub her lower belly and the area of her ovaries.

Shakti, allow the sensations to expand through your pelvic area and your body. You can help to spread the energy by massaging your breasts and other regions that feel sensual and erotic.

STAGE 6: ORGASM OF THE GODDESS SPOT

Shakti, don't feel that you need to have a G-Spot orgasm, or vaginal orgasm, as this may create unnecessary tension and disappointment. In this session, you are getting to know your G-Spot and its response to stimulation.

However, if you do come close to orgasm, you will find that you need

She is the primordial Shakti. She is the supreme, whose nature is unoriginated and undisturbed joy. She is eternally utterly incomparable, the sea of all that moves or is motionless, the spotless mirror in which is revealed the radiant form of Shiva.

—KAMA KALA VISLASA SUTRA

a lighter touch on your G-Spot. Communicate this to your beloved. The more the excitement, the less stimulation.

Continued light stimulation can bring a strong vaginal orgasm, with contractions deep inside your vaginal canal. There may be a release of ejaculatory fluid from tiny glands near your urethra. Relax and let it happen. These sensations can last one minute or five, perhaps even longer.

Shakti, continue receiving G-Spot stimulation until your appetite for sexual pleasure is satiated.

Acknowledge Shiva's generous contribution to your sexual awakening.

Close the session with a Heart Salutation.

Five Stages of G-Spot Stimulation

Here are five basic points to remember for stimulating the G-Spot:

1. Erotic foreplay
2. Stimulating the cleo
3. Finding the G-Spot
4. Mastering the strokes
5. Building arousal

Pointers

MOVING THROUGH LAYERS

Shakti, if you feel there is a lot of tension in the area of your G-Spot, or a sense of pain or burning, then keep the first session fairly short, say five minutes, or until you want to stop. Feel free to progress in stages that feel comfortable.

You may go through many layers of sensations in your G-Spot, some tense, some pleasurable. You may require three to four sessions before this spot becomes sensitive to pleasure.

Remember, female responses vary widely. Some women experience pleasure right away, some never feel anything special, while some discover other areas inside the vagina that are pleasurable when stimulated. I have discovered several such places, especially along the roof of the vaginal canal, on the same line as the G-Spot, between the opening and the cervix.

EACH SESSION IS A TEACHING

As I mentioned in the previous exercise, one of the biggest barriers to sexual pleasure is expectation. People tend to bring certain ideas to a particular exercise and, when reality does not match this expectation, they feel they have failed.

This is a misunderstanding. In my experience, there is always a deep teaching in each session, regardless of how it goes. The best approach is to come to each session totally fresh, not knowing what is going to happen. I am giving you a basic road map, but there are many delightful detours to be explored. You are moving into unknown territory.

EXERCISE: ALCHEMY OF THE BLENDED FEMALE ORGASM

Purpose and benefits

To give a woman the ultimate experience of prolonged sexual orgasm, blending the stimulation of her two principle pleasure spots in a subtle and ever-expanding orgasmic response.

Preparation

- Shiva, prepare the Magic Circle and create a beautiful atmosphere in the room. Check that you have plenty of lubricants handy and also a jug of water.
- Shakti, take a long, luxurious shower or bath, using your favorite oils, pampering yourself.
- Allow sixty to ninety minutes for this exercise.

Practice

STAGE 1: ENTERING THE GARDEN
Shiva, lead Shakti into the Magic Circle and help her to lie in a comfortable position.

When you are both settled, begin foreplay, lightly caressing Shakti's body, teasing and pleasuring her Yoni, gradually focusing on her cleo.

When Shakti is ready, begin to stimulate her cleo with a stroke that feels just right.

Let the index and middle fingers of your free hand rest at the door of Shakti's Yoni. Don't be in a hurry to enter. Wait at the door and let Shakti's arousal increase until your fingers are drawn inside her Yoni with a pulsating, sucking motion. This is the right moment to ask her "May I come in?" or, if you wish to be more poetic, "May I enter your sacred garden?"

Begin G-Spot stimulation. Find the best finger position, looking for the right pressure and stroke on her G-Spot.

Establish a rhythm of stimulating the G-Spot and the clitoris at the same time. Or, if Shakti prefers, you can alternate between the two.

STAGE 2: DOUBLE ACTION STROKES
Shiva, there are three basic strokes for stimulating Shakti toward a blended orgasm:

1. Leave your fingers anchored on her G-Spot, with little or no movement, while rhythmically stimulating her cleo.

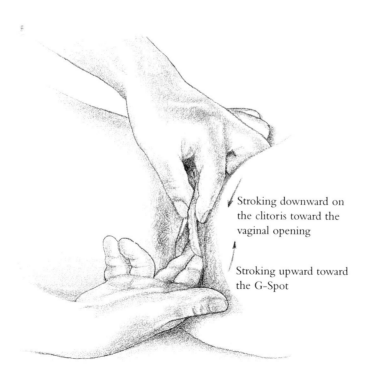

Double action strokes: pleasuring the clitoris emphasizing the downward movements; stimulating the G-spot emphasizing the upward movement

Stroking downward on the clitoris toward the vaginal opening

Stroking upward toward the G-Spot

2. Leave your fingers anchored on her cleo, with little or no movement, while vigorously stimulating her G-Spot.

3. Create a rhythmic, blended movement in both places. For example, you can run your fingers over her cleo down toward the mouth of her Yoni, while your fingers on her G-Spot push inward. In this way, the hands move in opposite directions, as if going toward each other, in a kind of double-action massage.

Or you can grip the shaft of Shakti's cleo with two fingers and stimulate the tip with a third finger, while the fingers of your other hand run in and out over her G-Spot.

There are many subtle variations to be explored as you learn to pleasure Shakti skillfully with combined strokes. It is as if the fingers of your two hands are having a dialogue with each other.

Shakti, it is your job to guide Shiva, saying how you want it, what combination works best, and when you want to explore a new variation. Good communication is essential to finding the right strokes. Remember to stay positive: "Yes, I like that. Now try this . . ."

STAGE 3: EXPANDING ORGASM

Once you have found the best combination of strokes, let Shiva know so that he can continue the same rhythm for a long time. You need regular stimulation so that you can relax and build slowly toward orgasm.

Shiva, the more intense Shakti's excitement becomes, the more regular your strokes need to be. When your partner seems to be coming close to climax, slow down, tease, give her the promise but keep her waiting. Build her arousal in steps, bringing her several times to a peak without going over the edge.

G stands for Growth, Good, Glorious, Goddess. Find the G spot, and you've found your way home.

—DR. ZANGPO

Shakti, you can generate a really exciting sensation that keeps spreading inside and out, like ripples that keep expanding until they cover your whole pond. Your body is moving deeper and deeper into relaxation, while your sexual excitement builds higher and higher.

Remember to use the Three Keys and the PC Pump to help enhance and spread your orgasmic sensations.

Your first orgasm is likely to be explosive, with pulsing contractions inside your Yoni and a great release of energy throughout your pelvic area. Afterward, it's possible to go on. You can have several orgasms, so it's important for Shiva to keep his hands in place, not moving, while the orgasm happens.

STAGE 4: INVOLUNTARY STREAMING SENSATIONS

Shiva, when Shakti's first orgasm has passed, slowly begin to stimulate the cleo and G-Spot once more, building toward even higher peaks of pleasure.

Shakti, now your orgasmic sensations are likely to be more subtle, like energy streaming, like a current of pleasurable feeling that keeps circulating and pulsing inside your pelvis and perhaps through other areas of your body. You are not doing anything. It is involuntary. It is happening to you.

You are entering an ecstatic state that is timeless, floating, deeply relaxed, and meditative, in which your body is so sensitive that very little stimulation is required. This can continue for as long as you wish.

One group participant described this state as follows:

> I had this incredible surprise: the orgasm was going on by itself. I had the impression of having tuned in to a new frequency of pleasure, as if ecstasy is available to me all the time, but I didn't know where to turn the dial to find the right wavelength.
>
> When the session ended, the sensations continued. I slowly tried to get up, always watching whether they would disappear. They didn't, so I started to whirl slowly, like a Sufi, turning on the spot with my arms held high.
>
> I had the impression that my orgasm was rising and falling up and down my body, from my feet all the way to my head, and through me from the center of the earth all the way to the stars.

Five Stages of Blended Orgasm

Here are five points to remember for creating a blended orgasm:

1. Stimulating the clitoris
2. Combined stimulation of the clitoris and G-Spot
3. Generating sexual arousal in steps
4. First orgasmic release
5. Ongoing, subtle sensations

Pointers

LETTING IT HAPPEN

In the beginning, good communication is required to find the right combination of strokes for stimulating the clitoris while simultaneously massaging the G-Spot. Later, it is helpful if Shakti can stop talking and simply relax, while Shiva maintains a steady rhythm, so that she can become completely receptive to this exquisite experience.

For this to happen, both partners need to have thoroughly trained themselves in all the various aspects of clitoral and G-Spot stimulation. Then Shakti can lie back and let it happen.

QUICKER ORGASMIC RESPONSE

One of the great advantages of this practice is that it is an excellent preparation for normal lovemaking. After experiencing blended orgasm, most women are able to enjoy much quicker orgasmic response during penetration with a penis.

Moreover, research has shown that expanding orgasm in this way balances the left and right hemispheres of the brain and enhances the production of endorphins, making people more relaxed, healthy, and happy, reducing tension and stress. This, surely, is magic in itself!

THE EASY APPROACH TO ORGASM

After practicing these methods of expanding orgasm for many years and learning how to integrate these wonderful experiences in my love life, I realize that my approach is somewhat different from other experts in the field.

For example, in their book *ESO,* Alan and Donna Brauer describe a three-level orgasm for women. The first level is characterized by rhythmic squeezing and relaxing pulsations around the entry of the vagina. The second involves involuntary contractions, pushing outwards, in the deeper part of the vagina and around the uterus. The third is a continuous stream of pleasure within the vaginal canal that happens effortlessly and which may continue for up to thirty minutes.

In my experience, orgasms do not necessarily follow a logical continuum from one step to the next. Each one has its own unique flavor, and I don't wish to create performance anxiety in my readers by saying "This is how it has to be."

Certainly, the Brauers' research is very valuable, opening up new fields of sexual understanding, but in the context of sexual magic, your attention needs to be focused on generating the maximum amount of orgasmic power as easily and as comfortably as possible.

It doesn't really matter how it happens. Whether your orgasm has three stages, one, or four is not so relevant. The real point is for you, the woman, to be able to have beautiful, expanded orgasmic responses that are free from pain or tension, pleasurable, and intense.

I love being female. I love being with a man. If I ground my sexual energy, I am here and now, otherwise I'm just roaming. Grounded sexual energy brings peace and nourishment to the soul.

—A Tantrika's Diary

These responses may last a few seconds, a few minutes, or half an hour, but duration of the orgasm is not the goal. The goal is for each individual woman to discover, with the help of her partner, all the orgasmic secrets hidden in her body and to unlock them one by one, in her own style.

Not only is this a magical experience in itself, it is also a very powerful aid to sexual magic, as we shall see later in the book. However, first we must focus on Shiva and the orgasmic pleasures that can be made available to him, for he has done well in honoring and pleasuring Shakti, and it is time for him to be suitably rewarded.

SHIVA'S MAGIC:
The Alchemy of Male Orgasm

Men, you are about to enter what I consider the greatest adventure in which you can become involved—greater than Columbus's discovery of the Americas, greater than conquering Mount Everest or landing on the moon. It is the adventure that consists in discovering, honoring, and cultivating the magical power contained in your Vajra—literally "thunderbolt"—your male sexual organ.

This power, when fully engaged, brings virility, dominion, and enchantment into your love life and a deep sense of kingliness to your being. Good lovers are the natural emperors of this world, for they are rooted in their manhood, at ease with themselves, and greatly loved and appreciated by their female partners.

Since ancient times the Vajra has been worshiped as a symbol of the fertility through which the earth grows new crops, through which herds multiply, through which the tribe feeds itself, prospers, and grows strong. Although this celebration of male sexual power may be difficult for a modern Western man to believe, it's true. Although many of today's men feel attacked simply for being men, it hasn't always been that way. You deserve your own special hymn, a "hymn to the Vajra," so relax and enjoy yourself while I sing a few verses for you.

Each spring, in Japan, your manhood is represented in large sculptures, blown up to gigantic proportions—a truly cosmic erection—and is paraded through city streets to celebrate the gods of fertility and renewal, with, of course, much song, wine, and sake. Dionysius, the drunken Greek god of ecstasy, also embodies phallic energy, helping people to dance, celebrate, abandon the rigid formalities of society for a while and let go into an uninhibited, orgiastic, and ecstatic state.

In Northern Europe, the horned god Pan, half goat and half man, is portrayed as a smiling, laughing deity who reigns over nature and the animal kingdom, walking around with a big erection, symbolizing constant enjoyment, a being who is always ready for sexual action.

These mythological beings represent dynamic energies that are part of you. They represent your own phallic strength and the qualities that exude from it such as manhood, power, potency, virility, creativity, courage, decisiveness, action, the ability to have a handle on events, to shape and control powerful forces.

If this eulogy sounds too good to be true, it is only because men are currently passing through a period of confusion about their role in relationship

A traditional phallic symbol in India, representing the qingham (penis) inserted in the yoni (vagina)

to women. Having acknowledged, to some extent, a brutish past in which they dominated and exploited women, many men are now trying to demonstrate that they can be as soft, gentle, and sensitive as their love partners.

Imagine their surprise, therefore, when they discover that women don't really want this newfangled masculinity—at least, not at the cost of losing the male strength they so much appreciate. True, they don't want to be dominated by aggressive and controlling male patriarchs, but neither do they want men to be so concerned about pleasing women that they lose their own sense of identity, strength, and purpose.

Small wonder, then, that today's male is a somewhat perplexed and angry creature. He can be forgiven for throwing up his hands in despair and saying "Okay, I give up! What the hell am I supposed to be, hard or soft, dominant or passive, masculine or feminine?" Then, before receiving a reply, he disappears into the local branch of the men's movement to share his woes with like-minded casualties of the "new sexuality" of the nineties.

All thoughts, all passions,
  all delights,
Whatever stirs this mortal frame,
All are but ministers of Love,
And feed his sacred flame.

—SAMUEL TAYLOR
COLERIDGE
Love

NATURAL MALE ENERGY

In answer to this dilemma, men, I have some good news for you. For a great many women—perhaps all women, in their heart of hearts—there is nothing more beautiful, exciting, and delicious than a man who is grounded in his sexuality, a man who is rooted in his virile, potent, natural male energy.

However, it is important to understand that when I use the phrase "natural male energy" I am referring to a very different phenomenon than the *machismo* behavior that has been accepted as manhood in the past. Natural maleness is not to be attained, for example, through popping steroids to gain a muscular torso, or through doing push-ups on a woman for half an hour without coming, or through acquiring a cool, casual image by cutting yourself off from your feelings. These are symptoms of unnatural maleness, of an acquired facade, a chauvinistic mask, a stereotyped *macho* image that is a sexual fraud.

The reason that so many men choose to cultivate such a facade lies in a deep-seated conflict between biology and society, between lust and law, between animal energy and civilized ideals. It is worth taking a look at these conflicting forces to see the dynamic in which our luckless heroes have been caught.

The biological force puts men in the same category as any pack of healthy male animals: hanging out in fraternal groups, horsing around, butting each other, testing each other's strength, feeling horny when the rutting season begins, and then beating each other up to see who gets first privileges with the patiently waiting females.

However, the rules of conventional society say that such animalistic behavior is, well, *animalistic,* and therefore unworthy of the civilized male. It also says that male sexual feelings must be strictly controlled and mostly repressed, especially during those seemingly endless years of adolescence when young men's bodies are full of raging hormones that demand intense sexual activity.

Further, the rules clearly state that men may act out their animal competitiveness only in certain specifically allocated theaters, such as the football field, Wall Street, and the occasional war. Otherwise they must hold back their instinctual energies and behave with social politeness and decorum, especially in the company of women.

This combination of seemingly contradictory forces, the animal and the social, has created a type of mutant maleness that is unique in the animal kingdom. The human male is supposed to look like a man, act like a man, but not behave like one. Not only must he repress his sexual and aggressive urges, he should, in addition, cultivate other unnatural qualities such as never showing fear, even when fear is an appropriate response, and never revealing any "weakness" such as weeping or feeling sad or helpless. Moreover, he should always be in command of himself and the situation around him.

Not surprisingly, this artificial condition has left men in a state of suspended animation, ready for action but usually not getting it, exhibiting their manliness and sexual potency yet rarely experiencing it as their personal reality. Under these stressful circumstances, the male sexual climax has become rather like a sneeze, a sudden release of pent-up tension, and the pleasure available to both man and woman is far shorter than it can or should be. That is why statistics show the average male orgasm lasts from two to ten seconds and occurs five to ten minutes after he begins to be excited. There is little opportunity for sexual magic in such an abrupt and speedy ejaculation.

In addition, man now has to deal with a feminist backlash to his long years of patriarchal rule. In the current war between the sexes, he is portrayed as the bad guy, the evildoer, the one who prowls around in the guise of a civilized human being, complete with suit and tie, but who is loaded with all kinds of dangerous hormones and nasty impulses that make him a

One cannot be strong without love. For love is not an irrelevant emotion; it is the blood of life, the power of reunion of the separated.

—PAUL TILLICH
The Eternal Now

potential sex maniac filled with a blind, unconscious lust that at a moment's notice can turn any woman into his helpless victim.

DRIVEN TO POWER IN ORDER TO MATE?

Men, if you think this assassination of your collective character amounts to gender overkill, I tend to agree with you. Certainly, you have abused your power in the past, but you may have been unwittingly assisted by an instinctive tendency in women to seek out, and mate with, those men who wield the most power.

As evidence, I refer to an intriguing global research project conducted by David M. Buss, a psychology professor at the University of Michigan at Ann Arbor. In his book *The Evolution of Desire,* Buss shows how, even today, the overwhelming majority of women around the world—spanning all nations and cultures—are still attracted to men who exude an aura of being able to take care of them, provide for them, protect and nourish them.

Why would women seek powerful men? According to Professor Buss, the answer lies in our evolutionary psychology, in an instinct for survival that developed over thousands of years of living as nomadic hunter-gatherers in an untamed and frequently hostile environment. Under such primitive conditions, Buss argues, women naturally gravitated toward mates who could best protect and provide for them during pregnancy and early motherhood, when their self-sufficiency was inhibited by their infants.

Over time, this ancient but successful strategy became hard-wired into our psychology. As Buss points out, "If women over evolutionary history have preferred men who have resources and have the power and status to control those resources, then over time they will drive the evolution of status-seeking, power-seeking mechanisms in men."

In other words, by making power a criterion for mating, our sisters in earlier times were sending messages to their menfolk that they needed to be big, strong, wealthy, and in command of the situation. The men, eager to adopt any behavior likely to impress the fairer sex, responded to these messages by developing characteristics of being chauvinistic, autocratic, and overbearing.

Buss's conclusions are controversial, but from a lay viewpoint they seem to make sense, bringing a more balanced perspective to the issue of responsibility for centuries of inequality between the sexes—although I would find it loathsome if his theory were used to justify any kind of male supremacist ideology.

The real issue here is not who is to blame for the ugliness and sorrows of our past, but how to liberate ourselves from the limiting habits, beliefs, and ideas carried over from earlier times so that we can discover our true capacity for sexual fulfillment.

Currently, as I say, men are suffering from a bad reputation among women. In an effort to restore the balance, many men these days are making Herculean efforts to satisfy their female partners sexually. Instead of leaping into the saddle for a quick ride in the grand urban-cowboy tradition, they have diligently read the sex manuals on how to satisfy a woman and are patiently and sensitively bringing their love partners to orgasmic climax before permitting themselves the ejaculatory release for which they secretly yearn.

This new attitude represents significant progress in terms of pleasure for women, but the man's orgasmic experience usually remains confined to the same quick genital convulsions that he knew before the historic words "female orgasm" were ever uttered. Moreover, the breathless gasps and moans of his beloved send him the unmistakable message that her capacity for sexual enjoyment is far greater than his own—something he did not have to face when he was the only one who mattered.

As a sexual being, man is still holding back, controlling and performing according to some socially acceptable ideal. The ideal may have expanded, so that now it includes satisfying the woman instead of ignoring her sexual needs, but man's ability to experience orgasm has not. So instead of being celebrated as an instrument for endless pleasure, his Vajra, his magical sexual organ, is often felt as a source of frustration and disappointment, especially in those delicate and often depressing moments immediately following ejaculation when all the man's juice is gone.

INITIATION INTO THE NEW MANHOOD

In terms of sexual magic, it is essential that male sexual power be reclaimed, honored, and expanded, so that the alchemy of charging a Magic Symbol with the combined orgasmic energy of a man and a woman who are entwined in deep Tantric embrace can happen at optimum power. The purpose of this chapter is to create a healthy, virile, male sexual energy that can meet the woman's energy in an ecstatic union, making powerful sexual magic.

The process for accomplishing this task is immensely enjoyable. It carries with it the added bonus of not making any new demands on the overburdened masculine ego by way of performance, achievement, or striving heroically toward some difficult and distant goal.

Rather, it lies in relaxation, in letting go, in allowing things to happen rather than forcing them to materialize on cue. To my male readers I would like to say: You have done enough; now it is your turn to lie back and receive.

In the following exercises, you will be invited to receive pleasure in a passive way, as your love partner stimulates first your penis, then your prostate gland, and then gives you a blended orgasm by stimulating both areas together. In this way, you will learn how to be deeply receptive, so that your sexual energy is not thrown outward in ejaculation but is absorbed inside your body, and your orgasmic capacity is expanded.

Through this exciting journey you have the chance to receive initiation into a new type of manhood, a new form of virility. This Tantric initiation may sometimes be difficult. It may take you through moments of not having an erection when you think you ought to have one, moments when you want to ejaculate and are being invited to keep the energy inside.

By mastering these challenges, you will come to experience a deeper sense of sexual potency. You will find yourself on an ascending curve of pleasure, rising to greater and greater heights of sexual fulfillment.

The most challenging part of this initiation into male sexual alchemy is to develop the inner strength that allows you to disassociate with your desire to ejaculate, your need to come, your impulse to release your sexual tension. The easier and more pleasurable part is to become receptive to an ever-widening pool of orgasmic energy that arises when your ejaculation is contained.

In the beginning you may feel that giving up your ejaculation, your familiar kind of genital orgasm, is no fun. You may get frustrated, even angry. It is an exercise in discipline, and you have to be willing to go through a period of delayed gratification in order to learn how to expand your sexual sensations, as you prepare for a whole-body orgasm instead of a localized genital one.

The payoff is going to be enormous, not only in the area of sexual magic but also in the field of normal lovemaking. Your new capacity to master your ejaculatory reflex means that you can decide when you want finally to let go, prolong your lovemaking ability, and allow you to satisfy your female partner fully as well as enjoy heightened orgasmic sensations yourself.

Raise your enjoyment to its highest power and then use it as spiritual rocket fuel.

—MAHA TANTRA ACANA

THREE STAGES OF EXPANDING MALE ORGASM

The exercises for expanding male orgasm are divided into three stages.

Stage 1

The woman stimulates the man's Vajra, or penis, finding ways to bring him close to ejaculation, then stopping just before the point of no return, allowing the aroused sexual energy to spread through the man's body.

Stage 2

Stimulation of Vajra is combined with external stimulation of the prostate gland, by massaging the perineum area, helping the man to broaden his range of sexual sensations.

Stage 3

Stimulation of Vajra is combined with massage of the prostate directly and internally, leading to a longer and more powerful orgasm.

This three-stage process allows the man to expand his orgasmic capacity in a series of steps, climbing toward sexual peaks, stopping each time before ejaculation, relaxing into the feelings that have been awakened, then climbing toward new and higher peaks.

Eventually, he comes to a place where there is no ejaculation happening but there is a continuous stream of orgasmic pleasure running through his sexual organs, his pelvic area, and his whole body. When he finally chooses to allow ejaculation, it lasts much longer, with much more powerful orgasmic sensations.

Before we move into the exercises, it will be instructive to examine the anatomy of the male sexual organ.

ANATOMY OF MALE SEXUALITY

The Vajra, or penis, is a relatively simple mechanism. It has no bones and no muscles, being composed mainly of spongy tissues. When a man is sexually aroused these spongy tissues become engorged with blood, stiffening Vajra and transforming it into a wonderfully energized, potent instrument of pleasure.

In today's male, the Vajra comes in two distinct styles: the unaltered model, complete with foreskin, or the circumcised version from which most or all of the foreskin has been removed. Both varieties have an equal capacity to satisfy sexually the owner and his beloved partner.

The shaft of the Vajra extends from the body just below the pubic mound and ends in a distinctive head or glans that looks rather like a smooth mushroom cap. Here, the texture of the surface changes as normal body skin gives way to the polished roundness of the head. The color of the head is usually several shades darker than the skin of the shaft beneath.

At the top of the head is a small opening that marks the end of the urethra, a small tube that carries the body's waste fluids from the kidneys to be expelled through the Vajra as urine. This tube also carries a mixture of fluid from the prostate gland and testicles, to be expelled through the Vajra as semen in sexual ejaculation.

On the underside of the penis, just below the point at which the skin of the shaft attaches to the head, there is a particularly sensitive area known as the frenulum. When correctly stimulated, this spot can be a great source of sexual pleasure and for this reason I like to think of it as the male equivalent of the cleo, or clitoris.

Below the Vajra lies the scrotal sac. This contains two oval-shaped testicles that manufacture sperm and the male hormone testosterone. The hormones are absorbed into the body, but the sperm are stored in special bags inside the scrotal sac known as epididymides.

When a man becomes sexually excited, the sperm travels up from the testicles through the vas deferens tube to the prostate gland. This small gland is shaped like a chestnut and sits inside the body, in the bowl of the pelvis, between the Vajra and the anus.

You can feel your prostate by pressing on the perineum point, halfway between your scrotal sac and your anus. You will feel a soft, spongy area. This is where your prostate is hidden. When your Vajra is erect your prostate feels like the root of your erection, as if it were part of the same organ. Anatomically, this is not so, but in terms of how it feels there is a definite connection between the two.

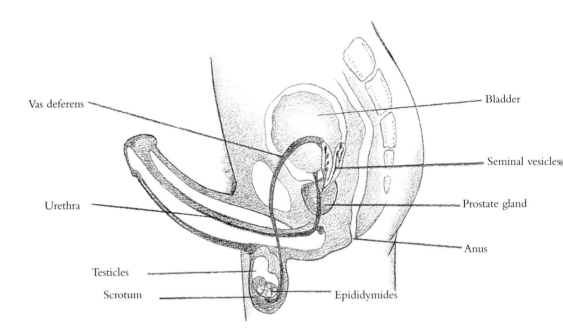

Vas deferens

Bladder

Seminal vesicles

Urethra

Prostate gland

Anus

Testicles

Scrotum

Epididymides

Anatomy of the male sexual organ

If the man's frenulum can be compared to the woman's clitoris, then his prostate gland can be compared to the G-Spot, because it offers deeper and more lasting sensations of sexual orgasm. Both these areas will be explored in the exercises that follow.

At the moment of sexual climax, muscular contractions around the prostate discharge a mixture of sperm and prostatic fluid through the urethra and out of the head of the Vajra.

EXERCISE: STIMULATING THE VAJRA

Purpose and benefits

Men, in the following exercises your love partner will be pleasuring your sexual organ in new and delightful ways, bringing you a whole new spectrum of sexual sensations and expanding your orgasmic capacity in preparation for sexual magic. She will bring you close to ejaculation, then help you to relax and let this energy be absorbed in your body before moving again toward a new and higher peak.

For monogamous couples, here is a great opportunity to bring fresh excitement and depth to your sexual routine, varying roles and behavior that may have become fixed, boring, or dull. Now you can reawaken your enthusiasm and energy for each other as sexual partners, enhancing each other's pleasure a thousandfold.

This practice is also very suitable for—although certainly not limited to—men in their fifties, sixties, and seventies, because this kind of stimulation does not depend on having a full erection, nor does it involve the sexual athletics that are sometimes required during sexual intercourse, such as frequently changing body positions and supporting your weight on your arms, shoulders, or knees for long periods of time.

Shiva, the success of this wonderful session depends on your ability to become receptive, letting go of your traditional role as leader, initiator, and producer of sexual pleasure and experiencing instead the more feminine qualities of surrender, receptivity, and trust. However, you need to remain in charge as the one who leads and instructs Shakti how to give you pleasure, guiding her actions, giving her continuous feedback on what she is doing.

Shakti, this exercise offers you a great opportunity to cultivate a sense of self-confidence and power. You are the co-creator, the equal partner, the giver, the provider of ecstasy. You will enjoy this exercise more if you understand that you are doing it for yourself, if you can say "Yes, I'm curious, excited . . . I want to learn how to master the art of giving a man pleasure . . . I want to know how his sexual organ responds . . . I want to see him moan with ecstasy at my touch . . . I want to feel my skills as a lover, as the one who initiates these feelings in him while remaining centered on myself."

However, be alert that you do not fall into the trap of overwhelming Shiva and taking control of the exercise, as this may inhibit his ability to express what he needs and fully experience his pleasure. Allow him to tell you how to stimulate his Vajra and follow his suggestions exactly.

Shiva and Shakti, the success of this exercise will depend on your ability to establish and maintain a nourishing heart connection with each other. I emphasize this because some couples may be tempted to skip over the early stages of the exercise in their eagerness to explore direct stimulation of the Vajra. But the initial steps, especially those bonding the two lovers through the heart, are of great help in paving the way for a successful session.

Preparations

- Stimulation and massage of the Vajra requires lots of good-quality lubricant. Water-based lubricants tend to dry faster than oil-based ones when applied externally. My personal preference is to use a pure, organic oil such as olive oil, which can be applied in abundance and has no harmful effect on the Vajra's delicate skin. It can also be used to massage other areas of the body. Alternatively, any good-quality, organic massage oil will serve your purpose.

- Create a special code word for Shiva to use when he comes close to the point of ejaculation and wants Shakti to stop stimulating his Vajra. He can say "now" or "stop" to indicate the moment when Shakti should cease all stimulation.

- Shakti, this time you are the one who creates the Magic Circle for Shiva. Bring any objects that have a strong male connotation like drums, male sculptures, feathers, photos, phallic symbols, and so on. Create an intriguing atmosphere through incense, candles, and subtle lighting. You may also want to bring a humorous and appropriate toy, like a model of King Kong. Be sure to wear something sexy, like a see-through blouse, or be naked except for a beautiful *lungi* around your hips and a flower in your hair. Whatever your choice, make sure your clothes allow your arms and torso to move freely.

- Shiva, give yourself time to have a luxurious shower, cleaning yourself thoroughly, especially your genitals and anus. Put on your favorite cologne and prepare to be pampered by Shakti. Make sure that your bladder is empty.

- Shakti, check that your fingernails are trimmed and smooth.

- Allow sixty to ninety minutes for this exercise, making sure there will be no interruptions.

STAGE 1: MEETING THROUGH THE HEART

Shakti, bring Shiva into the Magic Circle. Help him to feel welcome, relaxed, and at home. You may want to dance together for a few minutes, to rid yourselves of any tension.

Greet each other with a Heart Salutation.

Enjoy a long Melting Hug. Breathe deeply, in synchronicity together as you do so.

Sit facing each other on cushions.

Shakti, place your right hand on Shiva's heart, then take his right hand and put it on your own heart. Gaze softly into each other's eyes, harmonizing your breathing, listening for each other's heartbeat. Breathe slowly and deeply. Feel the love and trust that is flowing between you as you embark on this new and exciting adventure.

Shakti, dip your fingers in some special oil or perfume and bless Shiva's three main chakras. Touch his pubic mound and give your blessing, saying "May the door to your pleasure open wide for you this day."

Then anoint Shiva's heart center with oil, saying "May our hearts merge in love and trust."

Touch his third eye lightly with your middle finger, saying "May your orgasm expand your vision and understanding."

Shakti, when the blessing is complete, help Shiva to lie comfortably amid the cushions in a half-sitting position. Sit between Shiva's legs. Slide your legs under his and put pillows on your thighs so he can rest his knees on them (see illustration). Or you may prefer to kneel, Japanese style, with a cushion under your thighs. Some women like to sit at the man's side, close to his body. Some prefer to use a massage table so that the man is lying down while the woman is standing.

In my experience, however, the most intimate position is when Shiva reclines on big pillows and Shakti sits between his legs, close to the Vajra, although you may need to change the position of your legs from time to time during the exercise.

Shakti, slowly open Shiva's robe, exposing the front of his body.

Begin to caress his whole body, touching him everywhere, encouraging him to breathe deeply with his mouth open. Breathe in synchronicity with him.

If Shiva seems too serious, give him a tickle session, blow in his ear, nibble an ear lobe, lightly bite his throat, suck his toe, tease his body with your breasts, run your hair over him, creating an atmosphere of lightness and humor, inspiring him to trust and relax.

Massage his chest, gently squeezing and teasing his nipples. Then slide your hands under the small of his back and vigorously massage the sacrum area. Many sexual tensions are held in the V-shaped point where the back meets the buttocks.

Cup Shiva's testicles, his balls, in one hand, touching his perineum with the tip of the middle finger. In this position, the flat of your hand can press against the Vajra (see illustration). Place your other hand on Shiva's heart center, in the middle of his chest.

Yang can function only with the cooperation of yin, and yin can grow only in the presence of yang.

—The Yellow Emperor

In this position, gaze softly into his eyes, bringing all your love and attention to this being. He is the only one, the special one, and all your energy is focused on him. Allow this moment to wash away any intruding thoughts or distractions.

Shiva, open yourself to the love of your partner. Feel yourself becoming receptive, like a glass waiting to be filled with rich, dark wine.

STAGE 2: STROKES FOR STIMULATING THE VAJRA
Shakti, when you feel ready, ask Shiva, "Shall we start the session now?" If Shiva says "yes," you can begin to stimulate his Vajra, using all or any the following strokes.

The X-Stroke   Shakti, begin with the X-stroke, a beautiful and easy way to approach the Vajra that was developed by two close friends of mine, Terumi and Leonard Leinow.

Rest the palms of your hands on Shiva's knees. Your left hand rests on his right knee, and your right hand rests on his left knee.

Keeping your right hand motionless, slowly move your left hand up Shiva's right thigh, across his Vajra and genitals, being sure to touch them, then over his belly to his left nipple. In this way, you are caressing him in a diagonal direction from right knee to left nipple.

By the time your left hand is passing over Shiva's genitals your right hand has begun a similar journey, traveling slowly up Shiva's left thigh. As your left hand reaches its destination, your right hand is caressing Shiva's genitals on its way to the other nipple. Your left hand comes back to Shiva's knee and begins a new journey as your right hand travels over his belly and reaches his right nipple.

It may sound complicated, but in practice this stroke is very easy. Take time to develop an even flow of X-strokes, making sure your hands caress Shiva's Vajra as they pass over it.

The Twelve O'Clock Stroke   This stroke directly caresses the Vajra.

Caress upward, from the balls to the tip of the Vajra, with the flat part of your hands and fingers, giving alternating strokes with your left and right hand in a smooth, continuous series of movements. Shiva's Vajra should be lying on his belly for this stroke. Use lots of oil.

This stroke is particularly pleasurable because Shakti's hands are passing over the frenulum, on the underside of Shiva's Vajra, where the head meets the shaft.

Twelve-o'clock stroke

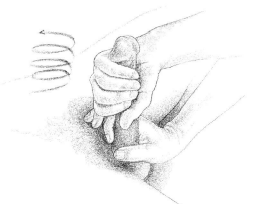

Spiraling the stalk

Strokes for stimulating the Vajra

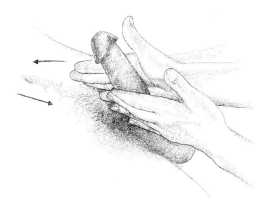

Making fire

293

Growing the Stalk   Cover Shiva's Vajra with lots of oil. Hold the base of the Vajra with one hand, pressing down slightly, then stroke straight upward from base to the tip with the other hand.

Spiraling the Stalk   Hold the Vajra at the base with one hand, then turn your other hand around the Vajra in a circular movement, beginning at the bottom and winding your way up to the head. When you get to the top, caress the whole head with the palm of your hand, using plenty of oil.

The Carousel   Hold the Vajra with both hands and rotate them in opposite directions around the stalk. Move your torso backward and forward in harmony with the movement of the hands.

Shakti, this stroke involves your whole body. Rock backward and forward from your pelvis, inhaling and exhaling deeply as you move back and forth, while rotating your hands around the Vajra.

Doing this stroke while looking in the eyes of your partner can be both delightful and playful, and has been likened to riding a carousel in an amusement park.

Making Fire   With the palms of your hands held vertically, facing each other on either side of the Vajra, press against the stalk and rub your hands backward and forward as if trying to start a fire by rubbing a stick. Start at the base of the Vajra, work up to the head and then down again.

Drumming the Vajra   Hold the head of Shiva's Vajra against his belly with the index and middle fingers of one hand, then lightly dance the fingers of your other hand over the back surface of the Vajra. You can play it like a small drum, using the whole underside of your fingers, not just the fingertips.

Stroking without the Hood   If Shiva has not been circumcised the head will be protected by his foreskin. It's nice to stimulate the head with the foreskin covering it. When he gets more excited, gently pull back the foreskin and directly stimulate the head, lightly massaging up and down with lots of lubricant.

STAGE 3: BUILDING SEXUAL AROUSAL

Now it is time for Shiva to begin a steady climb toward his first sexual peak. The easiest way to do this is through prolonged, rhythmic stimulation of the Vajra.

Shakti, liberally oil Shiva's Vajra and then hold the base with one hand. With your other hand grasp the stalk, surrounding it with your palm and fingers, and begin to stroke the stalk firmly up and down. This is the basic stroke that most men need to rise toward their sexual climax, but there are several variations.

Your stroke can move up and down the stalk, or it can include the head as well. You can alternate between stroking the stalk and stroking the stalk and head together.

Another option is to find a stroke that allows your thumb to press on the frenulum as your hand moves from the stalk to the head. At the end of the upward movement there is a kind of "snapping" or "flicking" movement with the wrist that can send a delightful pulse of pleasure into the frenulum.

Shiva, teach Shakti the strokes that really do it for you. Give her as much feedback as possible on the rhythm, intensity, and speed that give you most pleasure, so that she can create exactly the right strokes.

Shakti, some men like to have a steady, ongoing stroke that is strong and quick, while others like more variation. Don't get discouraged if Shiva doesn't peak right away, or if he doesn't get excited quickly. Now he is in the receptive mode and it may be more difficult for him to peak. Stay centered, have trust in yourself, becoming familiar with the process of stimulating your man for long periods of time. Settle into a rhythm of stimulating Shiva's Vajra.

Many women are not used to giving strong, rapid stimulation in this way, so listen to Shiva's guidance. Let him tell you what pressure, speed, and intensity he likes. If he is not speaking, ask him, "Is this okay?" "Is this exciting?" You need close and accurate communication.

Shiva, you may come to a place during stimulation when your penis is getting insensitive. If you're not feeling much, ask Shakti to leave your Vajra alone and massage your body from your Vajra toward your chest, spreading the energy toward your heart center. Then, after a few minutes, she can gradually come back to the Vajra, teasing the stalk, tickling the frenulum, caressing the head, before resuming rhythmic stimulation.

STAGE 4: PEAKING WITHOUT EJACULATING
Shakti, you are now moving from a general pleasuring of Shiva's Vajra to a precise method of stimulation that brings him close to ejaculation, without crossing the point of no return.

Build up the pace, stimulating his Vajra in a more dynamic way that brings him toward his orgasmic peak.

Shiva, now is the time to become really sexy and aroused, reaching toward your preejaculation peak. Focus all your attention on the sensations in your Vajra. Go for your lust, your excitement. Move your body. Thrust upward with your pelvis so you can feel Shakti's strokes on your Vajra even more acutely. Exhale strongly through your mouth, pushing your energy down into your genitals. If it is helpful, do the PC Pump, squeezing the muscles around your perineum and anus in short, strong, rhythmic spasms.

Shakti, bring Shiva to an "almost climax," not quite reaching his point of ejaculation. This means that you need to cease all stimulation for at least three to five seconds before the ejaculatory reflex sets in. The following signs help you know when Shiva is getting close to orgasm:

1. His thigh and stomach muscles begin to tense.
2. His back arches, pushing his pelvis closer to you.
3. The testicles contract upward toward the body.
4. His breathing pattern changes. Some men breathe noticeably faster, others slower.
5. The head of the Vajra becomes darker in color.
6. The Vajra becomes very hard, the veins bulge, as it becomes engorged with blood.
7. The Vajra tends to feel incredibly alive and energized.
8. There is frequent emission of a clear fluid from the opening of the urethra.

Shiva, when you feel that your level of sexual excitement is peaking and bringing you very close to ejaculation, use the code word you have arranged with Shakti. Say "Stop!"

Shakti, stop all stimulation of the Vajra. Press strongly into Shiva's perineum point with the index and middle finger of one hand, while holding the Vajra with the other. This will help him not to ejaculate.

Or, if necessary, you can press firmly with the thumbs and fingers of both hands on the Vajra stalk, just below the head (see illustration). This technique is normally used only when Shiva has come too close to ejaculation and needs extra help in preventing it.

Shiva, breathe strongly and deeply, filling your lungs with air, helping the energy spread through your pelvis. Allow your whole body to relax each time you exhale, letting go of control, becoming receptive to the exquisite sensations in your genitals.

Shakti, your partner's desire to ejaculate will pass in a few moments. When you feel he is ready, ask "Shall I begin again?"

If Shiva says "yes," begin to stimulate his Vajra once more. Over the next twenty to thirty minutes, bring him to a peak of sexual pleasure between three to six times.

If you both feel it is appropriate, you can end the session by giving Shiva's Vajra the final blessing and stimulating him all the way to the point of ejaculation.

Shiva and Shakti, sit or lie quietly together for a few minutes, absorbing the powerful experience you have shared.

Shiva, be sure to express your appreciation to Shakti for giving you so much pleasure. Reward her with a Melting Hug.

Share your experiences of what happened during the practice.

Close with a Heart Salutation.

Five Basic Points for Vajra Stimulation

Here are five basic points to remember when stimulating the Vajra:

1. Develop a good heart connection.
2. Start with playful, erotic foreplay.
3. Explore various strokes on the Vajra.
4. Practice rhythmic stimulation.
5. Come to several peaks without ejaculating.

Pointers

DROPPING THE "STRONG, SILENT" IMAGE

Shiva, as you probably know, men are not used to talking before, during, or after sex, so it is quite a challenge for you to move away from this "strong, silent" mode of male behavior toward an easy attitude of continuous communication.

One good tip is to keep your eyes open, to look at your partner while she pleasures you. Or, if you feel you must close your eyes at certain times in order fully to enjoy the sensations arising in your sexual organ, alternate between keeping them closed and looking at your Shakti.

Sexual erection is comparable to water and fire. Water and fire can kill a man or a woman, or help them, depending upon how they are used.

—PAO
The Plane Master

It is very important that you be willing to describe what you are feeling, otherwise Shakti will not be able to develop the skills she needs to bring you to higher and higher ecstatic peaks. Talk to her about each different stroke: how it feels, how you want to be touched, whether the pressure should be strong or light, what kind of stimulation turns you on most.

Resist the temptation to say "That's fine" to everything Shakti does, as this does not help to build her skills. But remember to stay positive in your communication, respecting Shakti's willingness to give to you.

Shakti, when your man begins to relax and enjoy himself, sinking into a blissful trance, you may feel that you don't want to disturb him by asking questions. But it is important to keep communicating. Ask short, simple questions that can be answered with a few words, like "Does this feel good?" "Do you want it stronger?" "Shall I try something different?"

A SUCCESSFUL FIRST EXPERIENCE

A good experience of expanded orgasmic states comes from a subtle interplay of technique, creativity, and communication. Bob and Sarah, a couple who had been together for seven years, had experimented with several Tantric techniques but had never done the exercise I have just described. Bob tells the story of their first experience:

> I had a shower while Sarah prepared the space. Earlier, I told her about Margo's idea to use olive oil as a lubricant and we both agreed to try it. But, just in case, we had a variety of oil-based and water-based lubricants handy.
>
> I put on my favorite bathrobe and Sarah led me to the bedroom. She had covered the bed with a white satin sheet and placed a towel on the spot where I would sit, in case any oil dripped on the bed. An array of large cushions was stacked against the end of the bed so that I could recline in a half-sitting, half-lying position, in a very kingly manner. Music was playing and the atmosphere was relaxing and welcoming.
>
> It felt very good to lie there, watching Sarah take off her robe to reveal her shapely body. She did a spontaneous dance for me, which was just delightful, then came and sat between my legs. We did a Heart Salutation and placed our hands on each other's hearts. Then she anointed the three chakras with oil, making an invocation at each one, and started to massage my whole body lightly.
>
> Although I enjoyed this, I could also feel that I was getting impatient, thinking "Okay, this is nice, but when do we get to the real thing? When is she going to touch my Vajra?"
>
> Sensing this, Sarah asked me "Bob, are you worried about the time?" And I had to admit it was true, because we'd agreed on an hour for the ses-

sion and quite a lot of time had gone by already, so I was anxious that the really pleasurable part of the session would be cut short.

Once it was clear what was bothering me we easily solved the problem by agreeing to continue the session until we had completed all the stages of the exercise, which we figured would take between ninety to one hundred twenty minutes. Then I could really relax and enjoy each moment.

This was also important for Sarah. She told me that she really needed to feel a heart connection between us in order to enjoy what she was doing, and my impatience was making this connection difficult.

I liked it when she cupped my genitals in her hand and tuned in, gazing into my eyes. Then she began the X-stroke and pretty soon my Vajra was erect.

I soon realized that I liked a lot of oil on my Vajra. The more oil, the more erotic and pleasurable the sensations, so I often said "more oil" and Sarah would oblige.

Then she moved into an exploration of the different strokes. It was just delightful for me to have all this attention focused on my penis. For once, I didn't have to worry about giving pleasure to Sarah. I could just bathe in the luxury of her total attention and the sensations in my Vajra.

For Sarah, it was important to have the freedom to adapt each stroke to her own style, and some worked better than others. A favorite of ours was the carousel, which was not only erotic but also playful because the rocking and twisting motion really did remind us of riding a carousel at a fairground.

Throughout this time I felt very sexual, my Vajra was hard, but I didn't have any trouble preventing ejaculation. I wasn't close to orgasm, and this was probably due to the fact that once Sarah began to caress my Vajra I became very relaxed, enjoying the whole show.

But this became a problem when it was time for me to move toward an orgasmic peak. Sarah used the basic stroke, but I didn't feel any great excitement. I offered to show her how to do it, but then I found that it didn't make much difference. I was hard, but not able to approach the peak.

At this point, Sarah said that she didn't really enjoy doing the repetitive basic stroke for very long, so she started playing around with a whole variety of strokes, using lots of oil.

In response, my body started to move around in a very sensual kind of way. At first, I held back, embarrassed, thinking "well, this is how women behave when they're turned on, not guys," but it felt so good that I just gave in to it.

Sarah was doing all kinds of strokes on my Vajra and I was pushing my hips up towards her, arching my back, running my hands over my face and chest, sighing, moaning, grunting and suddenly I was getting really turned on, really excited.

To my surprise, Sarah was also getting turned on. She told me later that my movements released a surge of male energy through my genitals that she found very arousing. So she was very happy, pouring oil over my Vajra and my body, letting me press my hips against her stomach while she rubbed my Vajra between her breasts and squeezed my nipples.

It was getting pretty wild and exciting for both of us. I came to my first peak and said "now" and we both stopped moving. There was an exquisite sensation in my Vajra, but I could also feel how my physical movements had opened up energy channels inside my body. My pelvis, belly, chest, and throat all felt more open, more alive, so the pleasure wasn't just local. It was spreading.

I came to a peak about four to five times without ejaculating and then told Sarah that I wanted to go for the full orgasm. She was so excited by this time that she was squirming her buttocks on the sheet while pleasuring my Vajra, so with one hand I dipped my fingers in the oil and reached between her legs, pleasuring her clitoris while she brought me to a final climax.

We both came at the same time, laughing wildly, rocked by spasms of pleasure, with semen and oil running all over us. It was great. I have rarely enjoyed myself so much, and afterward we felt very loving and affectionate toward each other, like having a new honeymoon.

HEADING INTO A FORBIDDEN SEXUAL ZONE

Now that the "front" part of Shiva's sexual organs has been well taken care of, it's time to discover ways of generating sexual excitement in the "back" part. In the following exercise, Shakti will be massaging the perineum area between Shiva's testicles and anus, thereby stimulating the prostate gland that lies just beneath the surface (see illustration of male anatomy).

Before introducing the practice, it will be helpful to examine some of the social attitudes that inhibit a man's ability to experience pleasure in the prostate and anal areas. You will find that you are working against a lifetime of taboos and opposing ideas and impulses.

From early on, often in a premature manner, children are taught a form of "toilet training" that includes contracting the anal sphincter muscle and the muscles around the prostate in order to hold back their stool. Should they fail in this endeavor, an attitude of disgust and condemnation is almost invariably directed toward them, conveying a strong message that this kind of behavior is unacceptable. Soon, they learn that this area of the body is somehow dirty.

In addition, it has been established that emotional denial, especially denial of anger, is closely associated with the contraction of anal muscles. For example, your boss has been nasty or rude to you at work, and you find yourself feeling very angry but unable to express it. Automatically, you tighten the muscles around your anus. As you do so, your breathing tends to become shallow, your stomach gets tense, and all energy flow to the anal and pelvic area is cut off.

A third source of tension derives from the universally accepted "missionary position" style of lovemaking in which the man, lying on top of the woman, makes repeated thrusts, using his pelvis to propel his Vajra into the Yoni in a dynamic and powerful way. This kind of lovemaking can be great fun and highly pleasurable, but when used habitually, in a strong, repetitive way, it creates layers of tension around the buttocks and anus, especially in the area of the prostate where the thrusting impulse originates.

Fear of homosexuality provides yet another source of tension. The idea that pleasure can be gained from caressing and stimulating this area may feel threatening to a man who has cultivated an image of being strongly heterosexual.

Unpleasant and insensitive prostate examinations, which nearly all men have to endure at some time, also create tension. The impact of a doctor's finger being suddenly rammed into your anus lasts well beyond the initial shock and hurt. Moreover, in recent years, the prostate gland has become a major source of medical concern with the rising incidence of prostate cancer.

For all these reasons, the anal area has become difficult terrain to explore and enjoy. But this traumatic social conditioning can be changed. There is a new challenge ahead: to relax this tense, forbidden area and allow it to be healed, to be nourished, to become a source of great pleasure independently of any cultural judgments or taboos. It is time for all of us to recognize that this part of the male body needs as much care and attention as any other part.

EXERCISE: STIMULATING THE PROSTATE EXTERNALLY

Purpose and benefits

To deepen the male partner's experience of the receptive aspect of his sexuality by stimulating his prostate gland. The prostate is stimulated externally by massaging the perineum area, between the testicles and the anus. This practice paves the way for an experience of multiple, implosive orgasms as opposed to the explosive orgasm of normal ejaculation.

Stimulation of the prostate gives you, Shiva, an experience comparable to the female G-Spot orgasm. You will experience how sexual pleasure can spread from your Vajra to your prostate in the same way that a woman's pleasure spreads from her clitoris to her G-Spot.

Combined stimulation of your Vajra and prostate allows you to connect two distinct types of pleasure: outer-directed sexual sensations and inner-directed ones.

When you ejaculate, the muscles around your prostate have a reflex response, a series of pulsations or contractions that help to eject semen out through the urethra. By stimulating the prostate, you can experience a subtle, ongoing stream of pleasurable sensations that requires no ejaculation.

Preparations

- Be gentle and loving when exploring this area. When you receive a prostate massage there may be mild sensations of temporary discomfort, which are natural when sensitizing a neglected area of the body. It is best not to work directly on the prostate for more than five to seven minutes in the first few sessions.

- If you have recently experienced inflammation of the prostate, or had an infection in this area, or have a medical history of prostate problems, you should not do this massage unless you receive permission from your doctor.

- Shiva, be sure that you take a shower and thoroughly clean your genitals and anus. One of the most important aids to easy and comfortable prostate stimulation is for both partners to know that the anus is clean.

- Shakti, you may want to adopt the attitude of a medical student, focusing on achieving skillful stimulation through experimenting and sharing information.

- Shakti, create the Magic Circle while Shiva readies himself to receive the massage.

- Make sure your fingernails are short and smooth.

- If you wish, you can wear latex gloves as an added hygienic precaution.

- Use a lot of oil-based lubricant.

- Allow forty-five minutes for this exercise.

STAGE 1: FOREPLAY WITH VIGOROUS MASSAGE

Shakti, welcome Shiva to your Magic Circle.

Begin with a Heart Salutation and a long Melting Hug.

Shakti, take off your beloved's robe and help him lie down on his stomach. If you wish, you can work on a massage table.

Begin to give Shiva a deep, dynamic massage all around his buttocks, including his lower back, sacrum, and the tops of his thighs. This is an important preparation for approaching the prostate. Make your massaging movements from your hara—your center of balance, below the navel—using your whole body.

Be playful. Enjoy yourself. Massaging the buttocks can be rather like kneading dough in a bakery.

End by placing one hand on each buttock and shaking them vigorously for two to three minutes, then stroke down the backs of Shiva's legs from his buttocks to his feet. Tap the soles of his feet, grounding the energy.

STAGE 2: ROUSING THE THUNDERBOLT (VAJRA STIMULATION)

Shakti, when you have finished, ask Shiva to turn onto his back and recline in the half-lying position, propped against cushions or pillows.

Take time to tune in to Shiva, cupping his sexual organ with one hand while placing your other hand on his heart center. Gaze lovingly into his eyes, feeling the trust and excitement flowing between you. Tell him something wonderful, like "This is all for you. I love you; just allow yourself to receive."

Breathe deeply and harmoniously together.

Shakti, as with the stimulation of your G-Spot, it is important for Shiva to be thoroughly aroused sexually before you begin to caress his prostate. The engorgement of the Vajra helps any tensions around the prostate area to soften and relax.

Lubricate Shiva's Vajra with plenty of oil and begin to stimulate this power scepter in the ways you have already learned. Go through your repertoire of skills and strokes, bringing orgasmic delight to your partner, then settle into a steady rhythm that brings Shiva to a peak of sexual excitement.

Shiva, use your code word to stop just before the point of no return.

Shakti, cease stimulation, letting your hand rest on his Vajra.

Shiva, relax, breathe slowly and deeply, allowing your orgasmic sensations to be absorbed and spread through your pelvis. Now you are ready to move to the prostate.

Experience your individuality as a healthy leaf. You feel the sap flowing from the vine of your innermost self.

—The Bird Tribe Book

STAGE 3: MASSAGING THE PERINEUM AREA

Shakti, after stimulating your partner's Vajra for fifteen to twenty minutes, bringing him to several peaks, ask him, "Now I would like to focus on your prostate. Is this okay with you?"

If he says "yes," begin to explore the perineum area.

Shakti, begin by stroking the skin surface between Shiva's testicles and anus. Feel the mound just beneath the testicles that forms the root of Shiva's Vajra, then trace it back toward the anus, noticing when your fingers start to push into a soft, fleshy area. This is the perineum, where the prostate is located inside the body.

Feel the two big sitting bones of Shiva's pelvis, at the bottom of his buttocks, and trace these down toward the perineum. Again, you will find yourself pushing into a soft, fleshy area.

Shiva, you may discover that, because this area is not often touched, it may be quite insensitive. Give Shakti plenty of time to find her way around. The more familiar she is with this territory, the more pleasure she can give you later on.

Shakti, the following strokes are designed to loosen and relax the perineal area, bringing sensitivity and aliveness, releasing tension. You may wish to place a small cushion under Shiva's buttocks to make the area more accessible.

Pressing with Fingers Shakti, press with your fingers in the area between the testicles and the anus, feeling where it is hard, where it is soft. You may find that you can press quite deeply and strongly in the soft area that covers the prostate.

Use pressure from your index and middle finger to find the most pleasurable point, experimenting while your partner guides you: "Yes here, now try further up, down a bit . . ."

Shiva, as Shakti starts to massage, begin the PC Pump, rhythmically contracting the muscles around your perineum and anus as you inhale deeply through your mouth. Keep your throat open.

As you inhale, imagine that you are breathing down into your heart. As you exhale, imagine that you are pushing the energy down toward your pelvis. This will help to relax tension in every part of your body.

Guide Shakti. Tell her how it feels, how much pressure you need.

Pressing with Knuckles Shakti, make a fist and begin to press gently with your knuckles into the whole perineal area. Maintain close commu-

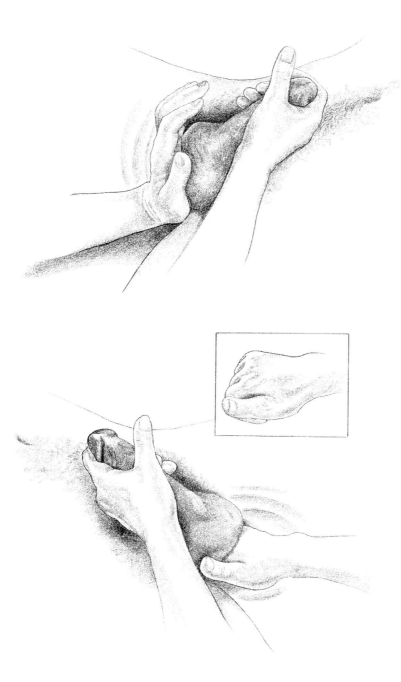

External stimulation of the prostate gland: vibrations applied on the perineum while pleasing the penis

External stimulation of the prostate: vibrating and pressing the fist on the perineum

nication with Shiva, asking him "Is this strong enough? How about if I do it like this?"

Once you know the point and the pressure, you will remember later on how to use a finger or knuckle to prevent Shiva from ejaculating in states of high arousal.

Vibrating with Fist   Make a fist and press with the flat area—between the first and second set of knuckles—against the perineal floor. Shake your fist, vibrating the whole area, sending tremors pulsing into the perineum. With your free hand, massage Shiva's chest and belly.

Encourage Shiva to move his body, push forward with his pelvis, let out sounds, so that the vibration can expand and spread into his pelvis and chest.

Vibrating with Both Hands   Slide your fingers under the base of Shiva's spine (the coccyx area) so that the heel of your hand presses against his perineum. Rest your left hand on Shiva's lower belly. Now you are holding his entire lower pelvis between your two hands. Using your whole body, moving from your hara, shake your hands so that this area vibrates.

STAGE 4: BUILDING SEXUAL AROUSAL

Shakti, now that you have energized the area around Shiva's perineum you can experiment with stimulating the Vajra and prostate together.

First, oil the Vajra and begin stroking the stalk, using your favorite style, bringing this magic wand to a state of erect alertness.

When the Vajra is erect, stimulate the perineum with your free hand, pressing firmly with your fingers or knuckles. Massage the perineum with a circular motion, or rubbing up and down, or giving quick pulsations on the spot.

Begin to massage Shiva's Vajra and the perineum area at the same pace. This steady, blended rhythm can help him build sexual arousal without getting too focused on the sensations in his Vajra.

Here is a good stroke to try: Take the Vajra in your right hand, holding it at the base. With your left hand, make a circle with your thumb and index finger containing the scrotal sack, just under the Vajra so that the whole sack lies in the palm of your hand as you press against the perineum with the flat part of your fingers, between the first and second set of knuckles.

Experiment with this position, stroking the Vajra with your right hand while vibrating the perineum with your left.

Shiva, tell Shakti how it feels—what degree of intensity, pressure, and speed you need.

The philosopher's stone transforms base metal into gold. In the heart of the jewel, love and passion can transform one into pure awareness.

—Tantric Alchemy

Here is an excellent tip: Shiva, in the initial stages, while Shakti is familiarizing herself with external prostate massage, you may want to stimulate your Vajra yourself. You can bring yourself to a sexual peak, expanding your awareness to include the new sensations created by Shakti. This can be very exciting for you and also gives Shakti more freedom to focus on the perineum area.

Shakti, if you find it difficult to caress the perineum while directly facing it, ask Shiva to part his legs wider so that you can sit at right angles to his genital area.

STAGE 5: COMBINED PEAKING

Shakti, bring Shiva to an orgasmic peak with strong, combined stimulation of the Vajra and perineum.

Shiva, really go for your pleasure, breathing strongly, rubbing your perineum against Shakti's hands by pushing down with your pelvis, moving your body, making sounds. Focus on your sexual sensations and seek to heighten them, encouraging Shakti to stimulate you in whatever way brings added excitement.

At the peak, stop, use the code word, cease all stimulation.

Shiva, relax your body, breathe slowly and deeply, focusing on the delightful sensations that are pulsing through your pelvis. Allow these sensations, even if they seem strange and new to you. Give in to them. Feel how the Vajra and prostate are complementing each other in this orgasmic dance.

Repeat this process as many times as you wish.

Bring the session to a close with a Melting Hug.

Shiva, thank Shakti for her willingness to give you new dimensions of pleasure.

Take a short break and then give feedback.

End with a Heart Salutation.

Five Basic Points for Massaging the Perineum

Here are five basic points to remember when stimulating the prostate externally:

1. Begin with vigorous massage around the buttocks.
2. Stimulate the Vajra before approaching the perineum area.
3. Explore various strokes on the perineum.
4. Give rhythmic, combined stimulation to the Vajra and perineum.
5. Practice peaking without ejaculating.

Pointers

BLENDING INTENSE EXCITEMENT WITH RECEPTIVITY

Shiva, the first problem you may encounter when Shakti massages your perineum area is that the more relaxed you become around your anus and prostate the less excitement you may feel in your Vajra.

You can counter this tendency by asking Shakti to continue to stimulate your Vajra while massaging your perineum, but if you do lose your erection there is no need to worry: this is a stage to pass through on the way to greatly enhanced orgasmic pleasure.

The focus of your attention should not be on maintaining an erection, but on exploring and enjoying the new sensations that are being created around your prostate area. Here, Shakti is helping you to open the receptive aspect of your sexuality.

When, with Shakti's help, you have acquired the knack of blending intense sexual excitement with relaxation and receptivity, you will be able to experience ongoing orgasmic pleasure that can last up to ten to twenty minutes. This happens when the area around your prostate and anus is relaxed and sensitized.

SPECIAL HYGIENIC PROCEDURE

We are about to move into the third and final phase of exploring the alchemy of male orgasm, in which Shakti will stimulate Shiva's prostate internally, by gently penetrating into the anal canal with her fingers and massaging the gland directly.

Before doing so, however, there is a special hygienic procedure that I encourage Shiva to practice. Many women are accustomed to using a vaginal douche, but there is a certain taboo about using the same technique for the anal passage, especially among heterosexual men. Such practices may stir uneasy feelings about homosexuality, or the risk of being thought a "sissy" by your partner.

However, I can assure you that this simple and straightforward method of cleaning your rectum will be greatly appreciated by your partner. She will be grateful for your hygienic care, for the knowledge that her role in this exercise is being fully supported by you. Moreover, a cleansing douche, or enema, using lukewarm water, will sensitize the area around your prostate and help you feel more pleasure.

Remember, no matter how shocking or embarrassing it may seem, this gesture of cleaning your rectal passage is really no different from cleaning the basement of your house. You are cleansing and purifying yourself of "emotional garbage"—in the form of tensions and armoring created by withheld anger, early toilet training, etc.—that has been stored in this area of the body since childhood.

In my experience of introducing many couples to this practice I have found that, in addition to enhancing male sexual pleasure, internal massage can help to soothe and reduce hemorrhoids; it also keeps the prostate gland healthy and energized.

EXERCISE: STIMULATING THE PROSTATE INTERNALLY

Purpose and benefits

To provide Shiva with the ultimate, blended orgasmic sensations by internally stimulating his prostate while at the same time stimulating his Vajra. This exercise gives Shiva the Tantric experience of balancing his own male and female energies: strong male energy is being aroused in his Vajra while more receptive, feminine sensations are being generated in his prostate area.

After this experience, Shiva can understand Shakti more fully, for now he knows what it is like to be pleasured through penetration.

Another benefit of this practice is enhanced sensitivity in Shiva's Vajra during contact with Shakti's Yoni in lovemaking.

It also provides the deepest and most powerful sensations of male orgasm that will prove invaluable in the practice of sexual magic.

Shiva, in this exercise you go to the very roots of male creative power, into the area where semen mixes with prostatic fluids, honoring and caring for this part of your earthly temple. In so doing, you will feel the added excitement of discovering an entirely new area of pleasure that has been previously ignored.

Linga and Shakti are shaped to one another, for how else could new life be born? Desire yokes man and woman in one passionate union.

—Kama Sutra

Preparations

- Shakti, for an internal prostate massage it is important that your fingernails be closely trimmed and filed to a smooth roundness, with no hangnails or sharp corners.

- You can purchase latex gloves to cover your fingers, should you wish to use them for the internal stimulation of the prostate. This will also protect the delicate and sensitive internal tissues from any rough spots on your fingers.

- Have tissues or paper towels handy.

⁊ Shiva, to clean your anal canal, purchase a small or "travel" enema bag at any major drugstore. Or ask Shakti to buy it for you. Use two cups of warm water, adding a few drops of a natural dermicide (such as essential oil of lavender) for added cleanliness. When you have finished, take a shower and prepare to be pampered.

⁊ Shakti, it is your job to prepare the Magic Circle. For this delicate exercise, take special care to create a nurturing, protective environment for Shiva.

⁊ Allow ninety minutes for this exercise.

STAGE 1: AROUSING THE VAJRA
Shakti, lead Shiva into the Magic Circle.

Begin with a strong rhythmic dance, jumping up and down, grounding the energy so that you both feel energized and centered.

Shakti, invite Shiva to recline on large pillows and sit close to his sexual organs, as in the previous exercise.

As with the external stimulation of the prostate, it is good to begin by stimulating Shiva's Vajra. This will engorge the area around the prostate with blood, relax any tensions, and increase Shiva's awareness of this invisible gland.

Make sure Shiva becomes thoroughly aroused, bringing him to a peak of sexual excitement by stroking his Vajra. Come close to the point of no return at least once.

It is important that you maintain contact with the Vajra throughout your exploration of the prostate, giving occasional stimulation, as this will help Shiva feel secure in his male sexuality and trust what you are doing.

STAGE 2: KNOCKING ON THE DOOR
Shakti, oil the anus and the cleft between Shiva's buttocks. Begin to slowly massage and caress the external part of the anus. Use plenty of lubricant. This can be a new and exciting sensation for Shiva but it can also be very scary, so don't be in a hurry.

Ask Shiva how it feels.

Shiva, if you are feeling nervous, do the PC Pump and rock your pelvis back and forth, breathing strongly through your mouth, making sounds. This dynamic preparation will help blood flow to the area, bringing fresh energy and vitality, and help dissolve any tensions.

Shakti, when you feel ready, leave your fingers on Shiva's anus, waiting at the door, and ask "Is it okay to move in?"

If Shiva says "yes," press gently on the anal opening with your index finger, using a lot of lubrication.

Shiva, by gently doing the PC Pump, squeezing the muscles around your anus and perineum, you will find that this movement sucks Shakti's index finger inside the anal opening.

STAGE 3: PENETRATING THE ANUS

Shakti, very slowly penetrate into the anus with your middle or index finger. As you do so, you may feel Shiva's sphincter muscle (the muscle surrounding the anal opening) become tense and rigid. If this happens, pause and wait for the area to relax. As the tension passes, wiggle your finger very gently for a few moments, then penetrate a little deeper. Go very slowly and sensitively, allowing the area to relax.

When your finger has penetrated about one inch inside, bend it in a crooked position and begin to rim the anal sphincter from within, pressing all around the anal opening from the inside. Press slowly. After a while, you can also begin to vibrate your finger a little.

Shiva, breathe deeply through your mouth while Shakti's massages the inner rim of your sphincter muscle. If you find many tensions in this area, you may feel you need to spend one or more sessions just relaxing this area. Do not try to push past any discomfort or pain. Be very gentle with yourself. Guide Shakti so that penetration and stimulation happen at a pace and rhythm that is comfortable to you.

STAGE 4: ENCOUNTERING THE PROSTATE

Shakti, you will know that it is okay to penetrate more deeply when you feel Shiva's anus is relaxed and comfortable. Now the muscles are getting used to your touch. Your penetration is welcome.

Keep exploring inside the anus. Ask Shiva "How does this feel?" Stay in close communication with each other.

Move your finger deeper into the anal passage, curving it slightly upward, until you encounter a round, firm body of tissue that is shaped like a chestnut. This is the prostate.

Shiva, you will probably notice a deep, unfamiliar sensation—it can be pleasurable, or it may just feel strange—when Shakti's finger presses against your prostate. When this happens, let her know that she has found the right spot.

Take plenty of time to explore the entire area.

Again, I would like to assure Shiva that there is no need to worry if you lose your erection. It is more important to develop a mutual understanding of the territory.

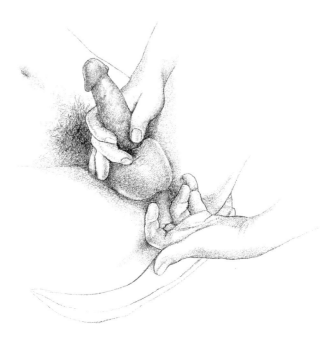

Simultaneous stimulation of
the prostate and the penis

Help Shakti locate the prostate and become familiar with its shape, size, and the degree to which she can press on it. Remember, you are the guide.

STAGE 5: STIMULATING THE PROSTATE

Shiva, in the beginning, the sensations you feel when Shakti presses on your prostate may not necessarily be pleasurable. They may feel strange. Or you may not feel much at all. Like the G-Spot, stimulation of the prostate sometimes takes two or three sessions to become a pleasurable experience.

Shakti, gently begin to stimulate the whole area of the prostate. There are three basic strokes for this type of massage:

1. Make a zigzag motion across the prostate and the surrounding tissue with your finger.

2. Move up and down the prostate with your finger.

3. Keep your finger on the prostate and then lightly shake your hand with a trembling motion, vibrating the prostate.

Shiva, you may want to do the PC Pump and rotate your pelvis slightly as Shakti stimulates your prostate. Or you may wish to be motionless in order to feel the sensations more accurately.

A good way to release tension is to ask Shakti to vibrate her finger on the prostate, while her other hand stimulates your penis. Or you may wish to focus exclusively on the sensations in your prostate, without stimulating the penis.

Breathe strongly through your mouth, sending fresh energy down to your pelvis. Give Shakti clear communication about how you want her to touch your prostate in order to bring pleasure and sensitivity to this area. Encourage Shakti to use strokes that help you feel your prostate the most.

Shakti, be gentle and use plenty of lubricant. In the beginning, prostate massage should continue no longer than five minutes, and always be aware to stop the practice if there are any painful sensations or a sense of soreness.

How to stimulate the prostate through the anus

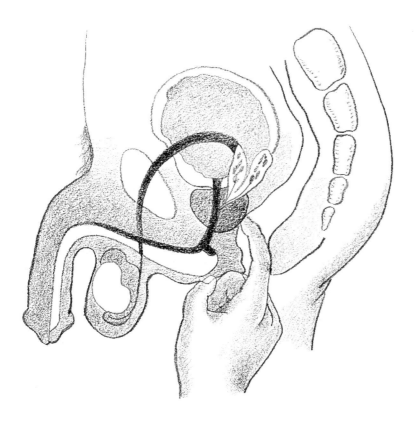

STAGE 6: BLENDED STIMULATION OF VAJRA AND PROSTATE

Shiva, when you begin to feel your prostate and become familiar with the territory, you can ask Shakti to begin to expand the experience by simultaneously massaging your prostate and stimulating your Vajra.

Shakti, experiment with keeping one finger on Shiva's prostate while, with your other hand, you begin to stimulate his Vajra. Use plenty of lubricant on both organs.

Here is a combined stroke that I call "Two Friends Meeting:"

Two Friends Meeting   For the purpose of describing this combined stroke, let us imagine that Shakti's right hand is holding the Vajra, while the index finger of her left hand is inside the anus, pressing gently against Shiva's prostate.

Shakti, first, strongly stimulate the Vajra with your right hand, keeping your left index finger motionless on the prostate. When pleasurable sensations begin to spread through the Vajra—it need not be fully erect—start your blended strokes: push inward into the anal passage with your left index finger, passing over and caressing the prostate gland, while at the same time stroking down the stalk of the Vajra with your right hand.

In this way, it seems as if your left index finger inside Shiva's anal canal is going to join your right hand at the base of his Vajra, like two friends meeting. Then, pull back with your finger while stroking up the stalk of the Vajra, like two friends parting, then push inward again while stroking down the Vajra, like two friends meeting, and so on.

You can vary this basic stroke in a number of ways, such as stroking the stalk of the Vajra while pulsing the prostate, or doing a zigzag motion around it.

Shiva, it is your job to give Shakti clear indications, telling her what works, how you want it, what pressures and rhythms feel good. Be as detailed as you like.

Remember, it may take several sessions before your prostate is sensitized and before Shakti has discovered exactly the right strokes to bring you to orgasm, so don't be in a hurry.

A good tip: As with the previous exercise, it can be exciting for Shiva to stimulate his own Vajra while Shakti applies rhythmic stimulation to his prostate. Experiment with this technique.

STAGE 7: MOVING TO A STREAMING ORGASMIC RESPONSE

Shakti, settle into a steady rhythm of simultaneous massage, using a combination of strokes that gives pleasure to Shiva.

Ask Shiva, "Are you ready to peak?"

If he says "yes," increase stimulation in both areas, holding the Vajra firmly, stroking up and down, while vibrating your finger on the prostate.

Shiva, you may want to use the Three Keys to intensify the sexual sensations that are spreading through your genitals and pelvic area: quicken and deepen your breathing, move your body with strong, pelvic thrusts, make sounds that express how you feel. Alternatively, you may want to deeply relax, becoming even more receptive to the exquisite sensations that Shakti is creating.

Go for your ecstasy, go for your pleasure, go for your excitement, in whatever way seems appropriate, reaching toward new orgasmic heights.

When you come to the moment just before ejaculation, use your code word. Say "Now!"

Two friends meeting. Giving the man a blended orgasm by stimulating the penis and the prostate simultaneously

Shakti, cease all stimulation, but keep your finger pressed firmly against Shiva's prostate, as this will help him not to ejaculate.

Shiva, now is the time to totally relax. Feel the orgasmic excitement that has been generated in your whole pelvic area. Give in to these incredible sensations, let them pulsate through your pelvis, your belly, your thighs, spreading out through your body in ripples of orgasmic pleasure. Breathe slowly and deeply.

When you feel ready, begin again. Ask Shakti to give blended stimulation to your two pleasure points. Continue in this way, moving toward higher and higher peaks of sexual excitement.

With each peak, the delicious ripples of sexual energy in your pelvic area will become more expanded, more intense, more continuous. Soon, you are likely to experience an ongoing stream of subtle orgasmic excitement that continues inside, with little stimulation required. Allow these orgasmic sensations to take you over. Let them flood your whole body. Become lost in them.

Now there is no need to hold back or control anything, because you are fully surrendered. You are not doing anything. It is just happening, as if you were softly floating, being carried on a river of orgasmic pleasure.

This is the streaming reflex that brings orgasmic ecstasy without any need for ejaculation. It can continue for ten to twenty minutes, even longer.

Shiva, if you wish to end the session with full orgasmic ejaculation, ask Shakti to give you this final pleasure. Or, if you prefer, lie quietly until your orgasmic streaming sensations fade of their own accord.

Shakti, after a while, ask Shiva if it is okay to retire, then very slowly withdraw your finger from his anus. Take off your latex glove with a paper towel.

After a while, sit up, give each other a Melting Hug.

Shiva, thank Shakti for her generosity in giving you so much pleasure.

Share what you have experienced together.

End with a Heart Salutation.

I never make love in the morning. It's not good for the voice. And besides, you never know who you're going to meet in the afternoon.

—ENRICO CARUSO

Five Basic Points for Blended Orgasm

Here are five basic points to remember when stimulating the prostate internally:

1. Stimulate the Vajra.

2. Gently enter the anal canal.

3. Explore strokes on the prostate.

4. Develop blended stimulation of prostate and Vajra.

5. Practice peaking without ejaculating until the orgasmic streaming reflex is triggered.

Pointers

PRACTICE MAKES PERFECT

Shiva and Shakti, while you are learning the techniques of blended stimulation you may come across moments when you feel you are not getting anywhere.

At such times you may think "Oh, it's no good," become discouraged, and feel the whole experiment is fizzling out.

Strong breathing through the mouth is a key. This is what keeps your body energized and helps you stay awake and alert, focusing on each step of the exercise, exploring quiet spaces as well as moments of intense excitement.

You can keep things interesting by experimenting with a variety of strokes. Sometimes it will help to focus exclusively on the Vajra, sometimes on the prostate, sometimes on combined strokes, sometimes on other pleasurable areas such as the entrance to the anal canal.

Supportive and positive communication is very important. Remember to communicate about sensations, strokes, feelings, energy. Avoid criticism, complaints, and impositions.

FEELING HEAT IN THE PROSTATE AREA

Shakti, when you penetrate the anus the first few times you may get an impression of an intense, fiery heat penetrating your fingers, coming from the prostate or from some other point inside the anal canal.

Heat is a sign that tension has accumulated at this point and is now releasing through your touch. If you keep your finger on the point where the heat is strongest, vibrating it lightly, you will usually find that the heat disappears after a few minutes and the area is now more relaxed.

POSITION CHANGES

Some men have difficulty lying on their backs for the whole exercise. They feel overwhelmed and even intimidated by the woman remaining continuously "on top of them" in a dominant position.

Shakti, if this happens you need to be willing to change position for a while. For example, Shiva can sit up while you keep your finger on his prostate. In this way he can feel that "I am open to you, but now I also want to show my power, that I am equal to you."

Other men very much enjoy the feeling of being in the receptive position and are quite happy to remain there for the whole exercise.

COMBINING ORGASM WITH SEXUAL MAGIC

Shiva and Shakti, you are to be congratulated on breaking through this major cultural taboo, entering through the anus to explore the world of expanded male orgasm, helping Shiva open to ecstatic sensations that most men never knew existed.

Now that both of you have succeeded in expanding your orgasmic potential you are ready to employ this tremendously vital, alive sexual power in the service of your sexual magic. How you do this is explained in the following chapter.

MAGICAL CONGRESS:
Fusing Sexual Orgasm with Magic

In this chapter, the art of sexual magic comes to a glorious climax, uniting your expanded orgasmic energy with your vision in a powerful Magical Congress. In this, the final step of sexual magic, you move with your love partner into sexual penetration and full intercourse, charging your Magic Symbol with your combined sexual energy and bringing it up through your joined bodies, passing through the seven energy centers. Through this intense alchemical process, the power of your Magic Symbol is refined and transformed, allowing you to connect with the universal, vibrating force fields of the Astral Network and manifest your heartfelt desire in the reality of your life.

The practice of Magical Congress brings together all the previous steps that you have learned in this sexual magic training, with the added spice of sexual penetration and lovemaking. It signifies your graduation as a student of sexual magic, giving you mastery over your life.

To be successful in Magical Congress you and your lover need to have embodied the skills of the preceding chapters: awakening your Inner Magician, healing sexual wounds, releasing your Wild Self, creating a magical vision together, channeling your sexual energy and expanding your orgasmic potential. In particular, you need to have mastered the art of staying on the threshold of sexual climax, peaking your sexual pleasure in expanding waves of orgasmic energy without ejaculatory release.

I would like to pave the way for your entry into Magical Congress by describing a session practiced by Marissa and Nicholas, two sexual magicians whose Magic Symbol of passion, freedom, and abundance was described in chapter 5. Their story provides you with a "sneak preview" of what you can expect later in the chapter as you move into the exercises. In particular, it shows how two love partners can select and synthesize the elements they need for a successful session of sexual magic.

Drop your will into the willingness to surrender.

—GANGIJI

Through studying and practicing the exercises in this book, you have acquired a great many skills and techniques. I have intentionally provided many options and alternatives in order to encourage you to establish a broad base for your practice of sexual magic, a base that is not only helpful and practical but also rich and diverse.

However, you do not need to draw on all your skills and knowledge in each session. Rather, you need to be able to select from an extensive "magical menu" the practices that suit your needs. This is one reason why Marissa and Nick's story is instructive. It shows you how to draw from your wealth of experience the elements you feel are most appropriate.

Another important aspect of the story is that it shows how two people make the transition from an ordinary working day into a night of sexual magic. This transition is a delicate art and a crucial element in their success. The natural tendency of any busy individual is to rush from one occupation to another without making a clear break between the two. As a result, he or she may carry the day's concerns, the stress, pressure, and speed of a busy mind, into the mysterious, esoteric practice of magic, which is sure to have a negative impact on the ritual. Note how Marissa and Nick avoid this pitfall.

In addition, you will see how these two practitioners use a self-pleasuring technique that offers a quick route to expanding orgasm. This process will be taught later in the chapter. Please remember as you read the story that Nick and Marissa have been practicing sexual magic for over a year. Their use of self-pleasuring is effective because they have spent many sessions helping each other to expand their orgasmic capacity through methods already explained in the previous two chapters.

Here, then, is their story:

MARISSA: We met at around five in the evening, a normal couple trying to connect after a day's work. Nick was sweaty, a day-old beard poking out of his chin—"rather unappetizing as a love magician," I thought, contemplating the practice session we'd tentatively arranged for the evening.

As for me, my head felt like the subway at rush hour, crowded with lists of things not yet done. I felt edgy, preoccupied, not really in the mood for sex magic.

What to do? The answer came as quickly as the question: go to nature, the great healer. We went to the beach, to walk along the water's edge, sit on the rocks, feel the fresh wind off the sea and the pleasant warmth of the fading sun, hold hands and relax. After a while, we had unwound enough to talk about practice.

NICK: I knew Marissa was thinking about the evening ahead, so I decided to air the question.

"So, what are we going to do tonight?" I asked.

"Well, I'd like to go with what we agreed to yesterday," she replied, referring to our plan to do Magical Congress.

"Okay, but I don't want to get into a big thing," I countered. "I have a major landscaping project to finish over the next two days."

I'm one of those people who almost always has to say "no" or "maybe" before I can go with "yes"—it's an old habit, a form of self-protection—but really I was looking forward to the session as much as Marissa.

MARISSA: We talked about which Magic Symbol to use. After a little discussion we chose our symbol for love and freedom in abundance, which we always seem to have fun with. It is a beautiful picture of a large silver cup overflowing with water, while above it two birds fly across a yellow sun. On the side of the cup is printed the message *Abundz,* our telegraphic form of the word "abundance," with a heart surrounding it. In the background, fountains of water shoot up over the cup in graceful plumes.

To us, this symbol means wealth in a very broad sense, a feeling of fullness and overflowing that, through the practice of sexual magic, makes us feel as rich as kings and queens.

By the time we got back from the beach we were pretty hungry, so I prepared a light salad with steamed corn and smoked tofu. We chewed slowly, taking our time so that our stomachs wouldn't feel too heavy for the practice ahead.

NICK: I prepared the Magic Circle in the living room while Marissa made supper. I enjoy this, and like to do it on my own: getting the lighting right, making the atmosphere seem mystical and sexy, placing the markers and power objects, putting a mattress in the middle of the circle, and all the rest . . . candles, incense, lubricants, tissues, and a decanter of water nearby.

The general idea is that when you walk in the room, you look around and go "Wow! This feels great, let's make love!"

MARISSA: We took a shower together, washing each other in a playful, sexy way. By this time, all tiredness from the day was forgotten. We were like two kids, off on an adventure. Then we perfumed each other, put on our kimonos, and entered the Magic Circle. It was 9:00 P.M., and we were ready for magic.

NICK: We faced each other across our mattress, greeting each other Japanese-style with a little bow, then walked slowly toward each other. As we met, I gently opened the front of Marissa's kimono and let my hands travel lightly over her neck, breasts, belly. She opened my kimono and we pressed our bodies together in a long Melting Hug.

MARISSA: We sat down. Nick placed the abundance symbol between us and together we invoked the qualities of each element.

"May the two birds fly together, bringing us freedom and flow."

"May the yellow sun bring us vitality and passion."

"May the our cup be filled to overflowing with abundant love."

We sat for a moment in silence, then Nick added, "We dedicate this ritual to attracting all that we need."

I added: "Wealth to live abundantly, an open heart to love generously, an overflow of joy, laughter, and playfulness in our daily lives."

We leaned back on our pillows, our legs spread wide, revealing more of our nakedness to each other, the Magic Symbol lying between us on the floor. I always find this part of the ritual very exciting. There is something delicious about exposing ourselves to each other in this way, as if we were somehow strangers.

NICK: Already, I was getting turned on, feeling excited, sexually aroused. I started self-pleasuring, stroking my Vajra, proudly showing my erection to Marissa while she gently caressed herself. She has this way of looking at me, with half-closed eyes, while she traces her hands over her body, her thighs, and breasts . . . a kind of "I want-you-so-much-but-keep-away" look that can drive me wild.

MARISSA: I was using one hand on my Yoni and the other on my nipples, caressing myself, driving myself deeper into my sensations. After a while, I brought myself to my first sexual peak, coming very close to orgasm. Nick did the same. Then we agreed to start working with our Magic Symbol. This can be a tricky moment for me, because I could just go on pleasuring myself, teasing Nick with my moans and groans, provoking him until finally he jumps on me. But it's also great to delay the passion, the climax, playing with the energy in a different way.

NICK: Looking at the Magic Symbol, I started to take in big draws of air through my mouth, doing the PC pump, imagining that I was sucking the symbol into my genitals. Marissa kept pace with me, matching my breathing. Then I closed my eyes and visualized the symbol inside my genitals.

MARISSA: This session seemed particularly sexual, so it was easy to visualize the symbol moving into my Yoni and mixing with my juices there. Then I slowly started to slide across the futon toward Nick, still pleasuring myself, arching my pelvis toward him, looking at him with big, appealing eyes.

That was all the invitation Nick needed to move toward me. As he approached, I slid my legs over his thighs until his Vajra pressed against the opening of my Yoni. We sat up, wrapping our arms around each other, kissing and licking each other around the face and neck.

I felt incredibly sexual. Again, it would have been easy to forget the ritual and dive into passionate lovemaking, but I kept telling myself there was no hurry.

NICK: As my Vajra pressed up against the lips of Marissa's Yoni, I started to visualize our Magic Symbol floating between our sex organs. I slowly penetrated, deeper and deeper, imagining my Vajra pushing the symbol inside Marissa. When I was fully inside, I had the sensation that the symbol had totally penetrated our first chakras. Then we began to blend the symbol with our sexual juices, connecting our excitement with the image of the overflowing cup, the soaring birds, the sparkling fountains . . .

We began to breathe together, sucking air into our lungs in big draws, and after a while Marissa started to guide the practice, saying "Now the symbol is in our second chakras," and we'd circle the energy with the symbol from the sex center up to the navel, in this way climbing steadily up through our bodies.

We were both totally absorbed in the practice. Sometimes we'd be very turned on, pushing close to the edge of orgasm but never quite into release. Sometimes the energy would reach a plateau and spread out in waves through our bodies. I felt we could have made love all night—there was so much energy available.

MARISSA: We brought our symbol all the way to the seventh chakra. Then I felt a strong urge to go for my full orgasmic release. I asked Nick if he was ready to come and he said "Sure, let's go for it." I was on top of Nick, riding him wildly, searching for the big peak yet still willing the symbol to be there in my imagination while the orgasmic energy was building, building, coming close . . .

As my body shook with spasms of release I allowed the image of the symbol to rise out through my crown chakra and hover in space above my head. Neither of us spoke, but I knew that Nick was doing the same. We held the symbol there for a few minutes, feeling it resonating with the Astral Network, then I said "Let it float away," and the symbol drifted away, becoming smaller and smaller, disappearing into infinite space.

Afterward, we just lay there, totally relaxed, seeing in our minds visions of a successful outcome, seeing us together, happy, nourished, contented, successful, financially satisfied, gratified, grateful for everything.

SELECTING YOUR MAGICAL MENU

Like Nick and Marissa, you can turn Magical Congress into an erotic, orgasmic art form. All you need is a background of practice and a "magical menu" from which to select tools and exercises suited to the way you feel.

Here is an example of what such a menu might look like. Just for fun, I have presented it in the guise of a restaurant menu so that you can develop a good appetite and savor the delicious tastes available in a good meal of sexual magic.

Setting the Table

Create a store of items from which you can choose things to make your Magic Circle beautiful. Select from a range of soft lighting, candles, incense, mood music, special markers, power objects (see chapter 2 for further inspiration). The right ambiance can make a huge difference. Vacuum the carpet. Close or open the curtains. Make your circle a little different each time.

Hors d'oeuvres

Physical activity.
Before sexual magic, choose some form of activity that will help you make a distinct break from daily tasks. Physical exercise and deep breathing are good. Go for a walk, dance wildly, jog, swim, chop wood, mow the lawn, sit in a hot tub, or take a hot shower that ends with a blast of cold water to clean away the dust of the day.

Connecting through the heart.
Often, it's important to have a little talk, to share anything that might otherwise stand in the way of good practice. For example, one partner may

need space to say "God, I've had a tough time at the office today, and I just want someone to tell me I'm terrific," while the other may confide, "I've been so focused on other things that I feel out of touch with you. Let's spend a few minutes lying quietly in each other's arms, not doing anything."

Soup du jour

Clarifying your intent.

Express your intent, your purpose in coming together.
Define your goals.
Choose the symbol with which you are going to work.
Select the tools, the exercises, that you will use to get there.
Be clear how long the session will last.

Starters

INVOCATION When you meet in your circle as magicians, create a simple ceremony, a moment of ritual greeting, that helps you to shift your consciousness from the level of your personality to your divine presence. For example, make a Heart Salutation to each other, and to each of the four directions, and say:

"We, _____ (your names) dedicate this practice of sexual magic to the goal of _____ (your shared vision)."

MEDITATION When contemplating the symbol you have chosen for sexual magic, you may need to select and practice one or more of the visualization exercises described in chapter 5 to help you imprint the symbol clearly in your mind. Remember, these exercises are always available to make magic more effective.

SEXUAL FOREPLAY Every successful union of two lovers in Magical Congress requires a "warm-up" period, or foreplay. Choose something unusual that gives you erotic pleasure. Give each other a short massage, do a striptease for each other, caress each other. Be playful, sensual, exciting.

Main Course

AROUSAL OF ORGASMIC ENERGY   Awaken your sexual energy and start to expand your orgasmic power. There are two basic options: either take turns to stimulate each other, or self-pleasure in front of each other.

CHANNELING ORGASMIC ENERGY   Bring your sexual energy and your Magic Symbol up through your body's energy centers, noticing the different qualities and experiences available at each chakra.

MAGICAL CONGRESS   Join together in sexual union. Take your Magic Symbol through your bodies as you make love and release it into the Astral Network at the moment of orgasm. If you are well prepared and have chosen correctly from your "magical menu" this will be a divine experience, a powerful invocation for sexual magic to manifest itself in your life.

Dessert

AFTERGLOW À LA MODE   Enjoy the sense of achievement and the deep relaxation that follows sexual magic, letting go, becoming receptive to whatever the universe showers on you. Bathe in the afterglow of your lovemaking and your magic.

MAKING YOUR OWN MENU

It is very helpful to create your own magical menu. Doing so will give you a readily available checklist that you can use whenever you are scheduling a session of sexual magic.

You will have your options available at a glance: what kinds of activities you may want to enjoy before the session, what props you can use to help create a magical atmosphere, what exercises are most attractive, and so on.

Here is an example of what such a menu might look like, when taken from a practitioner's notebook:

Sexual magic session scheduled for July 5, evening

Judy says she'll create the space before I arrive (surprise changes in decor anticipated!).

7:00—Meet, shower, change

7:30—Lie in hot tub, or maybe walk in woods

8:15—Talk about vision: probably use relationship symbol

8:30—Caressing and teasing session, with feathers; maybe erotic dance as well

9:15—Self-pleasuring session

9:35—Magical Congress

10:25—Celebration with chocolates and cognac!

Remember, keep your menu flexible enough to include any spontaneous changes in mood that may arise when the time comes to begin your practice session.

Reviewing the Basic Steps

Sexual magic is most enjoyable and effective when it becomes an art form—that is, when you are so familiar with the method that you can effortlessly direct your Magic Symbol up through your body on waves of orgasmic energy, passing through the seven chakras until, at the moment of sexual climax, your vision is released into the universe.

Mastery of this magical art depends to a large extent on being able to hold a clear image of your Magic Symbol and visualize its movement up through your Inner Flute, beginning at the sex center and ending at the Astral Network. This process needs to become so familiar that you can do it without tension, without stopping to think about what comes next. Such familiarity is gained through regular, weekly practice.

To review the basic steps that should be mastered:

In chapter 5, you learned how to create and hold a magic vision in the form of a symbol.

In chapter 6, you discovered how to channel your sexual energy, bringing your Magic Symbol up through your Inner Flute with a combination of breathing, movement, and visualization. You also discovered how to connect with the Astral Network, the mysterious, pulsating force field that links all human beings with the cosmos.

In chapters 7 and 8, you learned how to expand your orgasmic potential by stimulating each other's sexual organs.

Now you are invited to meet the next challenge: moving your Magic Symbol up through your body in combination with your greatly expanded orgasmic power and imprinting it on the Astral Network.

This blending of orgasmic energy with a Magic Symbol is a fascinating and exciting alchemy. You will experience how the symbol and the sexual energy become a single, living, dynamic force that changes or mutates as it passes through each of your seven energy centers. The whole quality of your sensations—whatever shapes, colors, textures, sounds, moods, or feelings you may be experiencing—seems to change and change again, as if the symbol is bringing new qualities to you, infusing you with love, freedom, fulfillment, understanding, ecstasy.

It is this alchemical transformation that gives your Magic Symbol tremendous force, making it more refined, lighter, more brilliant and clear so that in the final moment of release it can melt and merge with the Astral Network, sending your vision forth into the universe, rushing outward along millions of unseen currents of subtle energy. Such a dynamic call for manifestation is bound to be answered.

Now you are ready to explore the various ways of moving your Magic Symbol in this orgasmic way.

Man has no choice but to love. For when he does not, he finds his alternative lies in loneliness, destruction, and despair.

—An Existential Treatise

EXERCISE: CHANNELING ORGASMIC ENERGY WITH YOUR MAGIC SYMBOL

Purpose and Benefits

In this exercise, you take turns receiving sexual stimulation, generating orgasmic energy that you blend with your Magic Symbol and then channel up your Inner Flute through the seven energy centers to the Astral Network.

The practice begins by imprinting the image of the Magic Symbol in your body. This is important, because once you start to receive sexual stimulation it may become so pleasurable that you have difficulty focusing on the image of your Magic Symbol.

By imprinting the symbol on your mind, by saying "yes" to the symbol before erotic stimulation begins, you will ensure that it remains in your psyche, even during those moments when you cannot focus on it.

As a further aid to alchemy, you will be using the seven colors associated with your body's energy centers: red, orange, yellow, green, blue, purple, and white.

Preparations

- ⌖ Create your Magic Circle.

- ⌖ Choose an appropriate Magic Symbol.

- ⌖ Both partners, prepare yourselves with a refreshing shower.

- ⌖ Allow forty-five minutes for each partner to experience this exercise.

Practice

STAGE 1: MAKING YOUR INVOCATION
Shakti and Shiva, enter your Magic Circle and greet each other with a Heart Salutation.

Enjoy a Melting Hug.

Sit on cushions facing each other.

Place your Magic Symbol between you.

Place your left hand on your heart chakra, in the middle of your chest, and touch the symbol with the fingertips of your right hand. Together, spend a few moments looking at your Magic Symbol.

Raise your eyes to look softly at each other, acknowledging your love and appreciation for each other as fellow explorers.

Make an invocation for a successful session. You may want to say something like: "We take this symbol into our hearts. May this symbol bring abundance of love and wealth into our lives, joy and passion into our hearts. May this symbol remind us of the way we flow and move together, respecting each other's freedom within our relationship."

STAGE 2: IMPRINTING THE SYMBOL IN YOUR BODY
Decide which of you will be the first to receive sexual stimulation. I will describe the practice as if Shiva is going to stimulate Shakti.

Shiva, help Shakti to recline against some cushions in a half-lying

Integrating the Magic Symbol into yourself before sexual magic practice.

position. Gently spread her legs apart and sit between them, or, if you pre-fer, sit to one side in a way that gives you full access to her body, especially her sexual organ (check the positions in chapter 7).

Begin to massage Shakti's body from her sex center to her chest and throat. Use light, sweeping movements of your hands, brushing from her sex to her throat in one movement and then sweeping the energy down her arms and out of her hands.

Shakti, inhale deeply as Shiva sweeps the energy up your body, then exhale as he sweeps it down your arms.

Breathe in unison with Shakti.

Shiva, as you give this massage, whisper softly in her ear, reminding her of the various aspects of the Magic Symbol: what it looks like, what it means, what vision it represents . . .

Give your voice a magical, mysterious, seductive quality. Remember, most women love to have stories and secrets whispered in their ears, so enjoy this moment of confidential, intimate communication. Say "Yes! You can receive more, much more, so let the symbol penetrate every cell of your body . . ."

STAGE 3: CHARGING THE MAGIC SYMBOL
Shiva, begin to touch Shakti's body in a more sexual and erotic way, lightly caressing her nipples, her lips, her neck, turning her on.

Shakti, this is the moment to create a strong bond between your sexual pleasure and your Magic Symbol. Feel these caresses linking themselves to the symbol, becoming part of its magic.

Make the symbol part of everything that happens to you: it is the softness of Shiva's touch, it is his voice whispering in your ear, it is the love sounds you are making, it is the delicious shivers of energy that run up and down your body, the smell of incense, the music playing softly in the background . . . let it all be part of the magic represented by your symbol.

Shiva, you can help by reminding Shakti of the various aspects of your symbol. For example: "Let the birds fly free in your belly, let the sun radiate passion in your heart . . ."

STAGE 4: MERGING YOUR SYMBOL WITH YOUR SEXUALITY
Shiva, begin to stimulate Shakti's clitoris, her cleo, finding the stroke that she likes best and then developing rhythmic stimulation to awaken and arouse her sexual energy.

Shakti, visualize your Magic Symbol floating in your first chakra, your sex center. See the dark red energy of your sexuality spreading through your pelvis, flooding over your symbol.

Alternate your attention between your mounting pleasure and your Magic Symbol, focusing first on one, then the other. This is a good way to maintain strong awareness of both.

Shiva, bring Shakti to a plateau of high excitement, helping her to peak two or three times, coming close to the point of no return without orgasmic release.

Shakti, link these wonderful orgasmic feelings in your sex center with your Magic Symbol. Take all your orgasmic excitement and visualize that you are pouring it onto your symbol, almost as if you are ejaculating your sexual energy and shooting it over the symbol. But do not come to a full climax.

STAGE 5: BLENDED STIMULATION WITH THE MAGIC SYMBOL

Shiva, when you feel Shakti is ready, ask "Can I visit you inside?" If she says yes, gently penetrate her Yoni with your fingers, searching for her G-Spot while continuing to stimulate her cleo gently with your other hand.

Shakti, if you find yourself losing track of your Magic Symbol, remember to alternate your focus between your sexual sensations and the image of your Symbol.

Shiva, when you have connected with Shakti's G-Spot, begin blended stimulation of her G-Spot and cleo together, bringing her toward more sexual peaks.

Shakti, breathe deeply through your mouth, do the PC Pump, feel the symbol expanding and growing in your pelvis. Pour waves of dark red energy over the symbol, flooding it with orgasmic energy.

Giving sexual stimulation to your partner while he visualizes the Magic Symbol entering through his sex and passing through his Inner Flute and his chakras

STAGE 6: CHANNELING THE SYMBOL

Shakti, begin to move your Magic Symbol up through your Inner Flute. Inhale deeply, drawing your orgasmic energy with your symbol up from the first to the second chakra, located in your belly.

Exhale, letting your energy and symbol fall back to your first chakra. As you exhale, push out with your pelvis, connecting strongly with sexual sensations in your genitals.

Inhale, again drawing your orgasmic energy with your symbol up to your second chakra. As you do so, see the color orange spreading out through your belly, warming this area, bringing it alive.

Make a circle with the energy. Visualize the energy rising up your spine, then flowing forward through your belly and down to your sex center once more. Make circles with your arms and hands to emphasize the circular flow of your energy.

Keep Shiva informed of your progress, so that he feels included. Tell him, "Beloved, I am circling the symbol between my first and second chakras."

Greet the eager fingers of your lover with a slight push of your pelvis, reconnecting with your sex center as you exhale.

When you are ready, circle your orgasmic energy with your Magic Symbol from your first chakra to your third chakra, located in your solar plexus. Tell Shiva, "Now I am moving my symbol to the third chakra." As you do so, visualize the color yellow spreading through this part of your body.

Proceed in this way up through your energy centers, making bigger and bigger circles, from the first to the fourth, fifth, sixth, and seventh chakras. Notice the different sensations, qualities, feelings, moods, ecstasies that can arise at each of your seven energy centers.

See the color of the orgasmic energy change from yellow in the third chakra to green in the fourth, blue in the fifth, purple in the sixth and white in the seventh.

STAGE 7: CONNECTING WITH THE ASTRAL NETWORK

Shakti, when you are circling your orgasmic energy with your Magic Symbol from your sex center to your seventh chakra, you are ready to take the final step: connecting with the Astral Network, releasing your symbol into the vibrating force-fields of the universe so that they can respond to your desires, your visions.

This can be a magical experience in itself, because you are going to blend your Magic Symbol with a full orgasmic climax.

Ask Shiva to maintain a rhythmic, blended stimulation of your cleo and G-Spot that will bring you to full orgasm. Let him know that you are close to coming. Say "Yes, keep going, it's just right . . ."

Meanwhile, continue to circulate your Magic Symbol between your sex chakra and your crown chakra.

As you start to climax, as your body begins to pulsate with orgasmic release, shoot your Magic Symbol out of the top of your head with all your pleasurable, sexual, orgasmic energy.

See your Magic Symbol floating above your crown chakra, bathed in all those wonderful feelings that are now streaming through your body. Your symbol has arrived at the Astral Network flooded with your orgasmic power.

As your orgasm subsides, gently release your symbol into the universe. Perhaps you see it softly and silently dissolving. Or perhaps it is like a cloud, showering white rain in all directions until it is empty and disappears.

Breathing normally, feel that some of this energy is falling like white rain on your head, then trickling down through your body until it reaches your sex center, bringing you back to your roots.

Relax. Enjoy the afterglow. Touch Shiva's hands to signal that he can stop stimulating you. Allow yourself to bask in the energy that has been released, feeling that your Magic Symbol is sending back blessings and protection to you from the mysterious, invisible place where it has gone.

Enjoy a Melting Hug.

Be sure to thank Shiva for his generous efforts in helping you to reach this state of orgasmic bliss.

Share your experiences.

Take a short break and then change roles.

Close the session with a Heart Salutation.

Love should be a tree whose roots are deep in the earth, but whose branches extend into heaven.

—BERTRAND RUSSELL
Marriage and Morals

SHIVA'S TURN: CHANNELING ORGASMIC ENERGY

The process for Shiva is very similar.

Shiva, like Shakti, it is important that you receive a light massage prior to any sexual stimulation from your partner. This will give you time to imprint the Magic Symbol on your psyche and make it easier for you to hold the vision when Shakti begins to stimulate your Vajra, your penis, directly.

You can also alternate your attention between your sexual sensations and your Magic Symbol, enjoying the intense pleasure of arousal without losing track of your visualization.

EJACULATING MALE ENERGY

Here is an important hint that can help men combine their sex energy with their symbol: Shiva, during initial sexual arousal you will probably feel that your energy is flowing strongly toward the tip of your Vajra. This is natural. The sensation of your partner's hand stroking your penis from base to tip draws your attention toward this exquisite pleasure point in a rising curve of sexual excitement that would normally end in ejaculation.

But instead of throwing out your energy in a physical ejaculation, stay below the peak and imagine that your sexual energy is shooting out of the end of your Vajra and covering your Magic Symbol. In effect, you are ejaculating your energy without ejaculating physically, thereby charging your symbol with this powerful force.

BLENDED STIMULATION FOR SHIVA

As Shakti begins dual stimulation of your Vajra and prostate area, use pelvic movement, strong breathing, and your voice to maximize your sensations.

Allow these orgasmic sensations to become internalized.

Let your Magic Symbol and your energy become one, and begin to move them through your body.

After moving your Magic Symbol with your orgasmic energy through your seven chakras, you, too, can end with full orgasmic release as you connect with the Astral Network.

Pointers

CONSERVING MALE POWER FOR FINAL EJACULATION

While Shakti can enjoy several orgasms on the way to her final, orgasmic connection with the Astral Network, Shiva needs to avoid ejaculation until the last step.

It is just a woman's biological luck that she can experience several orgasms in succession without losing her sexual energy, whereas a man needs to conserve his sexual power for the *grand finale.*

SEXUAL HEALING THROUGH CHANNELING ORGASM

The practice of channeling orgasmic energy with a Magic Symbol can be tremendously beneficial for healing a variety of sexual problems, such as the inability to achieve orgasm, boredom with routine sex, or a sense of discomfort in the genital area.

You may recall the story of George, mentioned in chapter 3, who was having difficulties in being total in his lovemaking. After his dream of the

It isn't the action of higher forces, but rather a descent into the body, into cellular awareness, where the real changes will take place in matter, making an entirely new creation.

—The Mother
Aurobindo Ashram
Pondicherry, India

criminal and the policeman, I encouraged him to create a magical vision that permitted a much wider range of sexual responses, including wild, primal behavior during lovemaking.

He agreed and, as his symbol, chose a red triangle surrounded by flames, representing the sex energy in his first chakra and his desire to expand it.

He received an expanded orgasm session from his love partner, Lynne, during which he blended his sexual energy with his Magic Symbol and channeled them up through his body without ejaculating. This gave him a powerful energy charge that he was able to bring into a lovemaking session that immediately followed.

Riding this new energy, George became a wild man, growling, thrusting, rolling over and over with his partner, letting go of his usual restraint but continuing to visualize the red triangle burning inside him, the flames growing bigger and stronger. In his final climax, his ejaculation was very intense, giving him the sharpest sensations of orgasmic pleasure that he had ever known.

EXERCISE: SEXUAL SELF-EMPOWERMENT WITH A SYMBOL

Purpose and Benefits

This exercise offers a simple and effective way to prepare for Magical Congress, the ultimate practice of sexual magic. It is the art of awakening your own orgasmic energy by sexually pleasuring yourself.

Self-pleasuring allows two people to become sexually aroused simultaneously, as demonstrated in the story of Nick and Marissa in the beginning of this chapter. It offers a shorter route to high arousal than taking turns to stimulate each other. It is also an effective way of practicing sexual magic when you do not have a partner.

However, the practice of sexually pleasuring yourself in preparation for Magical Congress is effective only when you and your partner have spent several sessions expanding your orgasmic capacity through giving sexual stimulation to each other.

These longer sessions are essential for sensitizing your sexual organs, making each pang of pleasure sharper, sweeter, more intense, giving you the heights and depths of sexual experience that you need for great magic.

They are also needed for developing communication skills and teaching each other what turns you on. In this state of heightened sensitivity, you can move into self-pleasuring and create intense, fulfilling orgasmic sensations in a relatively short time, no more than ten to fifteen minutes.

In the following practice, you learn to combine self-stimulation with a magical vision, bringing your chosen symbol from your sex center up through your chakras with your sexual energy. It is best to practice this exercise at the same time as your love partner, watching each other self-pleasure.

Make God a reality and he will make you a truth.

—RABINDRANATH TAGORE

Preparations

- ⚘ Create your Magic Circle. Arrange cushions in your circle in such a way that you and your partner can recline on them while facing each other.

- ⚘ Place your Magic Symbol where you can both easily see it.

- ⚘ Bring a variety of sexual lubricants and tissues.

- ⚘ Both partners should take a refreshing shower and wear something soft, silky, and sensual that parts easily in front.

- ⚘ Allow thirty minutes for this exercise.

Practice

STAGE 1: TURNING YOURSELF ON

Enter your Magic Circle.

Greet each other with a Heart Salutation and a long Melting Hug.

Sit opposite each other. Recline on your cushions, facing each other. Spread your legs so that your feet are touching, or overlapping, those of your partner. Be sure that you are comfortable.

Take a few deep, relaxing breaths.

Look into each other's eyes, feeling the strong heart connection between you.

When you feel ready, undo your robe or gown, revealing the front part of your body.

Begin to caress your body, while gazing at your partner. Be sensual, erotic. Show your partner how you like to move, the places you like to touch, the way you like to give yourself pleasure.

Be creative. Moisten a finger and slowly slide it across your lips, make undulating movements with your pelvis, caress the inside of your thighs, without directly touching your sexual organ.

Don't be in a hurry. The more you turn yourself on, the more you can arouse your partner. Just for fun, make it a challenge to see if you can drive your partner wild with desire.

STAGE 2: CLIMBING TO THE PEAK

Touch your genitals, holding them in your hands for a moment, feeling their warmth. Feel that you are listening to this part of your body. How does it feel? What is it saying to you?

Begin to caress your genitals slowly. Stroke yourself, tease yourself, oil yourself with lots of your favorite lubricant. Slide your hands around your Yoni, your Vajra, making sure that your partner can see what you are doing.

Make sounds. Be sexy. Find those special ways to send tingles of sexual excitement running through your sex, pelvis, and thighs. Feel the pleasure.

You may close your eyes from time to time, if this enhances your pleasure, but be sure to open them again and look at your partner. It is important to maintain eye contact throughout the first part of this exercise.

Now you can start to go wild. Stroke your Vajra or Yoni in a strong, rhythmic way, arousing your sexual energy, climbing toward your first orgasmic peak. Arch your back, moan, suck the air into your lungs, showing your partner how aroused you are, how excited you are, how full of sexual pleasure.

Come to the point just before orgasmic release and then let stimulation cease, or slow down. Hold yourself at the peak, poised like a bird on the wing that is riding a high, invisible air current, relaxed, motionless, totally alert.

Breathe deeply, allowing the sexual sensations to expand and spread through your body. Close your eyes, as you feel a deep connection with your sexual organ.

If you are the first one to climax, wait for your partner as he or she also climbs to the peak. Remember, no ejaculation. There's more to come!

STAGE 3: CIRCLING YOUR MAGIC SYMBOL

Now you can begin to work together with your Magic Symbol. Place your symbol between you on the floor, just in front of your genitals. Make sure you can both see it, or perhaps you would like to use two copies of the same symbol, one for each of you.

Gaze at your Magic Symbol, caressing your sex, feeling the pleasure you are giving to yourself. Begin to arouse your sexual energy once more, starting slowly then giving yourself stronger, faster stimulation to bring yourself toward the peak.

Self-pleasuring while you visualize the Magic Symbol passing through your chakras

Just before reaching the point of no return, stop, squeeze your PC muscle, inhale deeply through your mouth, imagining as you do so that you are sucking your Magic Symbol into your sex center, your first chakra. Exhale, holding a vision of your symbol inside your sex center. Take several deep breaths, sucking the symbol into your first chakra until you feel comfortable with the vision of your symbol inside your sex center.

Close your eyes. Continuing to pleasure yourself, see your Magic Symbol inside your sex center. Feel the orgasmic pleasure and the symbol becoming one inside your first chakra.

Remember to use the chakra colors as an aid to alchemy. Visualize your aroused sexual energy as a dark red color that spreads through your sex and pelvis. See your Magic Symbol being soaked in red.

Now your challenge is to maintain a high state of sexual arousal without orgasmic release while visualizing your Magic Symbol.

Inhale, squeeze your PC muscle, bringing your symbol with your sex energy up to your second chakra, in your lower belly. Here, the energy turns into the color orange.

Exhale, letting the energy and your symbol fall back to your sex center. Repeat this several times until you can easily visualize or feel your symbol circling between your first and second chakras. Let the symbol rise up your spine, then flow forward through your abdomen and down into your sex again.

Inhale, bringing your orgasmic energy and Magic Symbol up to your third chakra. If it helps, place one hand on your solar plexus, while continuing to pleasure yourself with the other. Here, the energy transforms into the color yellow.

Exhale, letting the symbol fall back to your sex center. Circle your symbol between your first and third chakras.

Stay connected with your sexual pleasure. Stimulate yourself rhythmically and strongly. Use plenty of lubricant. Enjoy this feeling of giving yourself all the pleasure you love to feel. Be an artist, rising and flowing along the curves of your sexual delight, receiving encouragement from the presence of your partner.

STAGE 4: CONNECTING WITH THE ASTRAL NETWORK

Continue in this way, bringing your energy up your Inner Flute, circling your symbol through your chakras, bringing it higher and higher. When

When two people are at one in their inmost hearts, they shatter even the strength of iron or bronze, and when two people understand each other in their inmost hearts, their words are sweet and strong like the fragrance of orchids.

—I Ching

you reach the seventh chakra you can prepare for the big explosion, for full orgasmic release.

Bring yourself to full orgasm. At the moment of sexual release, send your Magic Symbol with your orgasmic energy out through the top of your head, connecting with the Astral Network.

Imagine your symbol floating above your head, while feeling the ecstasy of your orgasm pulsing through you, bathing you in pleasure.

Then, as your orgasmic sensations begin to fade, visualize your Magic Symbol moving away from your head, getting smaller and smaller until it becomes a tiny point in the distance, then disappears.

Begin to ground your energy. Breathing slowly and deeply, see your energy pouring down as rain, falling gently through your head, your neck, chest, belly . . . When it reaches your sex center, exhale strongly, pushing the energy down into your sex. Visualize the energy moving down from your sex center, through your legs and feet into the ground, the earth.

Lie quietly for a few minutes, relaxing and enjoying the afterglow of your climax.

Sit up and share a Melting Hug.

Share your experiences and close with a Heart Salutation.

HEALING THROUGH SELF-PLEASURING

Self-pleasuring alone or with a partner can be an immensely healing experience. For example, Denise, a twenty-nine-year-old novice in the art of sexual magic, was able to develop a new and healthier relationship with her Yoni when she practiced self-pleasuring combined with a magical vision.

Denise had a history of recurring sexual infections such as yeast invasions and unpleasant discharges. She was aware that in previous years she had abused her Yoni by indulging in indiscriminate sex with almost any man she dated.

Even though her habits changed dramatically and she was now enjoying nourishing lovemaking with a steady partner, Denise continued to suffer from minor sexually related infections. She decided to devote a magical vision to healing her Yoni, relating with her sexual organ in a new and more sensitive way.

She began by sitting in front of a mirror, looking at her Yoni, connecting with this shy, wounded part of her body and giving it a voice, as described in chapter 3. Her Yoni gave her a clear message that it was time to devote more care, attention, and love to this part of her body.

Deciding to use sexual magic as a healing force, Denise drew a Magic Symbol showing her Yoni as a beautiful flower, which she called "Passion Flower."

Denise continued:

> I wanted to wrap the flower in my heart, so in the symbol I drew a heart around my Yoni-flower. Then I put wings on the heart so that my Yoni could fly freely, without pain or difficulty.
>
> I began self-pleasuring with a strong, fiery breath and moved the symbol into my body at the first chakra. Each time I moved the symbol up to a new chakra it became more and more grand. By the time it reached my heart it had expanded and become very large so that I could see myself entering inside the symbol.
>
> It was three-dimensional and had a warmth and softness that I could feel. What this represented to me was my sexuality being fed by my heart with all the love and warmth it had been denied for so long. I could feel my heart feeding it, nurturing this Yoni-flower of mine.
>
> The symbol became an entire room, much bigger than me, and I was entering into it, moving through it, becoming one with it, feeling the dimensions, the texture, the warmth and reality of my blossoming Yoni-flower.
>
> Above the fourth chakra, everything became very light. When I peaked in the self-pleasuring, bringing the symbol all the way up to the top of my head, I was soaring on the wings of my Yoni and it was a very, very beautiful feeling. It still is, because each time I work with the symbol it becomes more and more vivid, more of a reality.
>
> I feel that this is going to have a very beneficial effect on my health, on the health of my Yoni in particular, because she already feels better, more loved, more included, more respected by me.

SELF-PLEASURING AND MAGICAL CONGRESS

When two partners self-pleasure together it is easy to move from a state of high orgasmic arousal into lovemaking with sexual penetration.

This is what Marissa and Nick did at the beginning of this chapter in their practice of Magical Congress. As Marissa explained, she was able to slide across the bed, still pleasuring herself, and sexually connect with Nick without breaking the stream of their orgasmic sensations. This continuous flow of sexual stimulation is important when preparing for Magical Congress.

However, as I describe the steps of Magical Congress in the following practice, you will see that I offer an alternative method of generating sexual arousal. This is a form of stimulating each other, done in such a way that lovemaking with penetration can immediately follow.

As a sexual magician, you are invited to explore all the options and select those practices that suit your style of creating orgasmic energy. Now, you are ready to begin the ultimate experience of sexual magic.

EXERCISE: MAGICAL CONGRESS, CLASSICAL STYLE

Purpose and Benefits

This exercise will bring together all the elements of sexual magic in a single, powerful ritual that can transform your life. For the first time, you are going to work with your Magic Symbol while embraced in deep sexual union. This alchemical fusion of your two sexual energies will greatly empower your symbol, invoking the outcome of your vision.

Magical Congress has two basic styles: classical and spontaneous. The classical style, which I am about to describe, is a type of Tantric yoga in the ancient tradition of Tibetan and Indian methods for awakening sexual energy and channeling it for higher purposes. It unfolds in a series of graceful and precisely orchestrated steps. Done correctly, it is an extremely powerful esoteric ritual that can produce spectacular results.

I will describe the spontaneous style later in the chapter.

Love is not what makes the world go 'round. Love is what makes the trip worthwhile.

—FRANKLIN JONES

Preparations

- Magical Congress is the culmination of your study of sexual magic, so it deserves a royal preparation. Take time to create a truly magical atmosphere in the room that you have chosen for your ritual. Use lighting, incense, and music to conjure up a world where fantasy and desire can become reality.

- Spend time preparing yourself, so that you feel clean, shining, and beautiful. Wear special clothing, decorated with feathers, jewels, or similar adornments. The more magical the preparations, the greater the impact of the ritual itself.

- Create your Magic Circle.

- Bring the Magic Symbol that you have chosen to work with.

- Prepare your favorite lubricants.

- Have a jug of water handy.

 ❧ Decide who is going to lead the alchemy section of the exercise, to guide the movement of your Magic Symbol up through your chakras (for the purpose of this description, I will choose Shiva as the leader).

 ❧ Allow at least sixty to ninety minutes for this exercise (personally, I like to set aside a whole Sunday afternoon and evening for it).

Practice

STAGE 1: MAKING THE INVOCATION

Come together in your Magic Circle.

Greet each other with a Heart Salutation and a long Melting Hug.

Place your Magic Symbol on the floor between you.

Together, make a grand and heartfelt invocation. Face each other across your symbol, raise your arms to the sky and declare, "We dedicate this Magical Congress to our vision of orgasmic joy . . ." adding the particulars of the vision that you have created.

After the invocation, light a candle on your altar and place your Magic Symbol before it, signifying that the ceremony has begun.

Slowly approach each other. Sensuously remove each other's robes, lightly caressing each other's bodies as they are exposed. Be playful, naughty, seductive. This ritual is potent and intense, but it does not need to be serious.

STAGE 2: DANCE OF WILDNESS

Put on dance music, preferably of a type that begins fairly slowly and then gradually gets faster, louder, and wilder.

Begin by stretching your body as you dance, flexing your limbs, your pelvis, your chest, back, neck, and head. Breathe deeply and strongly through your mouth, letting fresh air, fresh energy reach to every cell of your body.

Face your partner and dance together, letting your movements mirror each other's for a few moments. Perhaps you want to touch hands as you move in harmony, sometimes leading, sometimes following.

Now, as you dance, tune in to the image of some wild animal, as you did in chapter 4. This is an important key to successful magic. In my experience, the delicate moment when two love partners prepare to move deeply into ritual is also a time when old resentments, fears, angers, or frustrations can easily arise in one or both of them.

These negative feelings need not be taken too seriously. They are just part of the process, a certain aspect of your energy. As you will see, the animal in you can create something very beautiful out of them.

Let your animal feelings come out of hiding and grow in you. Become one with them and express them to your partner.

Move like an animal, make sounds like an animal, think and feel like an animal. Let a growling, cathartic, primal energy awaken in your belly, shaking and streaming through your hara in a wonderfully releasing and healing flood.

Keep a sense of theatrical playfulness. Don't be physically aggressive with each other. Be sure not to hurt each other in any way. Let the process unfold innocently, as children play at being animals. Improvise, as if you are participating in an actors' workshop.

Remember, all passionate loving contains a certain amount of aggression, and if this is expressed in a playful manner then your passion for each other will soon flow in a more loving way that will be suitable for Magical Congress.

STAGE 3: MOVING INTO A LOVING MOOD

After a few minutes, allow your aggressive animal energy to move into a softer, gentler, more loving mood, a more seductive type of energy.

If your partner has a hard time calming down, use your animal charms to soothe and seduce. Through tender sounds, help your partner transform any remaining aggressive energy into a more romantic mood.

Come close to each other and melt into an embrace. Close your eyes and hold each other, feeling the wild, delicious energy that has been released in your bodies.

STAGE 4: IMPRINTING YOUR MAGIC SYMBOL

Sit on cushions in your Magic Circle, facing each other. Place your Magic Symbol between you.

Close your eyes and breathe slowly and deeply, becoming more calm, centered, and relaxed. Breathe slowly and deeply.

When you feel ready, open your eyes and let your gaze rest softly on the Magic Symbol lying on the floor between you. Now is the time to remember that you and your partner share a common purpose, a common goal.

You have created this vision together. You have trained together in sexual magic, readying yourselves for this moment. Now it is your mutual

Your soul is plunged into the fire of divine love, like iron loses its blackness and then it grows white like heat, and becomes like the fire itself, and lastly it grows liquid, so too the souls of the lovers are made incandescent with divine love.

—Tantric Alchemy

intent to send this powerful vision into the universe to fulfill your heartfelt desires.

Let your gaze shift from your symbol to your partner. Look softly into each other's eyes, appreciating the trust and love that you feel between you, as you move into this great experiment. This is the crowning of your explorations. You have been adepts, initiates. Now you are both magicians, walking this esoteric path to creative manifestation.

STAGE 5: FOREPLAY FOR MAGICAL CONGRESS
Now you are ready for orgasmic foreplay, which paves the way for Magical Congress. At this point, you have two choices:

1. You can begin self-pleasuring while watching each other, as already described in this chapter.

2. You can stimulate each other through the following practice, which I call "See-Saw Stimulation" because each partner takes turns lying back and receiving while the other sits up.

Shiva, sit cross-legged in what I call the "open lotus" position (see *Art of Sexual Ecstasy,* p. 160) equivalent to a relaxed lotus pose in yoga.

Shakti, come to Shiva and sit in his lap, wrapping your legs around his body so that your feet touch each other behind his back. Then, when you are ready, let yourself recline backward so that you are lying with your back on the floor, your pelvis elevated, resting on Shiva's thighs.

This position can be experienced as a delicious moment of surrender, as you expose and open your sexual organs to Shiva for pleasuring (see illustration, p. 348).

Shiva, gently caress Shakti's body, brushing your hands from her thighs up over her belly, breasts and throat, then sweeping down her arms.

Let your caresses gradually become more sexual. Take plenty of massage oil and lubricate Shakti's breasts, roll her nipples between your thumb and finger, kiss or lick her nipples, slide your oiled hands over her belly and thighs, gently tug at her pubic hair, turn her on.

Shakti, as Shiva does this, visualize the Magic Symbol inside your body. Associate the symbol with these pleasurable sensations.

Shiva, now you can approach her Yoni, lightly circling the outer lips, using lots of lubricant, gradually focusing on her cleo, arousing her sexual

All come to me at last,
There is no love like mine;
For all other love takes one
and not another;
And other love is pain,
but this is joy eternal.

—EDWARD CARPENTER
Over the Great City

energy. As her excitement level rises, ask if you can slide your fingers into her vaginal canal, her sacred garden of delight.

Give blended stimulation to Shakti, listening to her guidance as to which strokes she likes best, bringing her to a sexual peak, stopping just before orgasmic release. Help the orgasmic sensations to spread through her body, massaging her pelvis, belly, and breasts.

Continue for about fifteen minutes.

Shakti, when you have been sexually aroused in this manner, sit up in Shiva's lap once more.

Now it is Shiva's turn to lie back, exposing his sexual organ to Shakti. Now it is his turn to receive pleasure.

Shakti, caress Shiva's body with long, sweeping movements of your hands, moving all the way from his legs and thighs up over his abdomen and chest to his throat, then down his arms.

Shiva, associate these pleasurable sensations with your Magic Symbol. Visualize the symbol inside your body.

Shakti, begin to massage Shiva's Vajra, remembering the strokes you learned in chapter 8. Excite him, stimulate him. Press against his perineum area with your free hand, vibrating the area, sensitizing his prostate gland. Bring him to a peak of erotic pleasure, stopping just before the point of no return.

Now you are both sexually awakened, ready for Magical Congress.

STAGE 6: MAGICAL CONGRESS—PENETRATION

Shiva, sit once more in the cross-legged position. Shakti, straddle Shiva with your legs and gently lower yourself into his lap until the tip of his erect Vajra is nuzzling the mouth of your Yoni.

Stop for a moment. Together, visualize your Magic Symbol floating between your sexual organs. Pause. Be meditative. This is an important moment in which you need to focus all your awareness on the point where magical alchemy is starting to happen.

Shakti, very gently and slowly, slide down into Shiva's lap, allowing his Vajra to penetrate inside your Yoni. As you do so, visualize the Magic Symbol entering you.

Shiva, as your Vajra slides into Shakti, visualize the Magic Symbol entering her Yoni.

Shakti, let Shiva's Vajra fully penetrate into your Yoni so that you are resting in his lap, his Vajra deep inside you.

Both partners, visualize the Magic Symbol inside Shakti's Yoni. As an

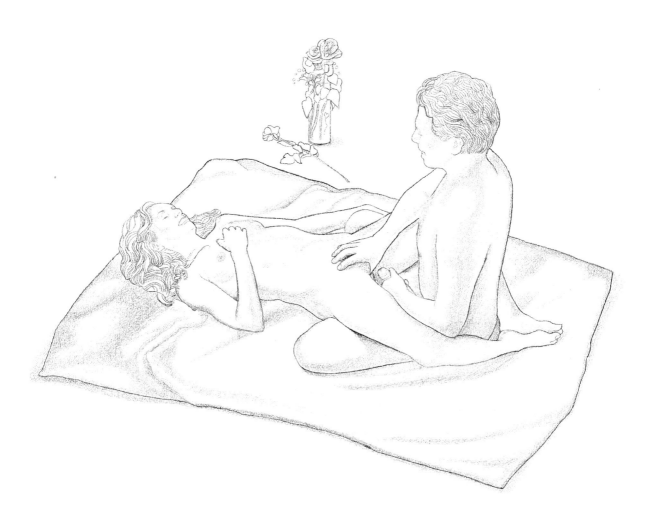

The see-saw method of stimulating sexual energy

aid to alchemy, see the color dark red spreading through your joined sexual organs and flooding the entire pelvic area.

Shakti, for a moment, explore what it is like to rotate and roll your pelvis around Shiva's erection. Practice the PC pump, milk his erection by squeezing your PC muscle and the muscles around your vaginal canal.

Shiva, you can also do the PC pump. Put your arms around Shakti, holding her lower back, so that she can make wide rotations with her body, caressing your Vajra as she moves.

Let your awareness of the Magic Symbol be like an undercurrent, or like background music, as you explore this Tantric position.

Magical Congress. Visualize
the symbol being pushed
inside the woman's vagina at
the moment of penetration.

Shakti, lean back and support yourself with your arms. Experiment
with a playful kind of friction sex, rubbing Shiva's Vajra inside your Yoni as
you raise and lower your pelvis. Remember, you can always sexually stimulate yourselves in this relaxed position during Magical Congress if you feel
you are losing your sexual connection.

STAGE 7: CONGRESS IN THE FIRST CHAKRA
Now you can begin the yogic practice of Magical Congress, moving your
symbol together up through your seven centers, charging it with orgasmic
power.

349

Sit close, your chests nearly touching, hands placed on your partner's sacrum area at the bottom of the spine, maintaining full sexual penetration.

Both partners, focus on the Magic Symbol floating inside Shakti's Yoni. Now you will begin a special breathing pattern to move the Magic Symbol up through your chakras. It is called "inverted breathing" because as Shiva inhales, Shakti exhales, and as Shiva exhales, Shakti inhales.

Shiva, inhale, visualizing that you are sucking the Magic Symbol out of Shakti's sex center, through your Vajra, into your own sex center. Feel the symbol come into your genitals.

Circulating the Magic Symbol through breath

Shakti, exhale as Shiva inhales, giving the Magic Symbol to Shiva, sending it out through your Yoni into his first chakra.

Shiva, now you exhale, sending the Magic Symbol shooting back into Shakti's Yoni with all your sexual energy.

Shakti, inhale, squeezing your vaginal muscles, milking Shiva's Vajra and sucking the Magic Symbol in through your vaginal canal, mingling it with your own juice as you receive it in your first chakra.

See the dark red energy of your combined sexual juices moving back and forth with the symbol, soaking the symbol with red.

Continue in this way for a few minutes. Communicate what is happening. Establish a clear image, or feeling, of the Magic Symbol moving back and forth between your sex centers.

STAGE 8: CONGRESS IN THE SECOND CHAKRA

When you are both ready, you can move to the next step of Magical Congress: bringing your Magic Symbol up through the chakras.

Shiva, you are going to guide the movement of the symbol. Place your right hand in the small of Shakti's back, at the level of the second chakra, while keeping your left hand on her sacrum. Shakti, you may wish to place your hands in a similar way, mirroring those of Shiva.

Shiva, tell Shakti, "Now we circle the energy between the first and second chakras."

Shiva, exhale, sending the Magic Symbol with your sexual juice shooting out through your Vajra into Shakti's sex center. Visualize the symbol and the juice penetrating Shakti and then rising up her Inner Flute to the level of her second chakra, where your right hand is placed.

Shakti, inhale as Shiva exhales, receiving the symbol from Shiva in your Yoni and drawing it up your Inner Flute to the second chakra.

Now the Magic Symbol is going to make a circle.

Shiva, inhale, drawing the Magic Symbol into your belly, then letting it fall down your Inner Flute into your sex center.

Shakti, exhale as Shiva inhales, giving the symbol to Shiva through your lower belly and visualizing it returning to his sex center.

Circle the Magic Symbol through your first and second chakras in this way, moving it into Shakti's Yoni, up her Inner Flute, through her belly, into Shiva's belly, down his spine, and into his sex center.

Stay in touch with your sexual feelings, pressing your genitals together, slipping and sliding around each other, letting these pleasurable sensations spread through the pelvis and up into your abdomens.

Now you can invoke the qualities of your second chakras. See the color orange spreading through your bellies, bringing warmth to this area. Feel the sensuousness, the juice of the lower belly, begin to awaken in this circle of sexual magic. Let your bellies greet each other, rubbing together, releasing bubbles of erotic delight as they share the Magic Symbol, soaking it with their energies as it circles through them.

STAGE 9: CONGRESS IN THE THIRD CHAKRA

When you are both comfortable with the inverted breathing pattern and circling the energy, you can begin to climb the Inner Flute, moving chakra by chakra up through your bodies, making bigger and bigger circles with your Magic Symbol.

Shiva, keeping your left hand on your partner's sacrum, move your right hand up Shakti's back to an area opposite her solar plexus. Say "Now we make a circle between our first and third chakras."

Shiva, exhale, shooting the symbol and your sexual juice into Shakti's Yoni and up her Inner Flute to her solar plexus, her third chakra.

Shakti, inhale, welcoming the Magic Symbol and sucking it up your Inner Flute to your third chakra, your solar plexus. Then exhale, giving the symbol to Shiva out through your third chakra.

Shiva, inhale, receiving the symbol through your third chakra and allowing it to fall down your Inner Flute to your sex center.

As you circle the symbol, invoke the qualities of the third chakra. Feel your power center begin to stir and unleash its strength as the symbol passes through it. Let your sexual energy take on a fiery, yellow hue as it rises to the third chakra, igniting the symbol, purifying it, making it shine with a healthy, radiant golden fire.

STAGE 10: CONGRESS IN THE FOURTH CHAKRA

Shiva, bring your right hand up Shakti's back to a point opposite her heart center, keeping your left hand on her sacrum. Say "Now we make a circle between the first and fourth chakras." Maintain the inverted breathing pattern.

Shiva, exhale, shooting the symbol into Shakti's Yoni and up through her Inner Flute to her heart. Then inhale, drawing the symbol into your own heart center and down to your sex.

Shakti, as Shiva breathes out you breathe in, sucking the symbol from Shiva's sex center into your first chakra and then drawing it up to your

As is the human body,
  so is the cosmic body.
As is the human mind,
  so is the cosmic mind.
As is the microcosm,
  so is the macrocosm.
As is the atom,
  so is the universe.

              —Upanishads

heart center, your fourth chakra. Then breathe out, giving the symbol through your heart to your beloved.

Invoke the qualities of the heart as you circle the symbol through this important chakra. See the color green spreading through your chest. Feel the nourishing warmth that the heart gives to your lovemaking, to your sexual magic. Feel a vast, peaceful space opening up between your armpits. Let your love, your acceptance, your compassion infuse your Magic Symbol with these precious qualities.

STAGE 11: CONGRESS IN THE FIFTH CHAKRA

Shiva, lightly place your right hand on the back of your partner's neck and touch the rear of her throat chakra. Say "Now we make a circle between the first and fifth chakras."

Shakti, inhale, pulling the symbol with your energy all the way up to your throat. Then make soft, sexual sounds in your throat as you exhale, passing the symbol to your partner. You may feel like purring, moaning, or sighing, as you vibrate your throat center.

Shiva, inhale, receiving the symbol from Shakti, sucking it into your throat and letting it fall to your sex center. Then exhale, shooting the Magic Symbol up her Inner Flute to the fifth chakra.

Invoke the qualities of the fifth chakra. See the color blue flooding your throat, healing, purifying, and transforming this area. Let your throats be open, relaxed. Make sounds, express your energy, your individuality, vibrating the fifth chakra. Give your sounds a sexual quality, uniting your first and fifth chakras.

STAGE 12: CONGRESS IN THE SIXTH CHAKRA

Press your foreheads gently together, so that your third eyes touch each other. Shiva, lightly touch the back of your partner's head with the fingers of your right hand, keeping your left hand anchored on her sacrum. Say "Now we make a circle between the first and sixth chakras."

Shakti, inhale, drawing the symbol up your Inner Flute to your forehead, at a point just between your eyebrows. Feel the energy pulsing in your third eye. Then exhale, passing the symbol into Shiva's forehead.

Shiva, inhale, receiving the symbol through your forehead and letting it fall down to your sex center. Then exhale, shooting the Magic Symbol up Shakti's Inner Flute to her forehead.

Invoke the qualities of the sixth chakra. See the color purple radiating out from the center of your head. Feel the lightness, the clarity, the space that opens up when the sixth chakra is activated. Let your Magic Symbol fly through this inner space, through this light, becoming more and more refined as it prepares to connect with the Astral Network.

STAGE 13: CONGRESS IN THE SEVENTH CHAKRA

Both partners, focus your attention on the crown of your head. Shiva, lightly touch the crown of your partner's head with the fingers of your right hand. Say "Now we make a circle between the first and seventh chakras."

Shakti, inhale, drawing your sex energy with the Magic Symbol up your Inner Flute all the way to the crown of your head. Then exhale, passing the symbol to Shiva and letting it fall down through his Inner Flute to his genitals.

Shiva, inhale, receiving the symbol from Shakti in your crown and bringing it down to your sex center. Then exhale, shooting the symbol up Shakti's Inner Flute to the top of her head.

Invoke the qualities of the seventh chakra. Here, you may begin to lose a sense of physical boundaries as your energy and your symbol start floating in white light, in a space that seems endless.

It might be tempting to stop here, in this silence and blissfulness, as you lose your grip on your sense of time and space, but there is one more step to take in order to complete your Magical Congress.

STAGE 14: CONGRESS WITH THE ASTRAL NETWORK

Both partners, reconnect strongly with your first chakras, stimulating your sexual energy. Shiva, say "Now we can go for full orgasm, for total pleasure."

Make love strongly, passionately. For a moment, don't worry about inverted breathing, or where your Magic Symbol is. Go for your pleasure, your passion, helping each other rise toward an orgasmic peak.

See if you can time your orgasms to happen simultaneously.

As you feel yourself approaching the point of explosive release, ask your partner "Can I come? Are you ready?"

Your partner may say "Yes, let's do it!"

Or perhaps your partner may say, "Wait a little—I'm almost there."

Or perhaps your partner is not close to orgasm but is so flooded with the orgasmic energy that he or she is happy to give you the go-ahead.

Be sure that you have an agreement, then move into full orgasm. Feel yourself being carried over the point of no return. Let go into full climax. Surrender to this delicious moment of pulsing ecstasy.

Allow the symbol to move
through you. Release it above
your head as the energy of
blissful union expands
through you in waves
of joy.

As your orgasm begins, bring the Magic Symbol with your orgasmic energy up through your body and out through the top of your head. It may seem as if you and your beloved have become a single body, with a single Inner Flute and a single symbol.

Let the Magic Symbol go shooting out through your head, mixed with all that beautiful orgasmic energy, connecting with the Astral Network.

Both partners, breathe slowly and deeply through your mouths, holding the vision of your Magic Symbol floating above your heads. Enjoy this timeless moment, this crowning accomplishment of your magical skills.

As the orgasmic sensations begin to subside, visualize your symbol floating away, growing smaller and smaller until it becomes a tiny dot, far away, then disappears.

STAGE 15: ENJOYING THE AFTERGLOW

Shakti, remain for a few moments sitting in Shiva's lap, resting against his chest, your foreheads lightly touching, staying sexually connected in a loose, relaxed way. If Shiva's erection has subsided, let his Vajra rest between your bellies.

Breathe gently together. Allow yourself to enjoy this space in which there is nothing to do, nothing to seek or accomplish, simply being intimate, feeling your hearts, appreciating your love for each other.

After a while, feel that some of the orgasmic energy that you have released starts raining softly down through your bodies as white light. Visualize it passing slowly down through the head, throat, chest, back to the sex center, and down into the ground, connecting you once more with the ground, the earth.

Slowly disengage your bodies. Lie down. Relax.

When you feel ready, sit up and enjoy a Melting Hug.

Congratulate each other.

Close the session with a Heart Salutation.

Pointers

KEEPING THE VARIOUS ELEMENTS IN HARMONY

When practicing Magical Congress the first few times, you may have difficulty keeping the various elements in harmony. For example, you may lose track of where you are in the chakras, or you may forget the breathing pattern, or you may lose your connection to your sexual energy.

One way of overcoming such problems is to adopt the theatrical practice of having a "technical run through" before the real performance. Go through the stages in a leisurely fashion, without sexual penetration, practicing the breathing and the alchemy until you feel comfortable with them. Then you can commence the full ritual from the beginning, including lovemaking.

Another potential difficulty in this exercise is a tendency to lose the heart connection with your partner because you are so focused on the technique. If this happens, take a moment to stop, relax, and look in each other's eyes, remembering your love for each other, before continuing.

Magic is the ability to affect change in conformity to the will.

—ALEISTER CROWLEY

During the ritual, it is important to keep a strong sexual connection in your first chakras. Sometimes you may need to pay total attention to your sex, temporarily putting aside your visualization of the symbol and the chakras. Shiva, hold Shakti's buttocks and pull her firmly toward you as you thrust with your Vajra into her Yoni, stimulating both sex organs simultaneously. Shakti, revolve your pelvis around Shiva's Vajra, sucking and milking it with your vaginal muscles. Be playful. Have fun.

Then, when your sexual juices are flowing strongly, you can return to the ritual. One of you can say, "Okay, now we can take up where we left off, circling the symbol from one to four."

CONGRESS WITHOUT ERECTION

It is possible to perform Magical Congress without Shiva having an erection, with his Vajra resting softly inside Shakti's Yoni. Indeed, it may be helpful in the beginning to practice congress in this way in order to become comfortable with the steps of circling the Magic Symbol with the breath, before including the sexual aspect.

If the Vajra comes out of the Yoni during the exercise, keep it pressed between your lower bellies. It is important that the Vajra not hang loose from Shiva's body, because this may interrupt the flow of energy.

VARIATIONS IN PRACTICE

I have guided you through what I consider to be the most effective method of classical Magical Congress. But there are many options available. For example, if you have difficulty keeping in synchronicity with each other after reaching a certain chakra, you may agree to continue the rest of the way independently. This is fine.

You may prefer not to end your Magical Congress in explosive orgasmic release but to retain the energy as you connect your symbol with the Astral Network. This is perfectly okay.

Trust your feelings. Trust your heart. Don't make the mistake of cutting your energy flow because you have a fixed idea how Magical Congress should happen. Avoid the performance anxiety of thinking that you have to do it exactly as described in this chapter.

You may also wish to make smaller circles, circling between the second and third chakras, the third and fourth chakras, rather than making circles that always include the first chakra. The advantage of small circles is that you do not have to visualize such big movements of energy. The difficulty is that, as you rise through the body, you may lose your connection with the sex center, and that is why I prefer to circle from the first chakra.

MAGICAL CONGRESS: SPONTANEOUS STYLE

You may feel that the practice of classical Magical Congress is rather formal and complex, like performing a difficult yoga posture in which you are required to synchronize body twists, breathing patterns, and visualizations all at the same time.

However, by understanding and practicing all these steps with your partner you are building a magical highway, a channel through which your energies can dance, flow, and transform on their own accord.

For this reason, I encourage people to practice classical Magical Congress before experimenting with the spontaneous style. Once you have mastered its intricacies, you have a solid foundation on which you can freely improvise without getting lost or confused.

With spontaneous Magical Congress you focus less on precise steps, more on the sexual and loving connection with each other, enjoying the intensity and aliveness that come from following the natural flow of your sexual energy, which can be different every time you make love.

For example, while moving your combined sexual energy up through your seven chakras, you may become aware that your energy feels particularly pleasurable in a certain part of your body—in your belly, for example. With the freedom of the spontaneous style, you can focus on this area for as long as you wish.

This offers a deep experience of the alchemy that occurs when your Magic Symbol and your sexual energy meet, merge, and mingle in one place. You can enjoy the warmth, the pleasure, the sensual sensations in your

In the Eastern religions and in mysticism, the love of God is an intense feeling of the experience of oneness, inseparably linked with the expression of this love in every act of living.

—ERICH FROMM

belly, using the Three Keys to intensify your experience and blending your Magic Symbol with the energy that is swirling and bubbling in this part of your body.

However, before you end your practice session it is important, even in spontaneous Magical Congress, to complete your journey through the seven chakras and connect with the Astral Network. This will ensure that the energy, love, and alchemical transformation that you have generated will resonate with the network and help to manifest your vision.

As an example of the spontaneous style, I offer these excerpts from a conversation with two seasoned sexual magicians, Stephen and Jackie, after a session of Magical Congress.

They began their practice in the formal manner, then started to branch out into different movements and visualizations.

JACKIE: On this occasion I felt very relaxed with Steve, enjoying an easy sexual connection with him that allowed me to experiment, to follow the energy in whatever way seemed most natural and inviting.

At first, we made circles of energy, from the first to the second chakra, then from the first to the third. But then I received a strong image of part of our Magic Symbol—a big wave with dancing dolphins. The dolphins were rolling and diving and playing in my belly. When I focused on this image, it was as if I became the dolphins, and this gave me a lot of pleasure and excitement, triggering a series of flowing, graceful movements as I made love. It was a totally fresh kind of feeling—very alive, very playful, watery, slippery, and sexual—and I understood how the symbol can transform the quality of my sexual energy when it appears in a certain place in my body.

STEPHEN: Different aspects of the symbol revealed themselves in different parts of my body—up and down my arms, whirling around in my chest—giving me a feeling of power and spaciousness. It seemed as though I was a vast, empty container in which all the various elements of the symbol could dance freely, and that felt very good.

I also realize that it's not always possible for me to visualize the symbol when I'm making love, and I simply accept that. Even when I can't visualize it, I can feel its qualities. I have a feeling for it, but I can't constantly hold a picture of it in my mind.

JACKIE: Another beautiful thing was that I found myself visualizing something like an egg of energy that encompassed both of us. I inhaled Steve's energy through my sex, mixing it with my own, bringing it up my spine to the third eye, and then, as I exhaled, I sent the whole energy through Steve's head, all the way down his spine and into his sex chakra. So it was easy to create an egg of light that included us both, moving our Magic Symbol around and around this circle.

I did that for the longest time; it was so enjoyable. Then, just at the right moment, when I was beginning to feel a bit disconnected from Steve, he guided us back into the formal practice and we took the symbol all the way up the chakras to the Astral Network.

STEPHEN: I sent the symbol out through my head at the moment of orgasm. Then, right afterward, it felt important for me to inhale strongly and hold my breath for a few moments. That helped to give me a vivid image of the symbol floating above my head, resonating with the Astral Network. Later, when I wanted the symbol to move away and disappear, I felt the need to exhale strongly several times, to almost blow it away from me.

After releasing the symbol I enjoyed being close to Jackie, holding her, breathing slowly. I felt this was very necessary. I remembered that in the past, when I didn't take these moments to rest and relax together, I sometimes left the practice feeling kind of empty and weird.

So it was good just to lie together. I felt whole, connected from head to toe. I could feel Jackie in a much gentler way, very loving. I think that's important for me.

JACKIE: I see the importance of using the same symbol for several sessions of sex magic, especially if it's something about our relationship. It triggers a whole new energy level between us.

One thing I experienced with the symbol during the time we were making love was, at some point, the symbol became very big and we were actually in a landscape surrounded by the symbol, sitting inside the symbol, making love inside the symbol. That was really nice.

STEPHEN: It's not that the symbol creates something in me. The symbol reflects something of myself, which is already there. It just needs to be validated.

MASTERS OF SEXUAL MAGIC

By mastering the art of Magical Congress, you have attained full status as sexual magicians. Now you have all the skills you need to make magic in your lives, empowering yourselves, shaping your destiny, creating whatever outcomes are appropriate to lead a fulfilling and joyful existence.

Now you are skillful players in a world of infinite possibilities. When you bring love and harmony into your own lives, you are simultaneously doing it for all mankind, bringing a touch of magic into this world, showing others how life can be lived, healing the planet with your joy. May your life be abundant and prosperous, and your bed filled with golden orgasms!

EPILOGUE
Awaiting the Outcome of Your Magic

Now that you have mastered the art of sexual magic, what happens next? How do you know that your magic is working? When will your desire for transformation and personal change be fulfilled? What are the chances of success?

First of all, it is important that you recognize the significance of your mastery of sexual magic. This is a great achievement, for both you and your love partner, something of which you can feel justly proud. With this mastery, the bulk of your work is done. Whatever difficulties you may have encountered in the practice are now behind you, and you are free to enjoy this beautiful, ecstatic art—to reap its plentiful rewards.

In the world of magic, there is nothing more powerful and attractive than a harmonious couple who co-create their success through sexual alchemy. Together, you have developed what Roberto Assagioli, the noted psychologist, has termed "skillful will," the ability to obtain desired results with the least possible—and most enjoyable—expenditure of your energy. Beyond simple willpower, you have harnessed your lovemaking and your imagination to support the magical transformation of your lives.

However, it's important to remember that sexual magic is an ongoing practice. It's not something that you do once, then sit back and wait for the heavens to shower their blessings upon you. It is regular practice of Magical Congress that impregnates your mind, body, emotions, and spirit with the vision of your desire, as expressed in your Magic Symbol. This symbol is a potent alchemical force that will work in a creative, positive, and purposeful way, provided that you continue your practice.

The moment that your symbol begins to resonate with the force fields of the Astral Network, the magical transformation starts to happen, although its manifestation may not be immediately apparent. Sometimes, the results of magic are instant and obvious; sometimes they take longer. There is no way of predicting the precise moment at which the alchemical process involving your psyche, your symbol, and your response from the Astral Network will culminate in the manifestation of your desire.

One indication that the network is resonating at the frequency of your Magic Symbol is a new and emerging sense of synchronicity in your life. Unexpected things start to happen that correspond to your vision. For example, you suddenly realize that you and your love partner no longer argue over a recurring, thorny issue, because you created a vision together of greater harmony in your love life. Or perhaps you bump into an attractive newcomer at the office, because you created a vision of meeting new and interesting people.

Another sign of magic at work is a growing feeling that you have more control over your life, greater influence over others and over your environment. People may say things to you that change your idea of how you are perceived, altering your self-image in positive and supportive ways. Events may suddenly unfold that open up new and exciting possibilities. It may not happen in exactly the way you imagine, so be alert and available to the new and the unfamiliar.

Some practitioners of sexual magic like to engage actively in the process of fulfilling their desires. For example, they feel they can help bring about the desired outcome by talking positively about it with their partners, speaking as if the transformation is about to happen, or as if it is in the process of happening, or as if it has already happened. They like to reaffirm their vision regularly, repeating affirmations on a daily basis, confirming that their desire is coming true. They are alert about the way they use language, taking care not to fall into old, negative attitudes such as "It's no good; it isn't going to happen."

In support of their efforts, these magicians sometimes make a list of daily actions, planning tasks that can help their magic happen, itemizing ways in which they can change their lifestyle, their routine, their patterns of relating and socializing, in order to help create the desired change. In so doing, they develop a growing awareness of those factors that help change come about, and those that tend to inhibit it.

For example, if you are using magic to stop smoking, then, in addition to your practice of sexual magic, you may want to repeat the affirmation "I enjoy having smoke-free lungs," or "I love to be healthy and free of the effects of cigarettes." You may also want to change your lifestyle in ways that make your desired outcome easier to manifest: not going to the places where you usually smoke, not keeping cigarettes in the house, not leaving ashtrays around to remind you . . .

In other words, you may want to look at every aspect of your life in concrete and practical ways in order to enhance your chances of a successful outcome. This active, participatory approach to magic can certainly be helpful as a "reality check," anchoring your magical practice in your daily life.

On the other hand, you may prefer a more passive, receptive approach, allowing the magic to work by itself, free of any additional efforts on your part. This, too, is perfectly valid, for the essence of magic lies in its mystery, the fact that it takes you beyond the ordinary world of cause and effect. That is why it is such a wild and wonderful phenomenon.

Another way to approach this issue is to create your Magic Circle, sit quietly in the center, and visualize yourself returning to your Sanctuary and meeting your Inner Magician. Having established communication with this magical being, you can ask for insights and guidance on how to ground your magical vision in your daily life. Your Inner Magician may simply say, "Just wait, be patient and receptive; it is happening by itself," or you may be given practical suggestions, things to do, plans to carry out.

There is one practice that I personally enjoy very much and that seems to help the manifestation of my own magical visions. It is the art of making myself empty, creating space inside myself for the new, the fresh, the unexpected to happen.

For me, this emptiness arises most easily in meditation. Sitting quietly with my eyes closed, breathing in a slow, relaxed manner, with no disturbance from the outside, my mind begins to quiet down. Just by sitting silently, being alert, watching the thoughts passing through my mind without trying to do anything about them, the mental traffic slows down, fades and disappears, leaving only a silent, empty space behind.

If I allow this emptiness, this nothingness, to continue for a few minutes, then, slowly, slowly, a profound feeling of well-being begins to arise from deep within me. I start to feel good about myself for no particular reason. I feel more settled, balanced, content. Most important of all, this inner space gives rise to a new sense of availability, of flexibility, open-mindedness, a pleasant sense of anticipation that something is about to occur in my life without any fixed idea of what exactly it is.

I find this meditative space particularly helpful in those moments when my partner in sexual magic is away and when I don't particularly feel like generating orgasmic energy myself through self-pleasuring.

At such times, I will go to a silent room in my house, or to a quiet spot in the garden, and move into meditation. When the space of emptiness opens up inside I will enjoy resting in it for several minutes, as if I am floating in a vast, creative womb, where anything can happen. Then I begin to focus on the vision I have created and want to be manifest in my life. I will visualize the Magic Symbol, I will see the symbol gently floating up through my body, passing through the seven energy centers—all within the context of a vast, silent, surrounding emptiness.

In other words I continue to be the magician, invoking the power of magic, but I do it in a very silent, meditative way. For me, this is the perfect complement to the intensity and orgasmic ecstasy of sexual magic, a valuable support that allows me to stay tuned in to the practice by myself.

In the case of "single" magicians who send visions of new love and romance out into the cosmos, I have had reports of positive results from people who, in addition to their practice of sexual magic, focus their attention and energy on loving and nurturing themselves: taking care of their bodies, eating healthy food, going to the hairdresser, enjoying a massage, making sure they feel radiant and upbeat when they go to social functions, finding all kinds of ways to generate a sense of well-being and self-esteem. In this way, they feel they are preparing themselves for the rapturous moment of meeting their new beloved.

One friend of mine whom I introduced to sexual magic enjoyed great success by focusing all her attention on the unseen, imagined, longed-for lover. As her Magic Symbol, she painted an abstract picture that conveyed her feelings about this person, which she hung in her living room. Every evening, she would enter the room and sing love songs, gazing at the picture, or dedicate a dance to him and then whirl around the room as if she were in his arms. This, she reported, worked wonders—she is now happily involved with a new love partner.

So, as you can see, there are many ways to await the outcome of your sexual magic. Perhaps the greatest secret of helping your magical vision become reality is not even to think about it. This applies especially to love partners who, having trained in sexual magic, are ready to move deeply into the practice of Magical Congress on a frequent and regular basis.

If you can drown yourself in Magical Congress, if you can be so lost in the orgasmic delight of sexual magic that you simply forget about the outcome, there is no surer method of success. This sounds paradoxical, but it's true.

Let me explain. You practice sexual magic in order to fulfill a certain desire. But if you are too focused on the result, on the goal, then you are not capable of bringing your total energy into your practice of sexual magic. Part of your mind, part of your attention, will be directed into the future, toward the result you are trying to achieve. This creates a split in your energy that weakens the power of your magic.

Totality is the key to success. If you can be fully absorbed in the art of your magical lovemaking you will find that you are naturally becoming a great magician. And you can safely let go of any concerns about the outcome because your Magic Symbol is already performing this function for you. Your symbol already carries the healing, the transformation, the harmony, the goal for which you long. That is its function, its purpose. You are free to pour your total attention and energy into the magical ritual of lovemaking with your partner.

To conclude: My idea of good magic is best portrayed by a pair of skilled lovers who have practiced carefully and have mastered all the steps that lead to Magical Congress. Now they no longer need to think about the individual exercises; it all comes naturally—as a creative, artistic, alchemical dance in which they can joyfully lose themselves, rising to higher and higher experiences of orgasmic delight.

They become so absorbed in their craft, their ecstasy, their magic, that when they finally look around and notice that their vision has manifested itself, it comes almost as a surprise.

"Oh, look!" they exclaim. "It happened, and we were having such a great time, we didn't even think about it!"

This is sexual magic *par excellence.*

RESOURCES

Now that you have enjoyed this book, you may wonder: "What's the next step?" My suggestion is: take action. In the context of a loving and safe environment, with a group of people who support the idea of reaching their maximum potential as magicians in the art of love. More than 15,000 people worldwide have already participated in seminars in the Art of Sexual Ecstasy and the Art of Sexual Magic. I invite you to inquire about the seminars and share with me the many ways to heal and expand your relationship, and to enjoy a great love life. The seminars offer a safe, supportive, and insightful experience.

For information about the seminars and training programs, private counseling, and products, please contact:

SkyDancing Institute
20 Sunnyside Ave. Ste A219
Mill Valley, CA 94941
Tel: 415-927-2584
or: 1-800-974-2584

In Europe contact:

SkyDancing Institute Germany/Austria
Schoenbergstrasse 17
D-83646 Bad Toelz
Germany
Tel: (49) (0)8041-74648
Fax: (49) (0)8041-74649

SkyDancing Institute Francophone
C.P. 233
1066 Epalinges
Switzerland
Tel/Fax: (41) (0)21 784-2033

SkyDancing Institute Switzerland
Aman Schroeter
Langgrutstrasse 178
8047 Zurich
Switzerland
Tel/Fax: (41) (0)1 493-4847

John Hawken
SkyDancing Institute—UK
Lower Grumble Farm
New Bridge, Penzance
Cornwall TR 208 QX
England
Tel: (44 736) 788 304
Fax: (44 736) 786 260

Special programs are available for same sex and gay individuals and couples who are interested in introducing loving, ecstatic sexuality to their lives. Contact:

SkyDancing Institute
Gay Tantra Institut
Kraustrasse 5
D-90443 Nuernberg
Tel: (49) (0) 9112448616
Germany

Products by Margo Anand

"SkyDancing Tantra: A Call to Bliss" (CD with Steve Schroyder and Vinit Allen). A unique blend of sounds generated from the spaciousness of Tantric meditation. Using voice, flute, saxophone, and synthesizer, it is conceived as a background induction for expanded states of consciousness. For order information please call (415) 455–4945.

The Art of Sexual Ecstasy (with music by Steven Halpern). A guided meditation on erotic touching and awakening your inner lover. Distributed by Inner Peace Music. To order call (800) 909–0707.

Audiotapes by Margo Anand are available through Sounds True Recordings. To receive a copy of the Sounds True Catalog or to order the tapes listed below, please call (800) 333–9185 or write Sounds True Catalog, 735 Walnut St., Boulder, CO 80302.

The Art of Sexual Magic. A comprehensive training on the tantric art of healing sexual wounds, creating relationships, growing spiritually, and making dreams reality. Guided by Margo with music. Nine hours.
6 Cassettes in Binder   Order #F036 $59.95

Sex Magic Meditations. Margo gently guides the listener through four powerful meditations that help expand and deepen one's experience of sexual magic. Three hours.
2 Cassettes   Order #A283 $18.95

Mail Order Sources for the Music

All Rajneesh-related music and meditation tapes are distributed by Osho America, Box 12517, Scottsdale, AZ 85267. Tel.: (800) 777–7743.

Gabrielle Roth music is distributed by Raven Records, P.O. Box 2034, Red Bank, NJ 07701. Tel.: (201) 642–7942.

Raphael and Kutira music is distributed by Kahua Hawaiian Institute, P.O. Box 1747, Makawao, HI 96768. Tel.: (808) 572–6006, Fax: (808) 572–0088.

Ariel Kalma music is distributed by Astral Muse, 315 Alilolani Street, Pukalani, HI 96768. Tel.: (808) 572–6096, Fax: (808) 572–3830.

Nightingale Records is distributed by Meistersinger Musikproduktion, Bamberger Str. 4, 8550 Forcheim, Germany. Tel.: 011-49-91-80808.

"Ecstatica, Sound Track for Lovers," by Ramana Das and Marilena Silbey, is distributed by U-Music, P.O. Box 613, Fairfax, CA 94978.

Shanti Prem: "Music for Lovers." Distributed by Bildklang Studio, Pavillon, 74575 Bartenstein, Germany. Tel.: (49 7936) 757.

Anugama, particularly "Exotic Dance" and "Shamanic Dream," are distributed by Nightingale Records, Meistersinger Musikproduktion, Bamberger Str. 4, 8550 Forchheim, Germany. Tel.: 011–49–91–80808.

Constance Demby: "Aeterna," "Novus Magnificat," and "Sacred Space" are distributed by Sound Currents, P.O. Box 1044, Fairfax, CA 94978. Tel.: (415) 459-2041.

You can obtain all quoted titles that do not have their own special references from Backroads Distributors, 417 Tamal Plaza, Corte Madera, CA 94925. Tel.: (800) 825-4848.

Music List for Special Processes in the Book

For The Laughing Pelvis exercise (Chapter 4): "The Mystic Rose" (a wonderful tape of laughter): Distributed by Osho Chidvilas, P.O. Box 3849, Sedona, AZ 86340. Tel.: (800) 777-7743.

For the Fire Meditation (Chapter 8):

- Deep Forest
- Vangelis, "Antarctica" and "1492" (Atlantic Records)
- Gabrielle Roth: "Waves"
- Soundtrack for "Baraka" (BMG Distributors)

Chapter 6: Chakra Breathing Meditation tape. Distributed by Osho Chidvilas. Tel.: (415) 381-9861.

For the Chakra Wave Meditation:
"Totem," "Waves," and "Bones" (Gabrielle Roth)
"1492" (Vangelis) (Atlantic Records)

Chapters 7 and 8:
"Oceanic Tantra," "Angels of the Deep" (Raphael and Kutira)
"Gourmet Sax," "Flutes for the Soul" (Ariel Kalma)

INDEX

ABOUT THE AUTHOR

Margo Anand is the author of *The Art of Sexual Ecstasy*. She has developed a unique path to sexual bliss called SkyDancing Tantra. She has helped to establish SkyDancing Institutes in eight countries including the USA. She has taught the Love and Ecstasy Trainings around the world to more than ten thousand people for the last fifteen years. Her passion has been to explore and teach that Eros is the source of our creative power and the key to magic: the power to transform, create, and manifest our dream.